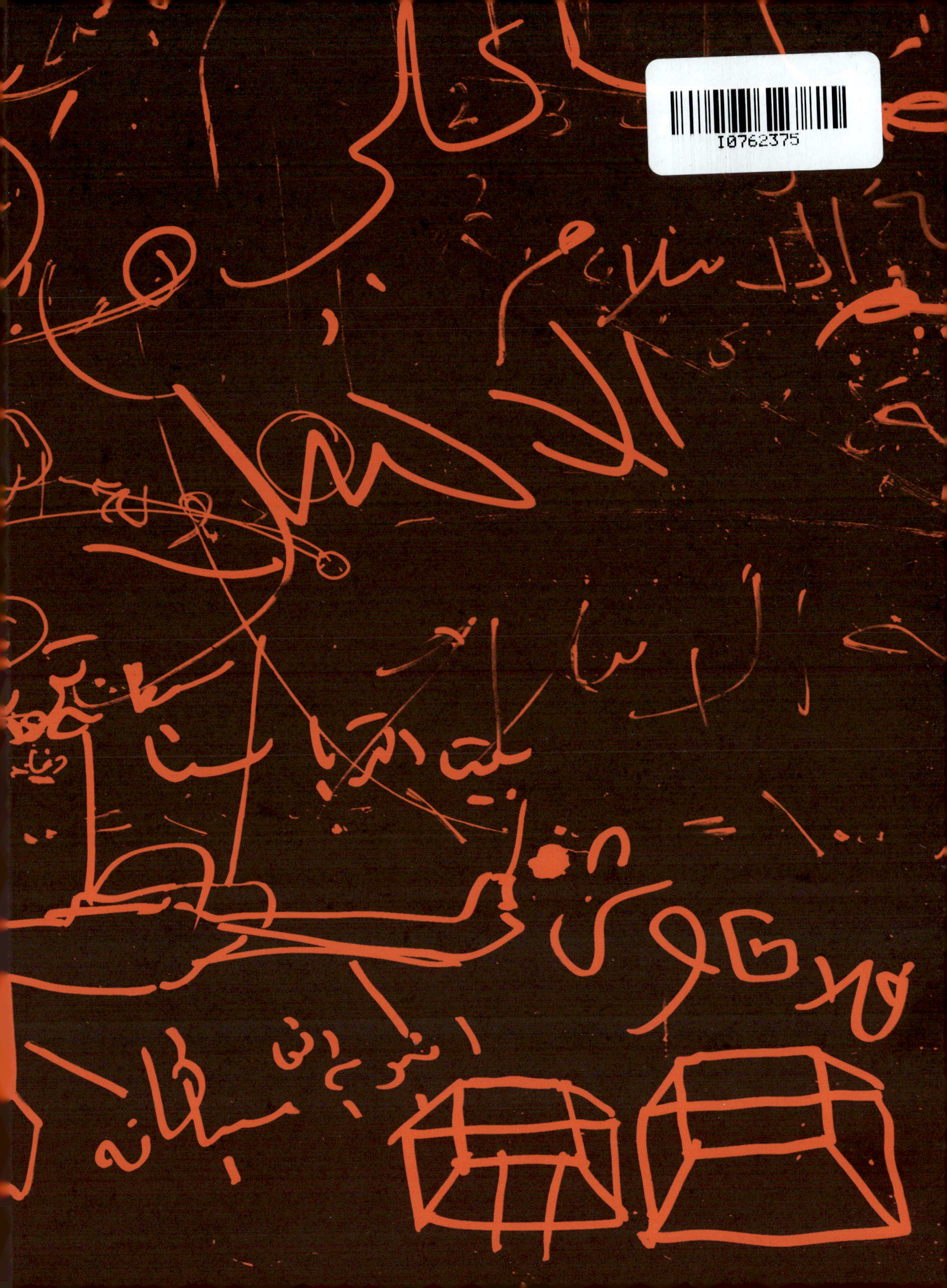

WE DON'T SAY GOODBYE

LORENZO MELONI

GOST

'LA STORIA INSEGNA, MA NON HA ALLIEVI.' **'HISTORY TEACHES, BUT IT HAS NO PUPILS.'**

Antonio Gramsci

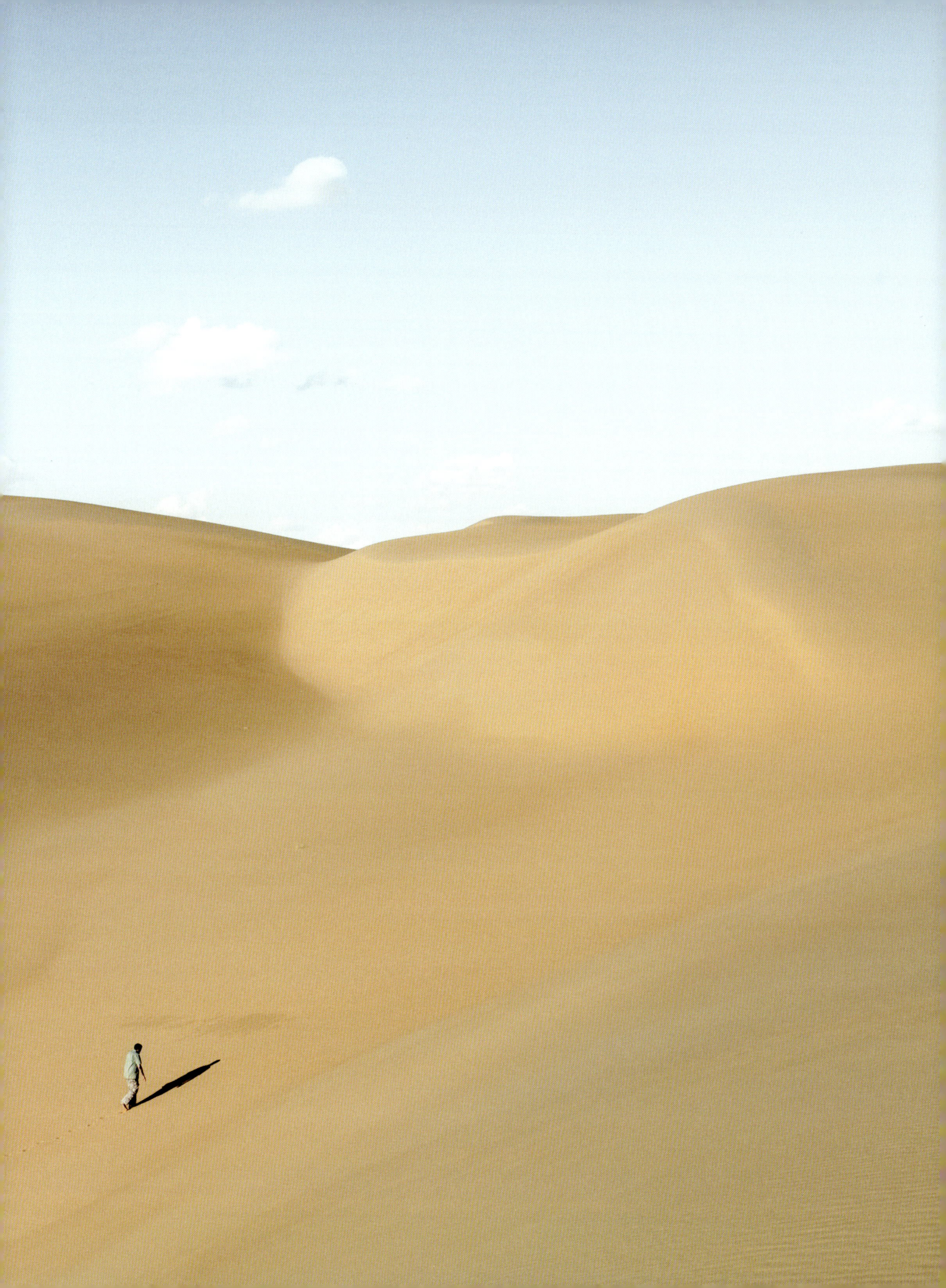

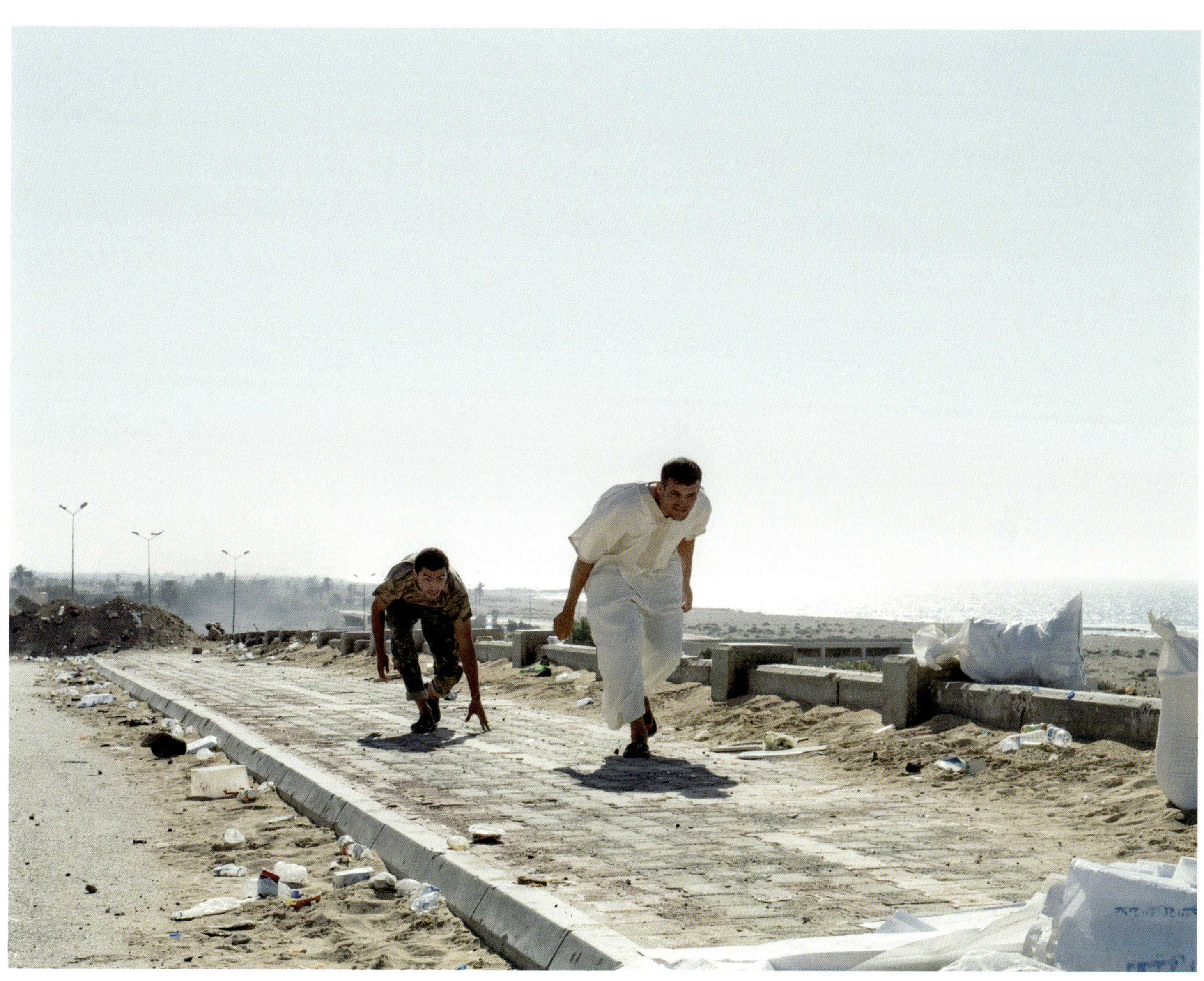

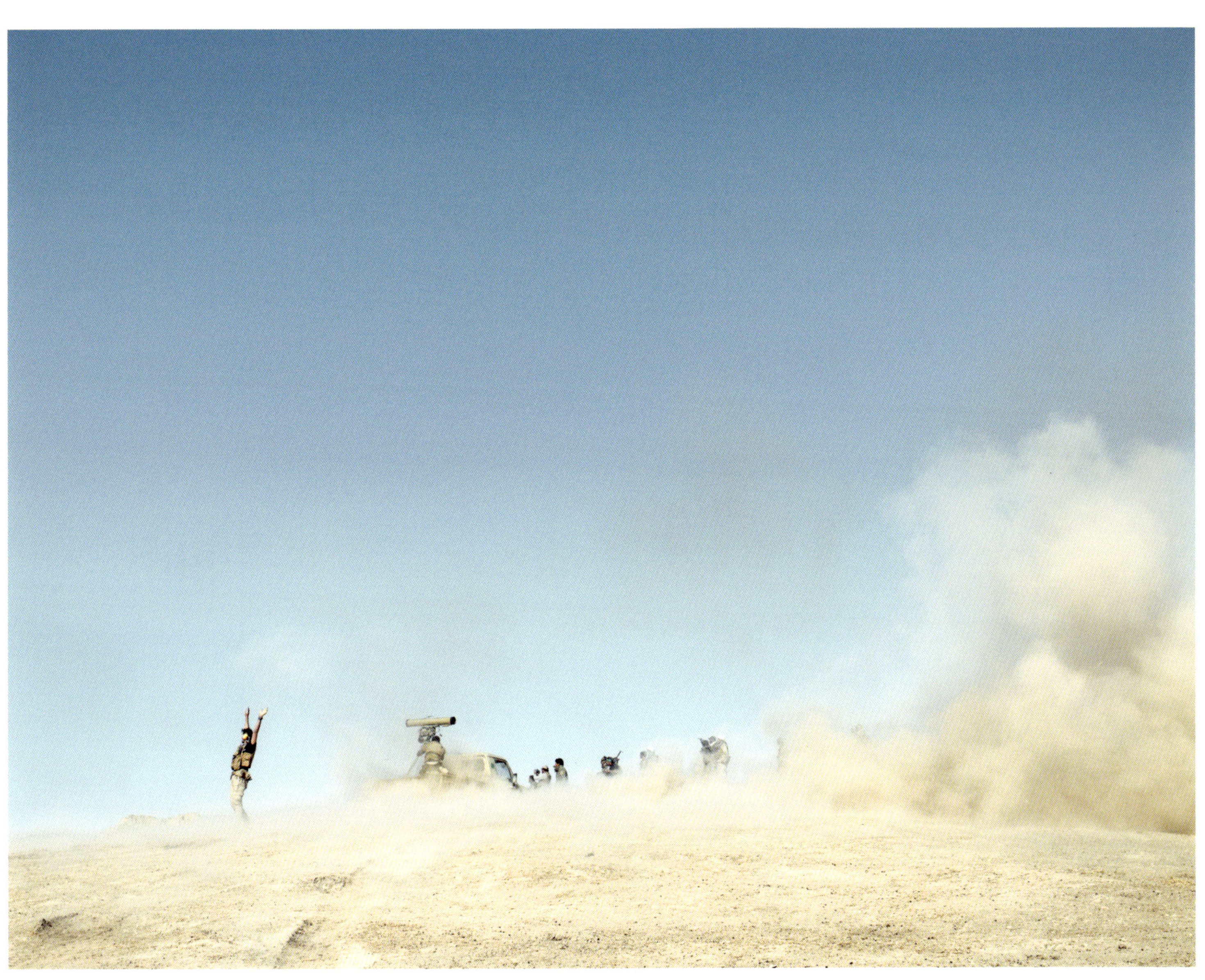

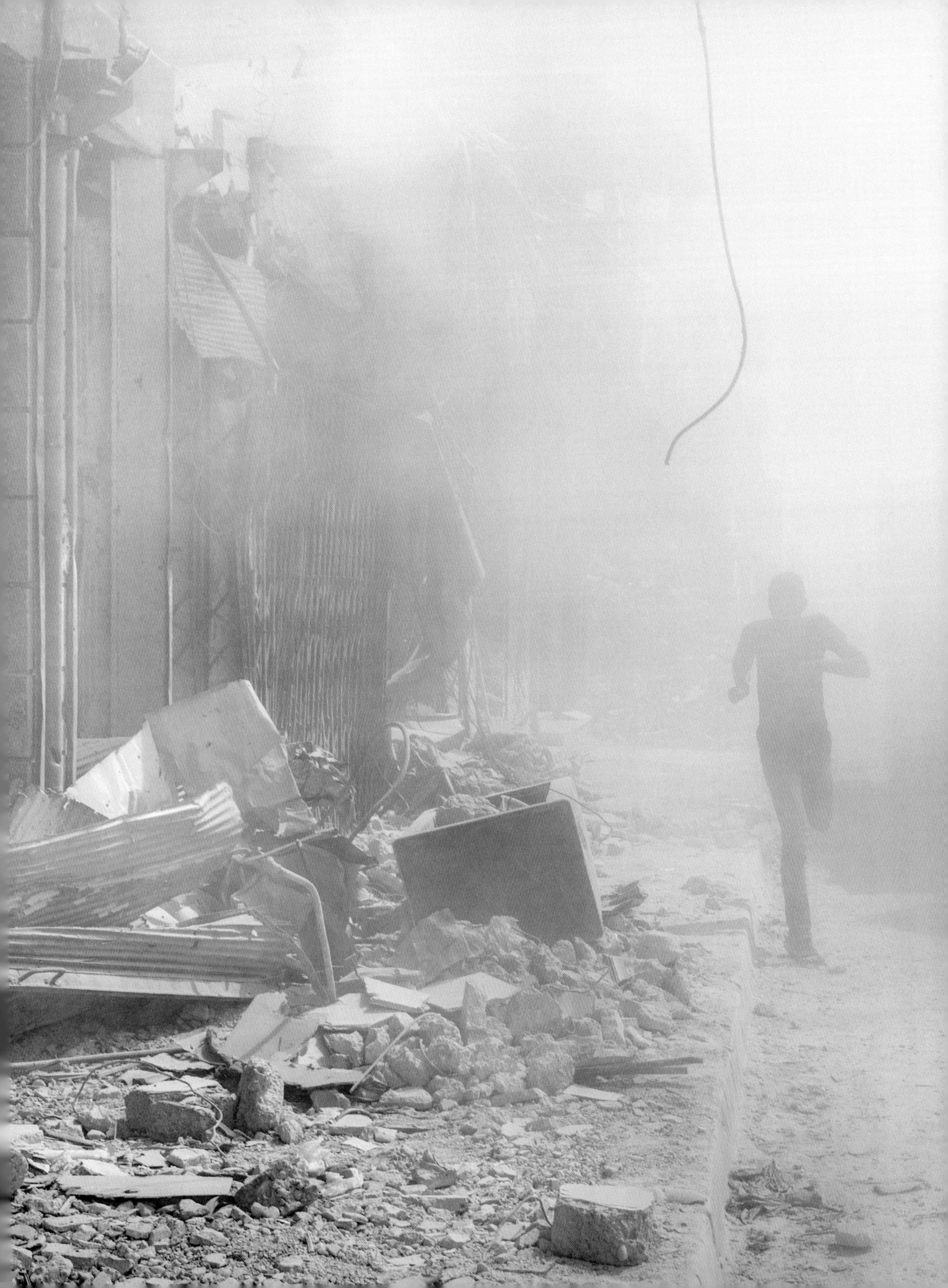

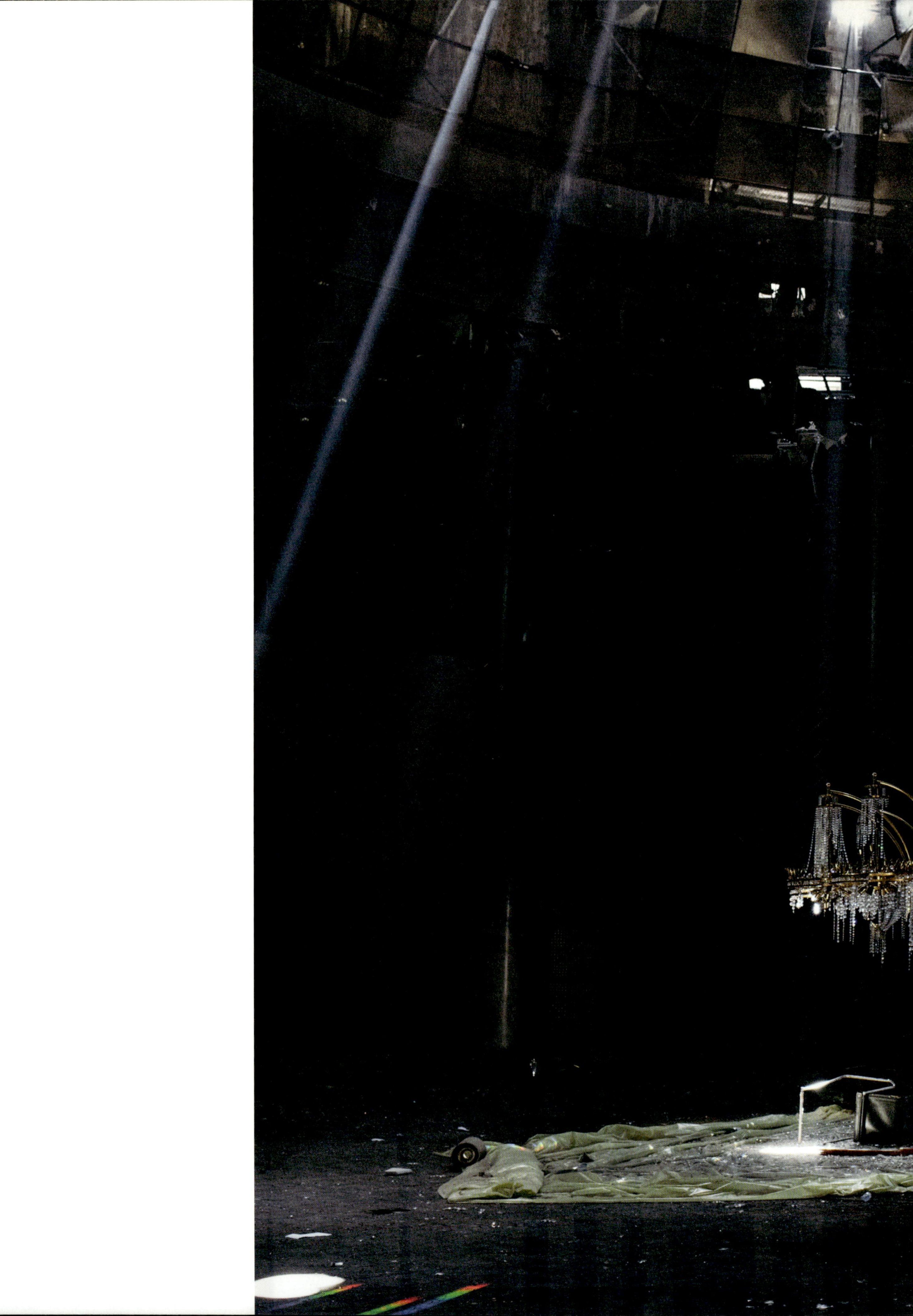

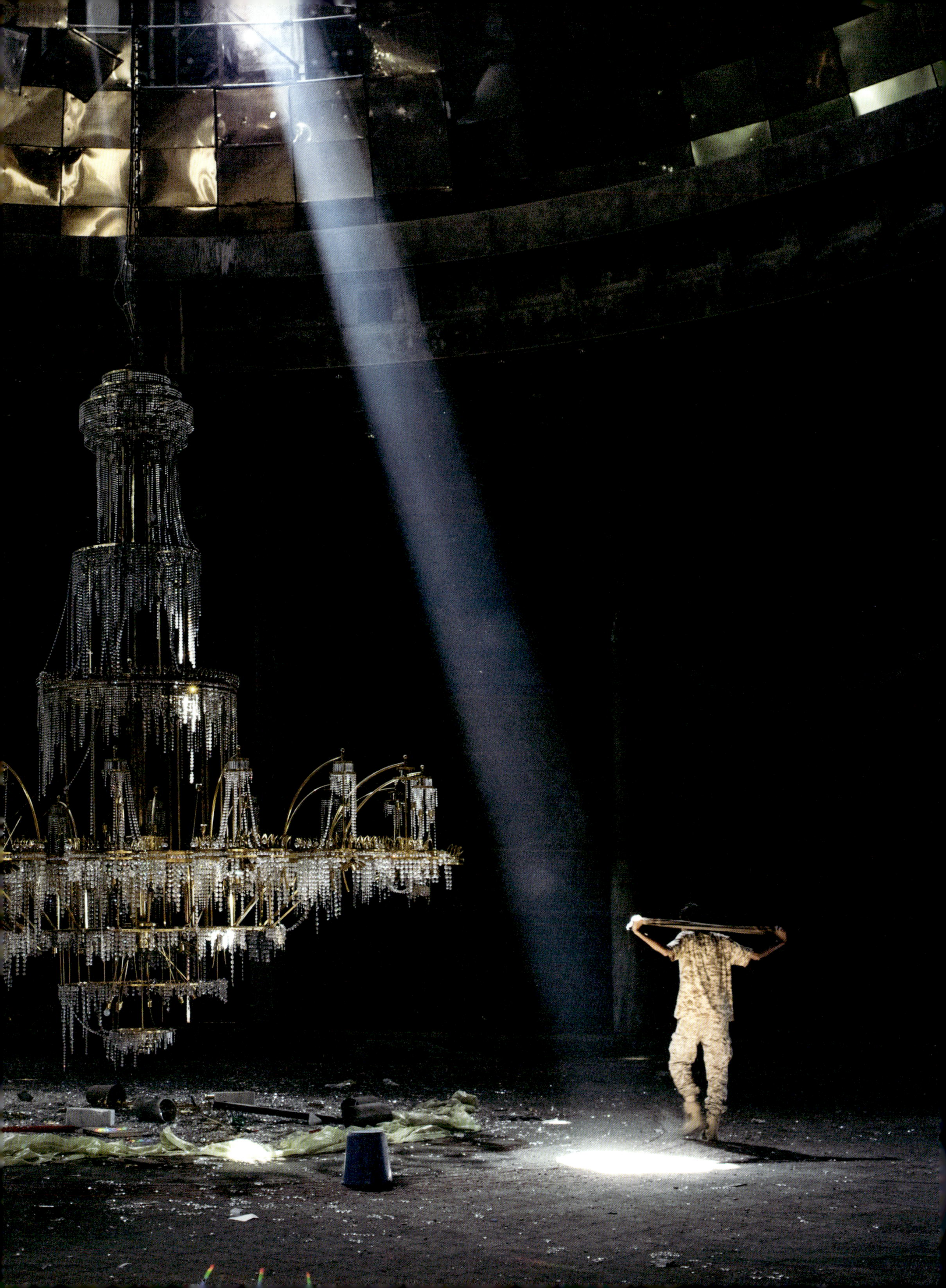

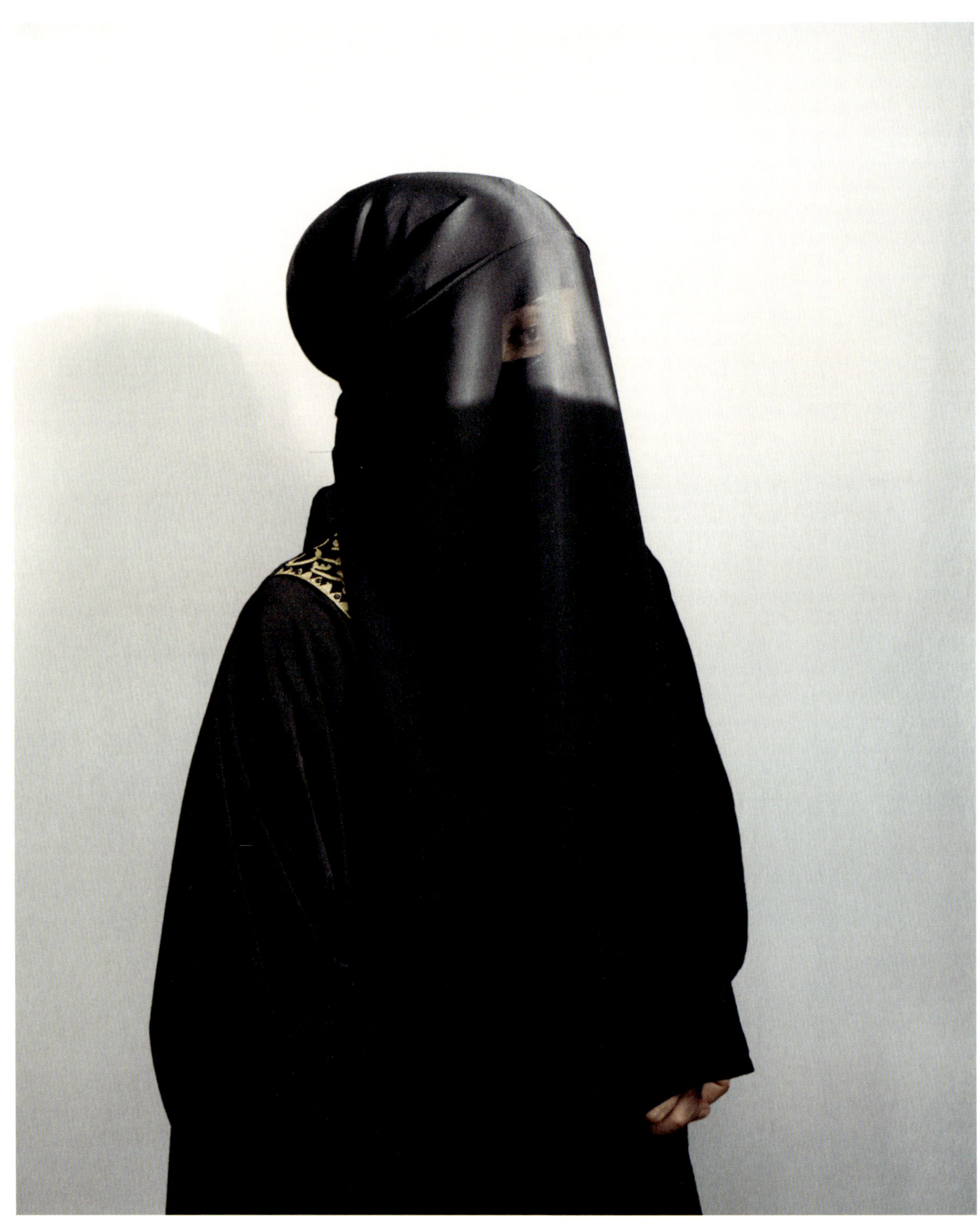

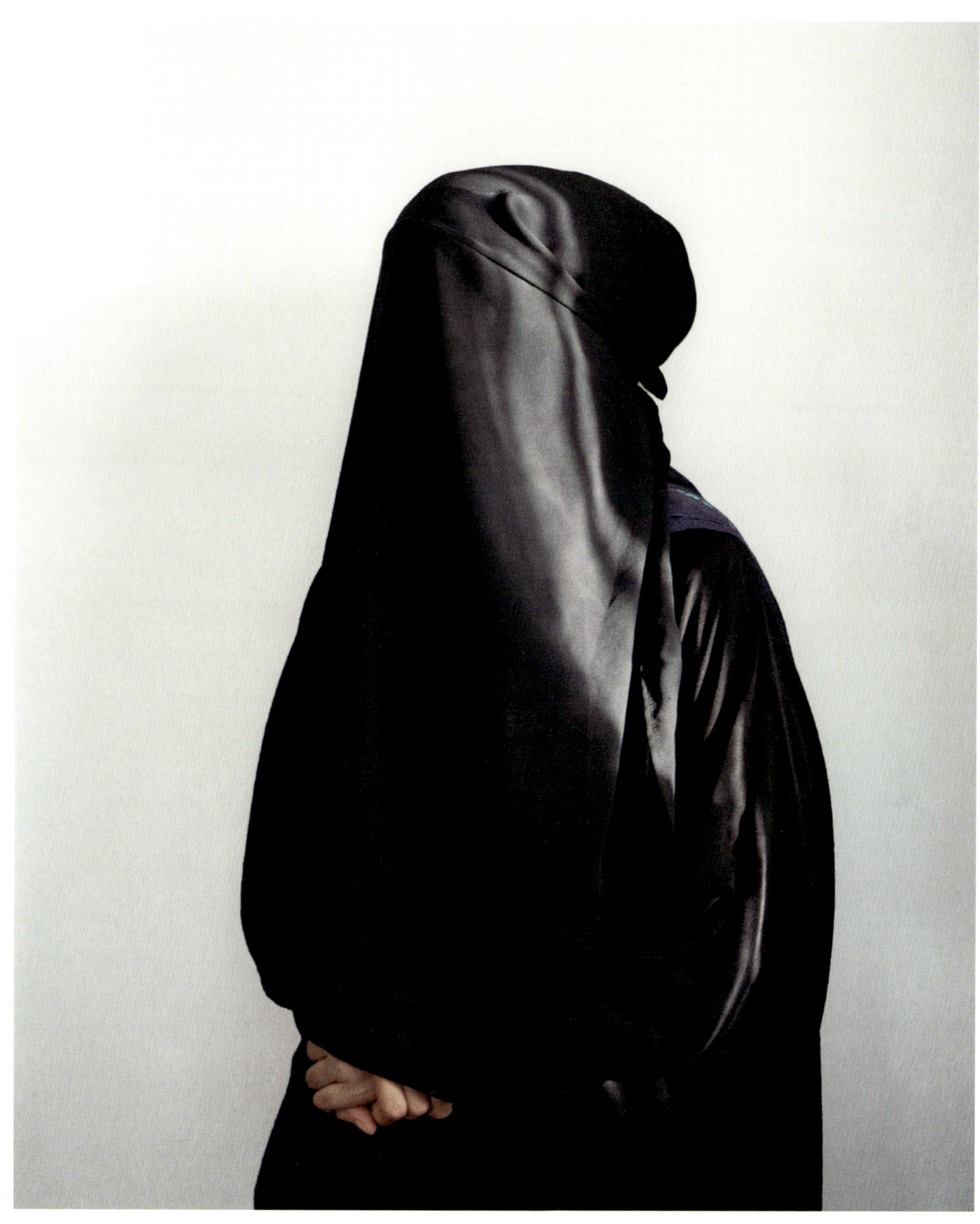

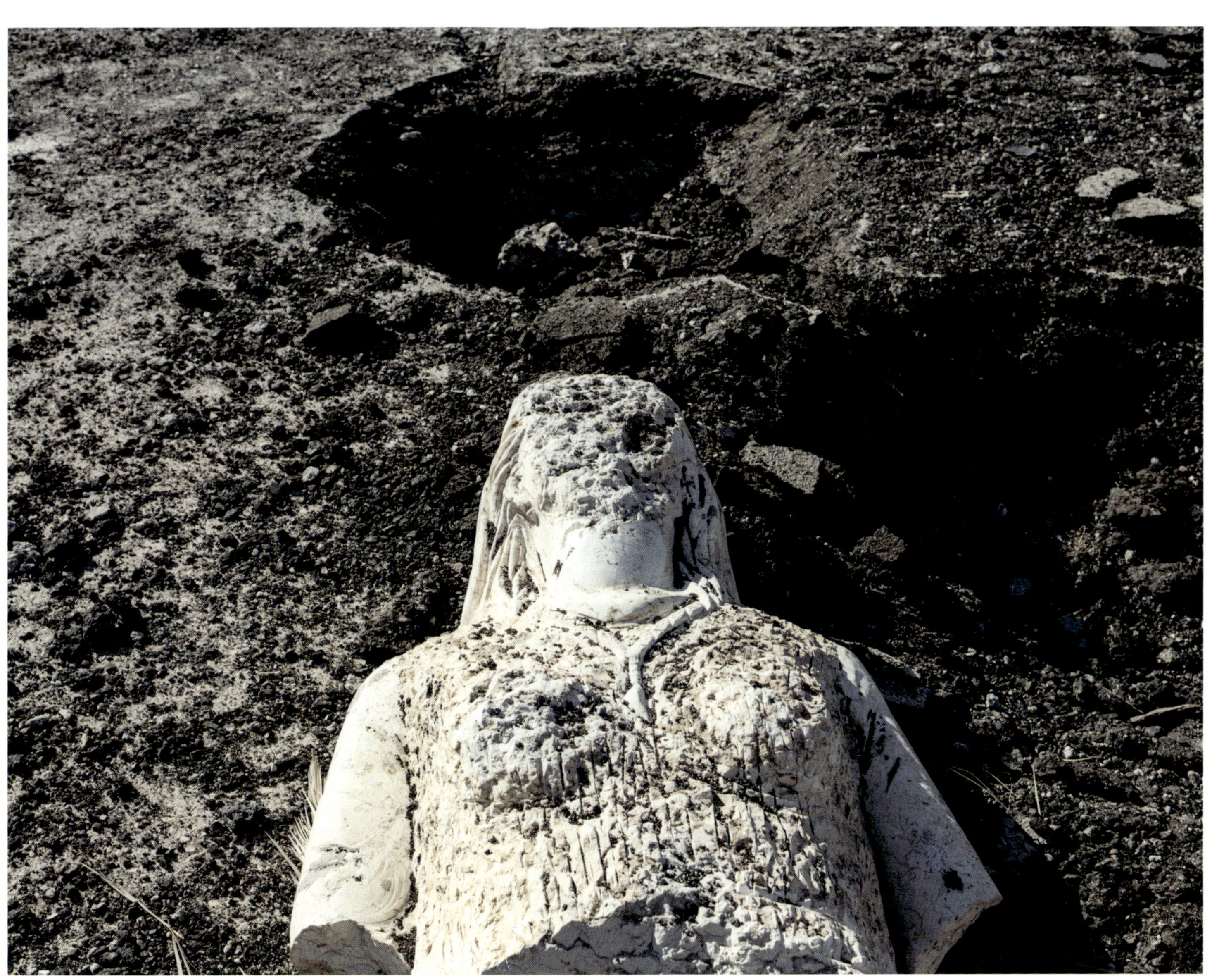

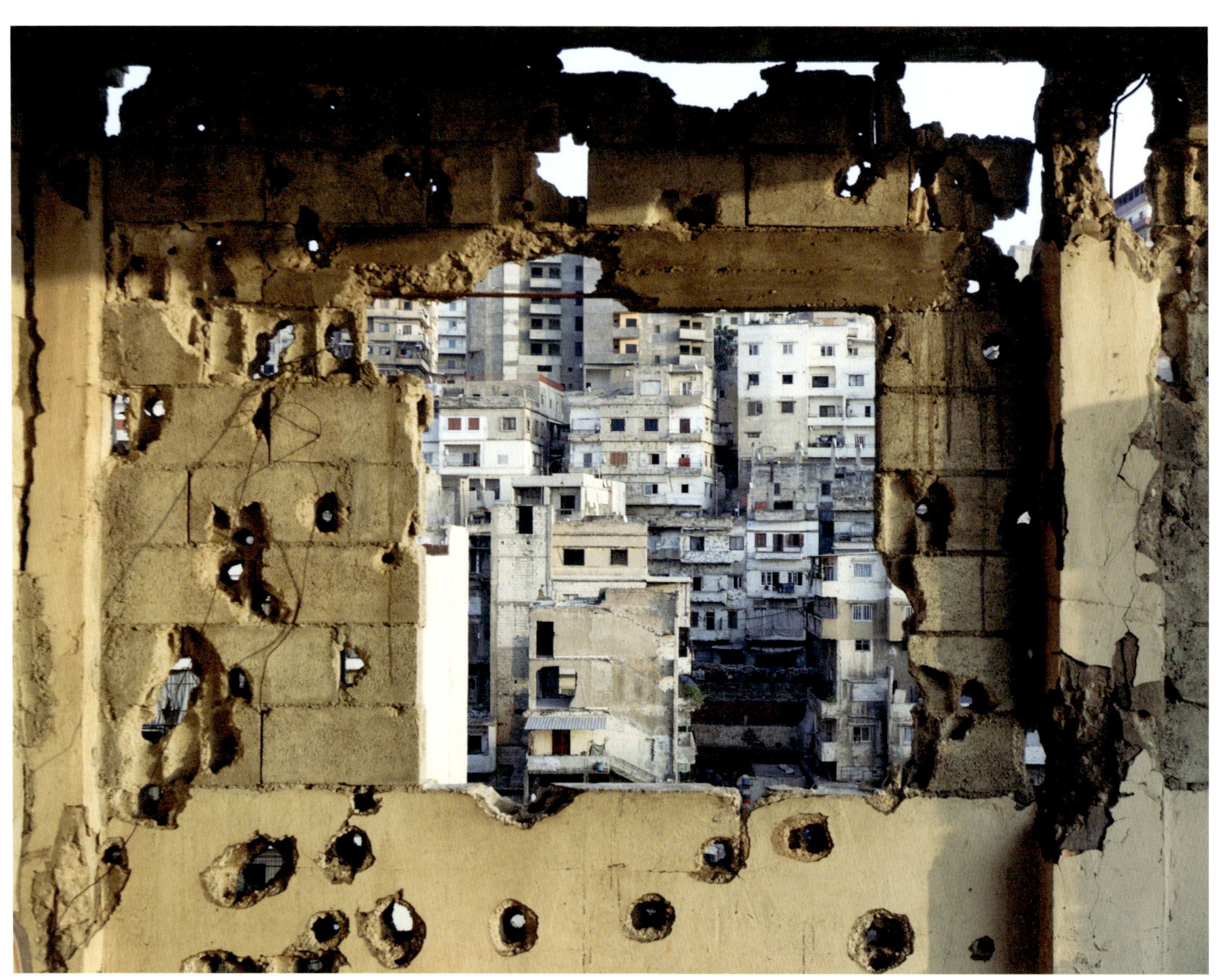

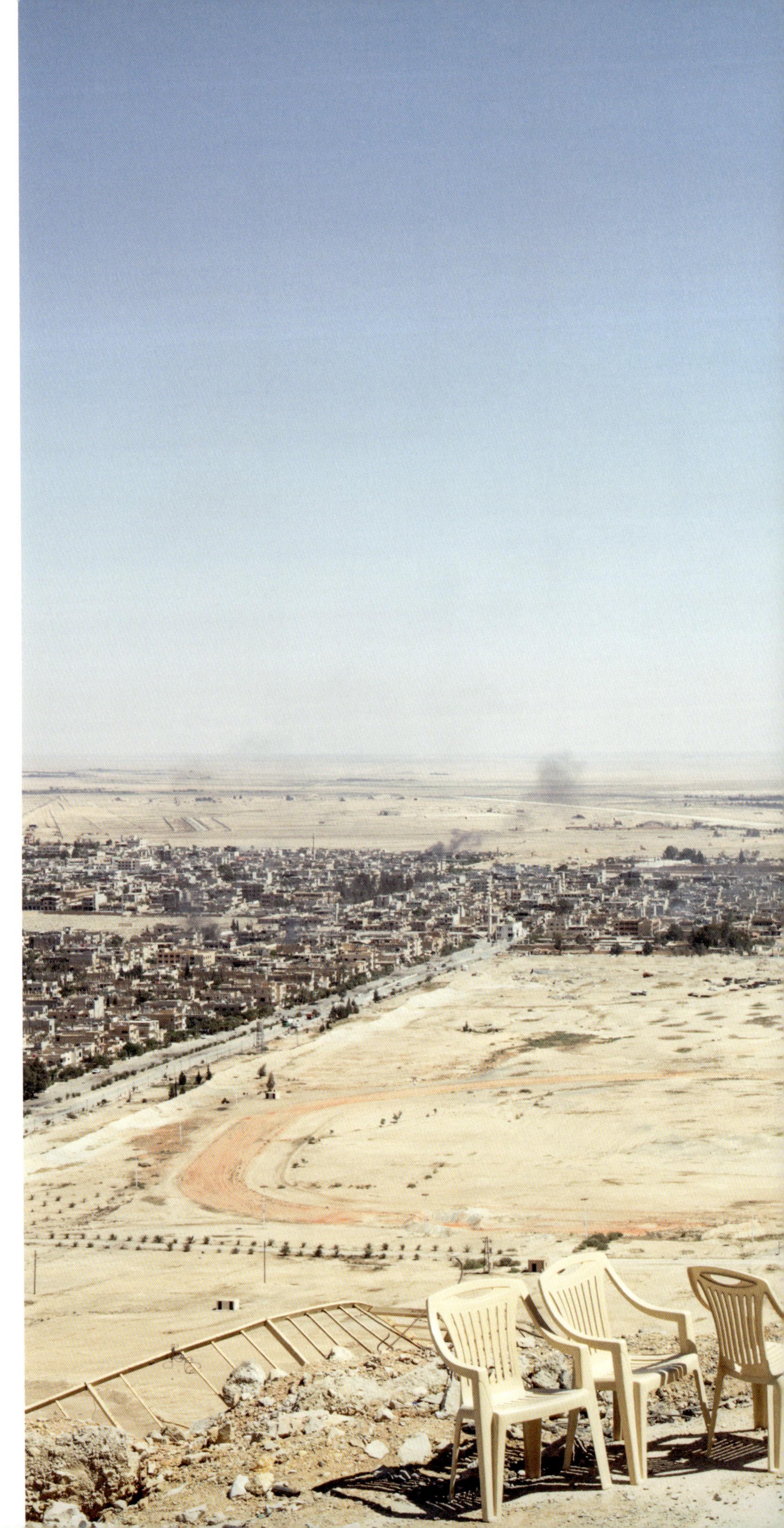

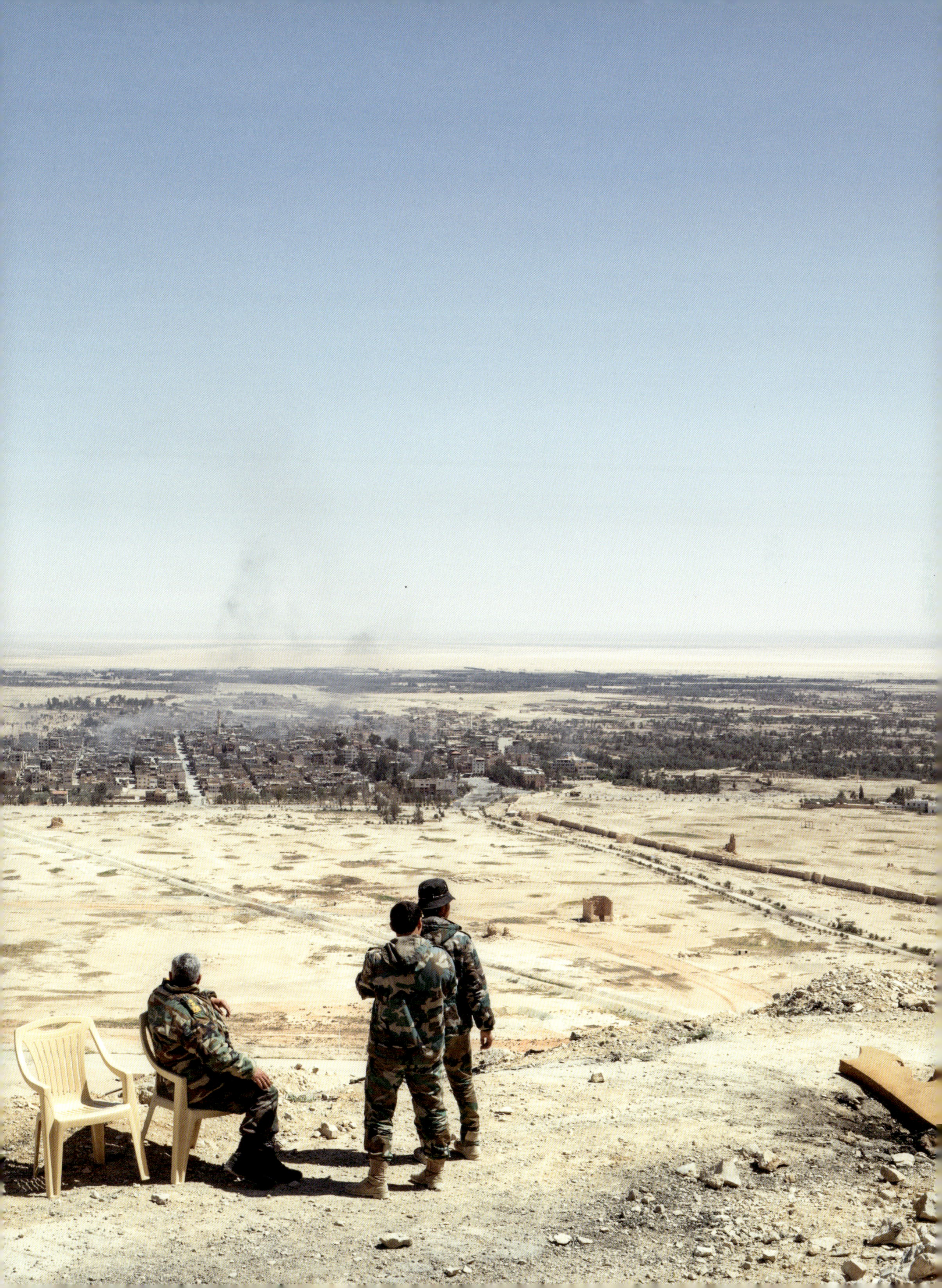

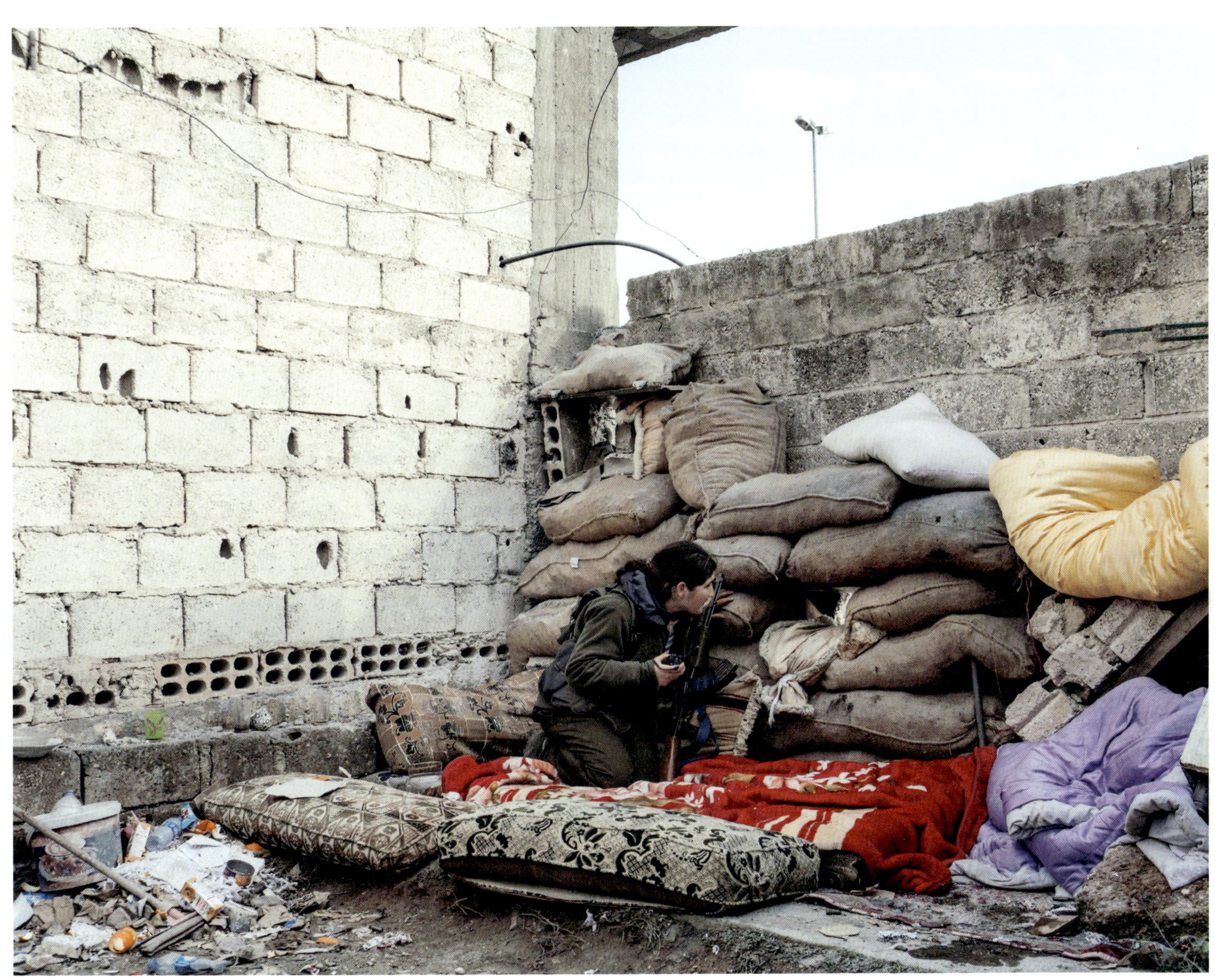

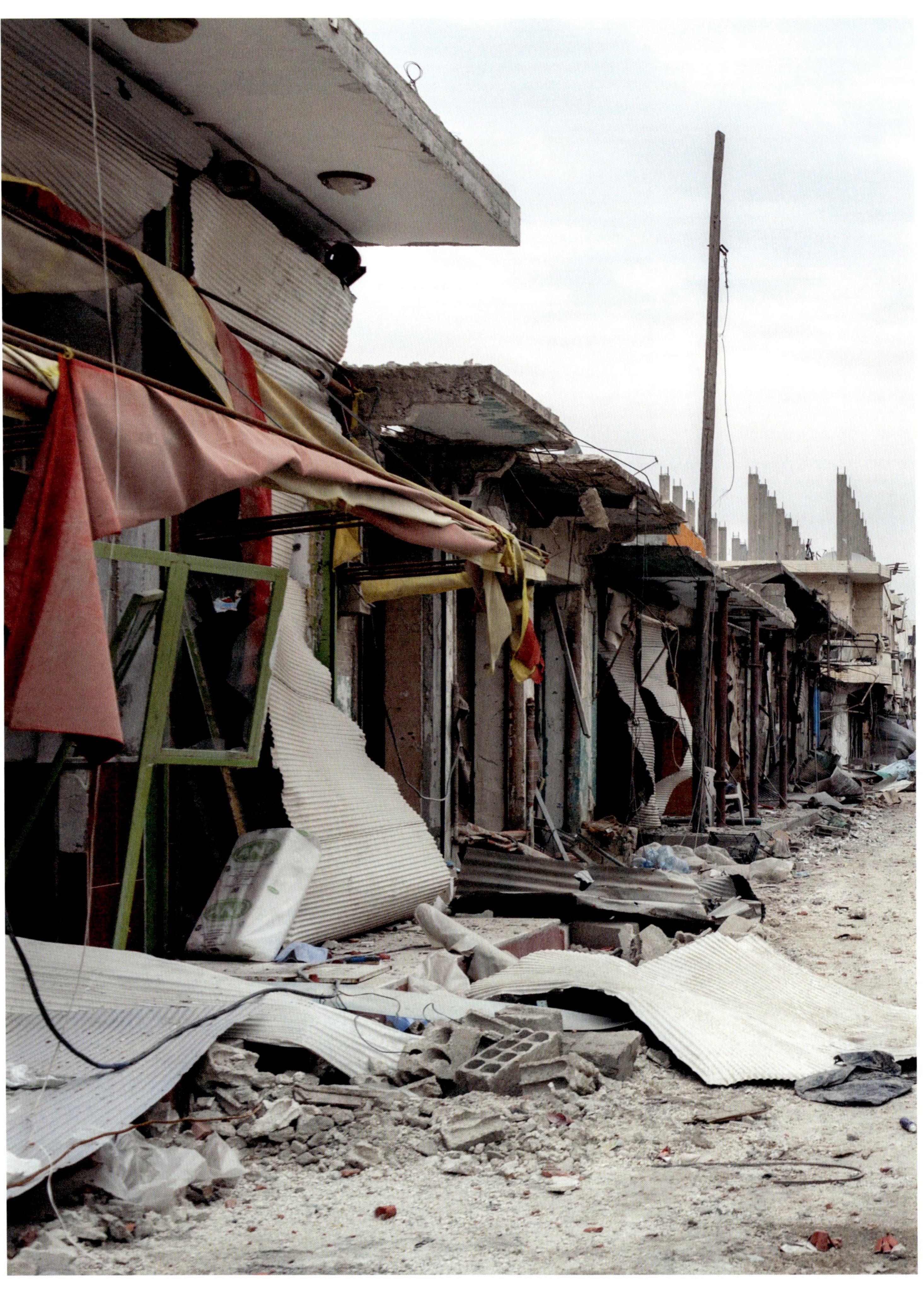

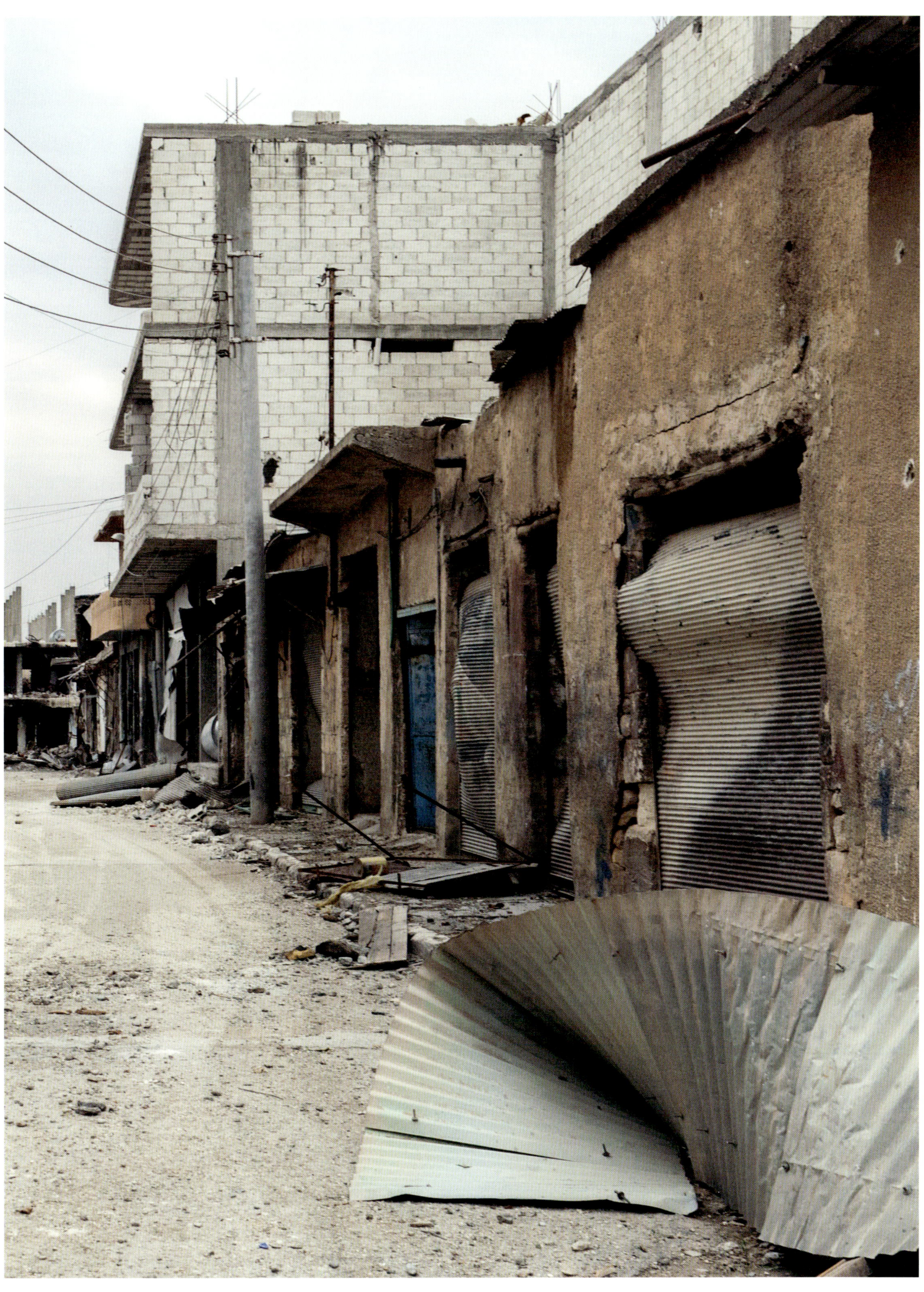

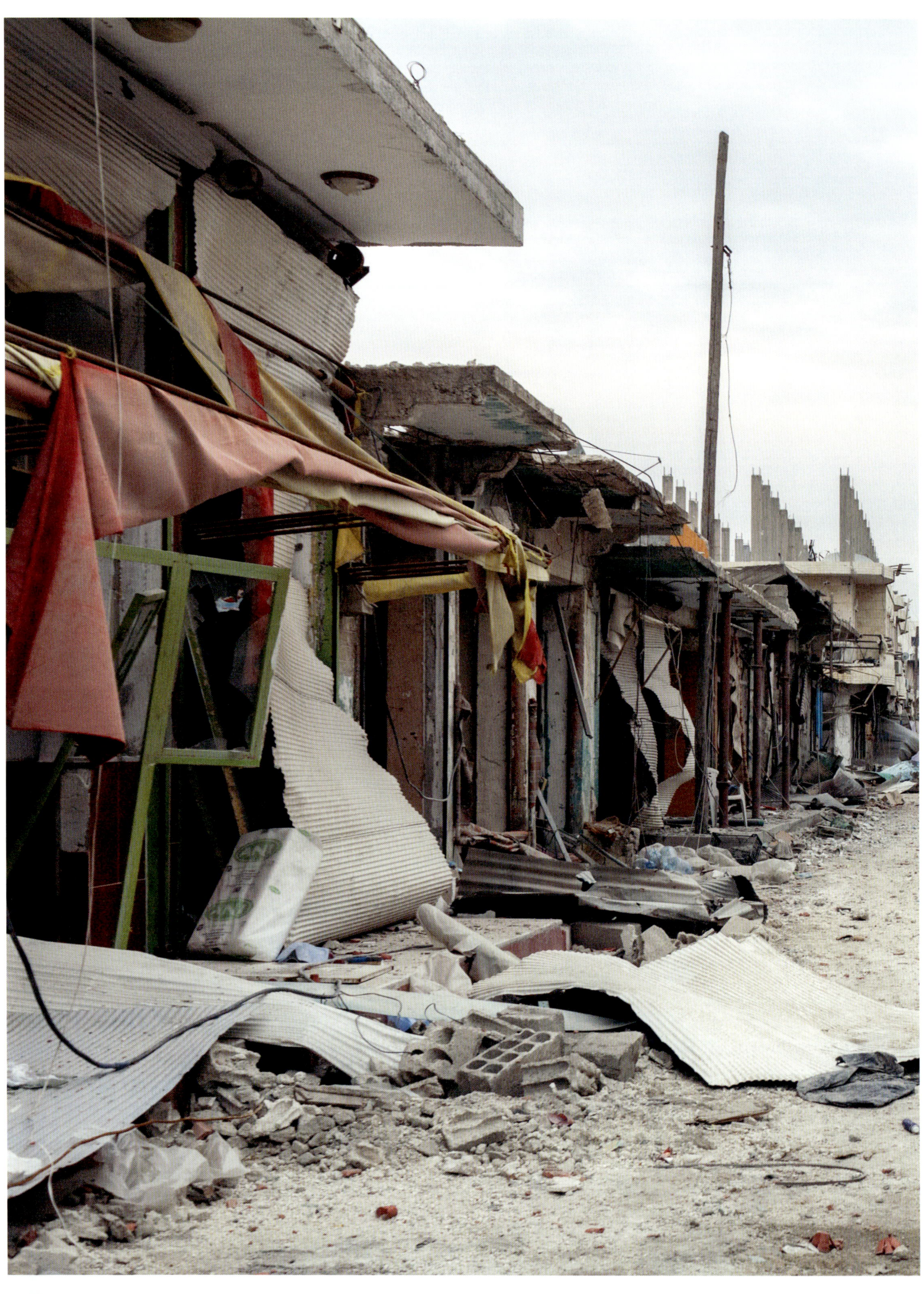

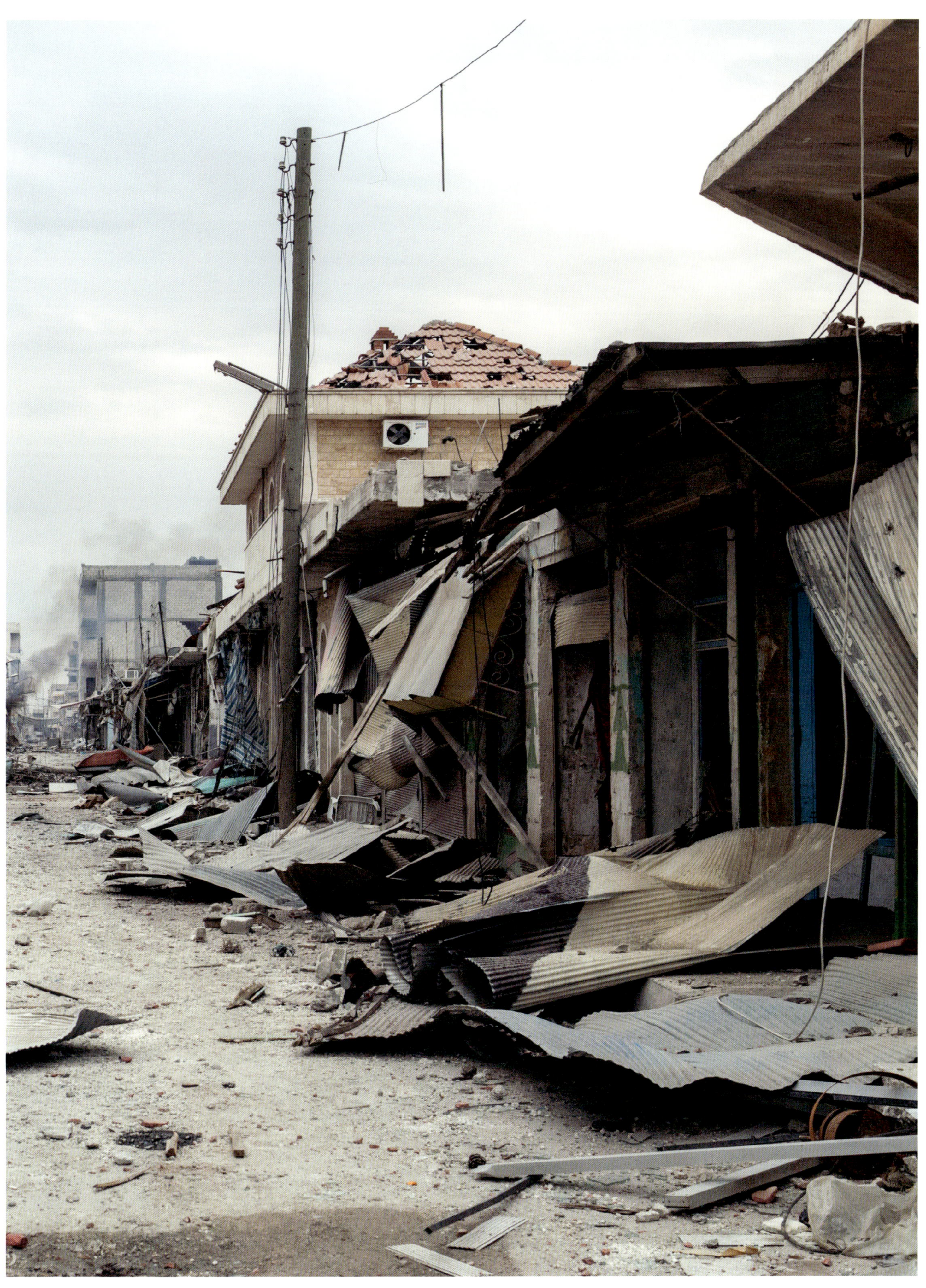

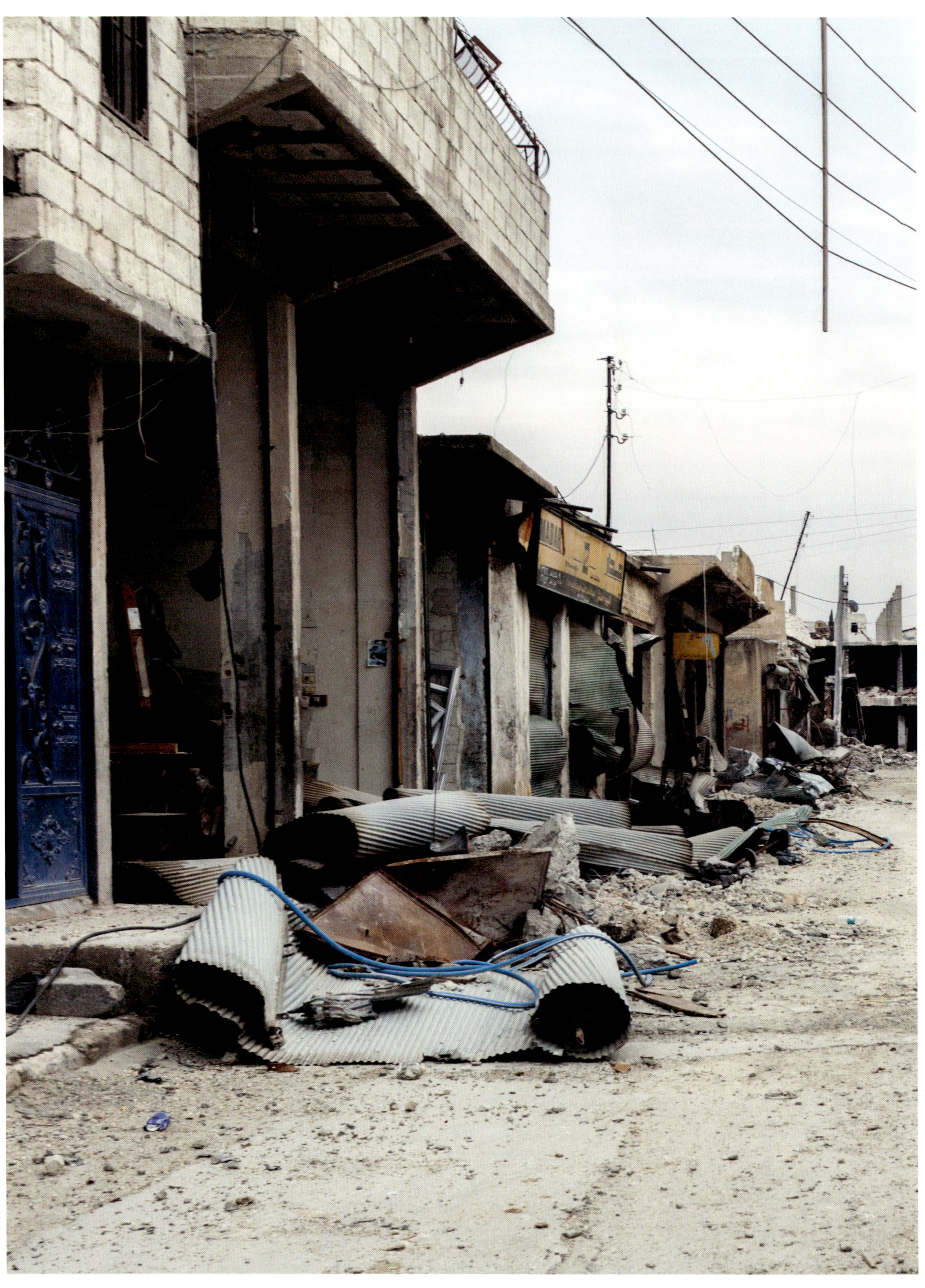

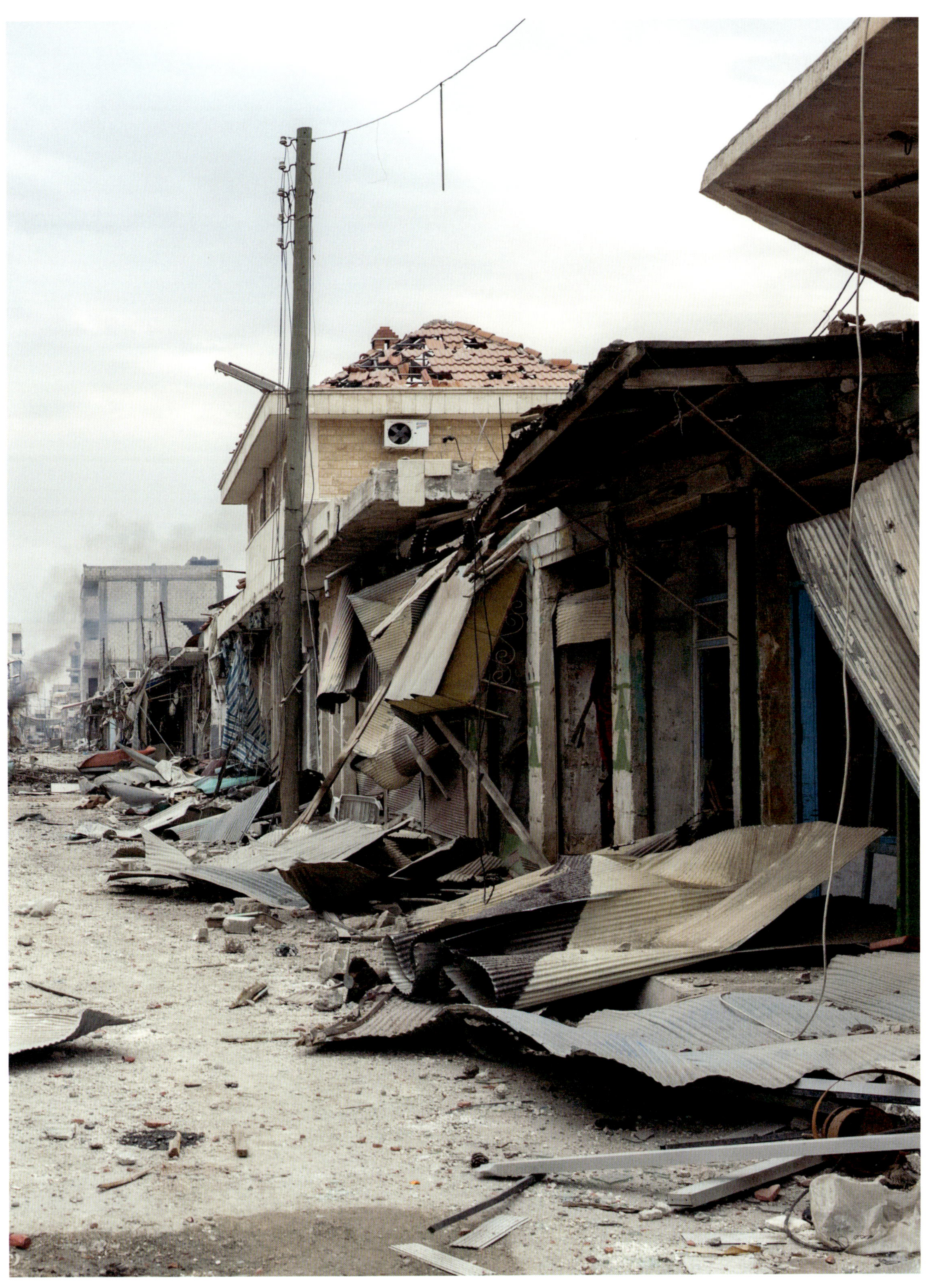

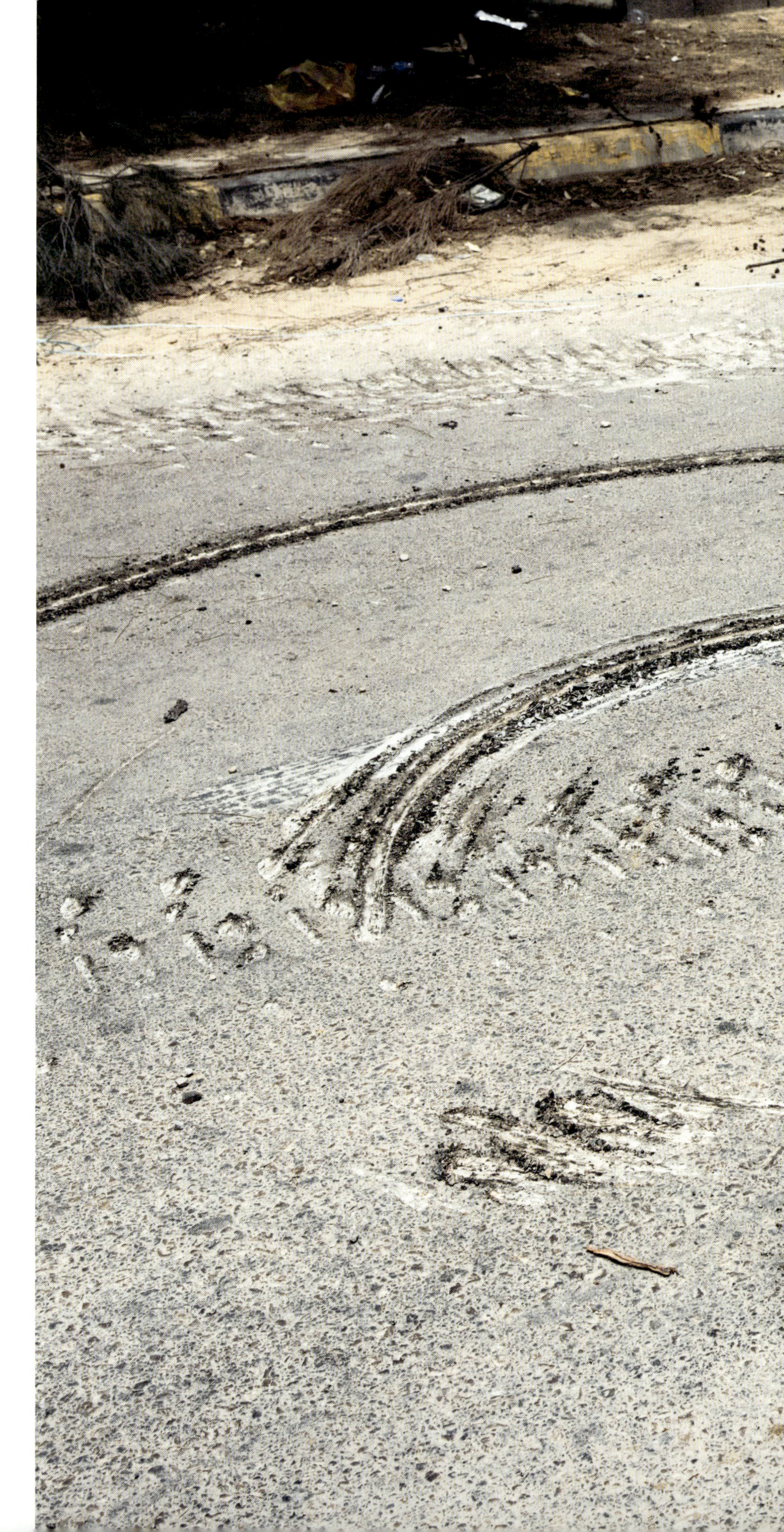

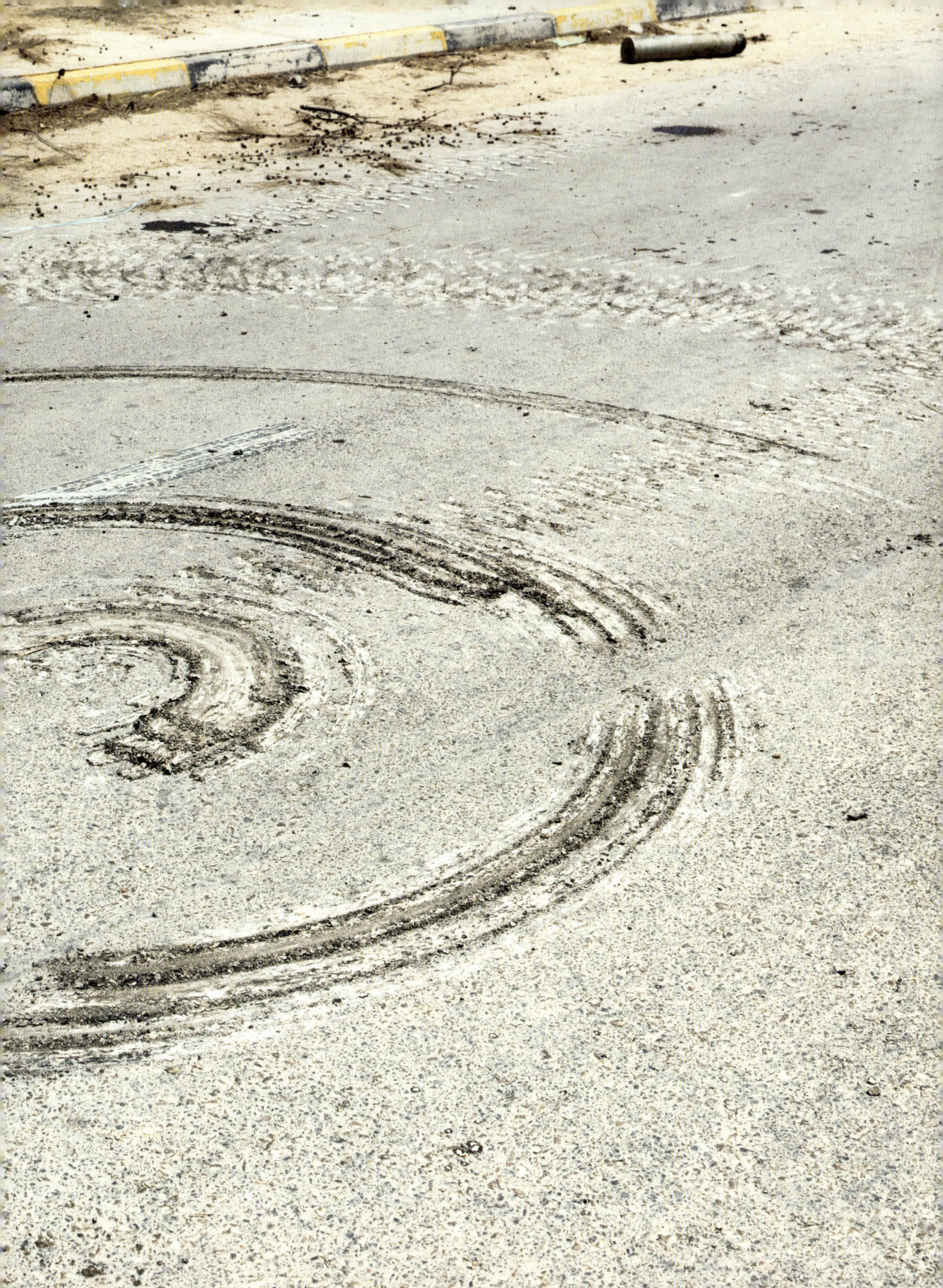

'HISTORY REPEATS ITSELF AND THE LOGIC THROUGHOUT THE AGES DOES NOT CHANGE.'

'PEOPLE CHANGE, ACTORS ARE CHANGED, TOOLS EVOLVE, BUT THE STAGE OF THE EVENTS IS CONSTANT AND THE STORY OF THE CONFLICT IS THE SAME.'

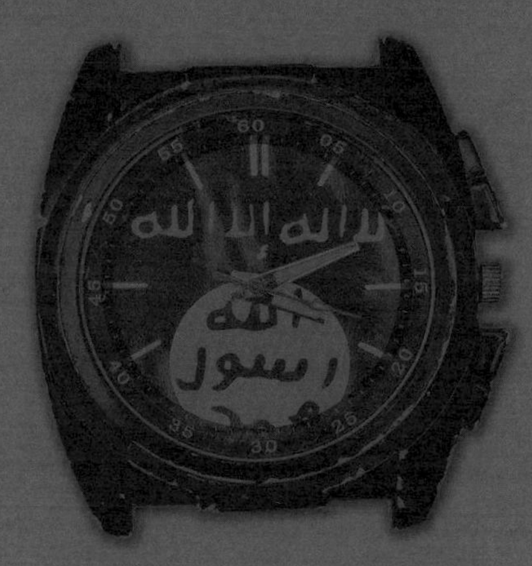
لا اله الا الله
الله
رسول

STEEL BACK MADE IN P.R.C. STAINLES

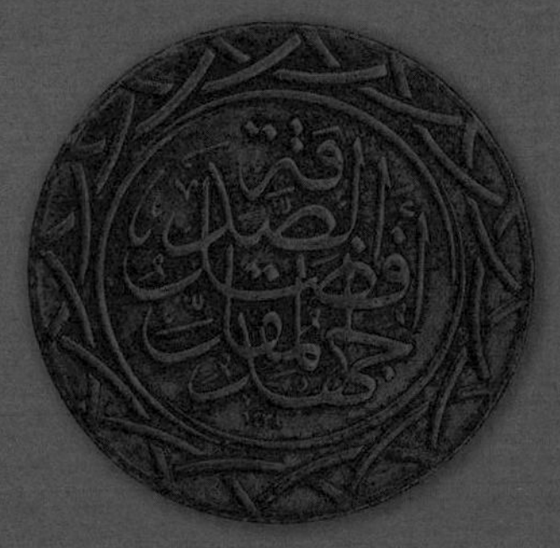

'DO NOT WORRY ABOUT MONEY OR ACCOMMODATIONS FOR YOURSELF AND YOUR FAMILY. THERE ARE PLENTY OF HOMES AND RESOURCES TO COVER YOU AND YOUR FAMILY.'

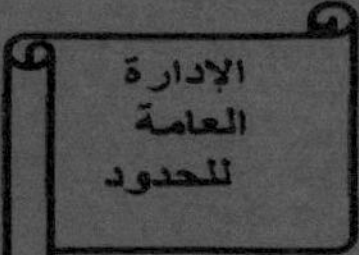

بسم الله الرحمن الرحيم
الدولة الإسلامية في العراق والشام
الإدارة العامة للحدود

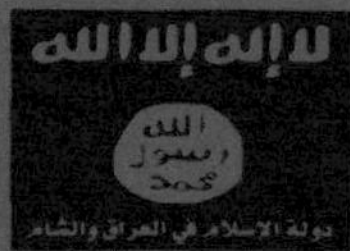

بيانات مجاهد

1	Name:	
2	Jihadi name:	
3	Mothers name:	
4	Blood type:	
5	Date of birth and nationality:	
6	Marital status:	
7	Address and place of residence:	
8	Level of education:	
9	Level of sharia knowledge:	
10	Job before coming:	
11	Countries you travelled to and duration:	
12	Border post you entered and contact:	
13	Recommended and by who:	
14	Date of entry:	
15	Did you on jihad before and where:	
!6	Fighter/suicide/ingemasi(fight till death)	
17	Specific skills:	
18	Current place of work:	
19	What did you leave at deposit office:	
20	Level of obedience:	
21	Address that we can contact:	
22	Date and place of death:	
23	Notes:	

مسوول الحدود

الدولة الإسلامية في العراق والشام _ سري _

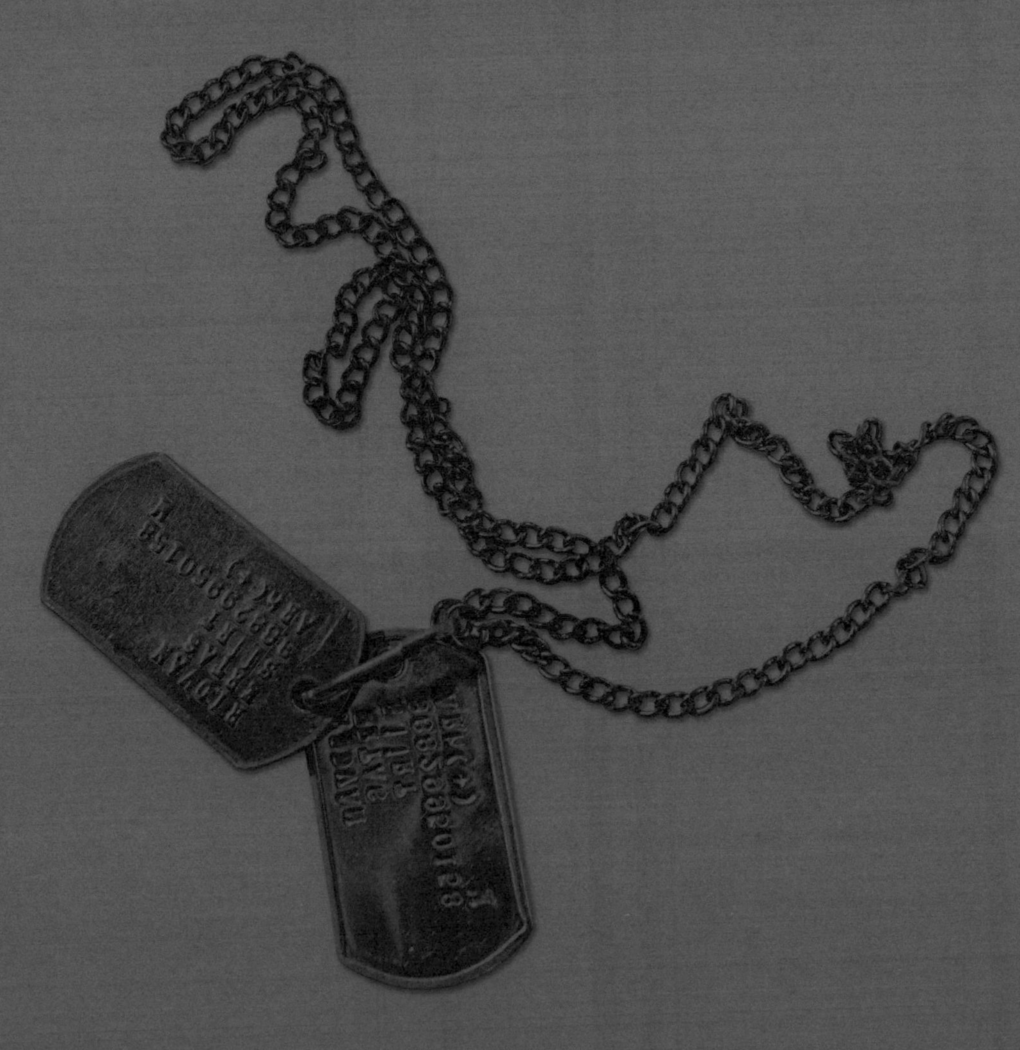

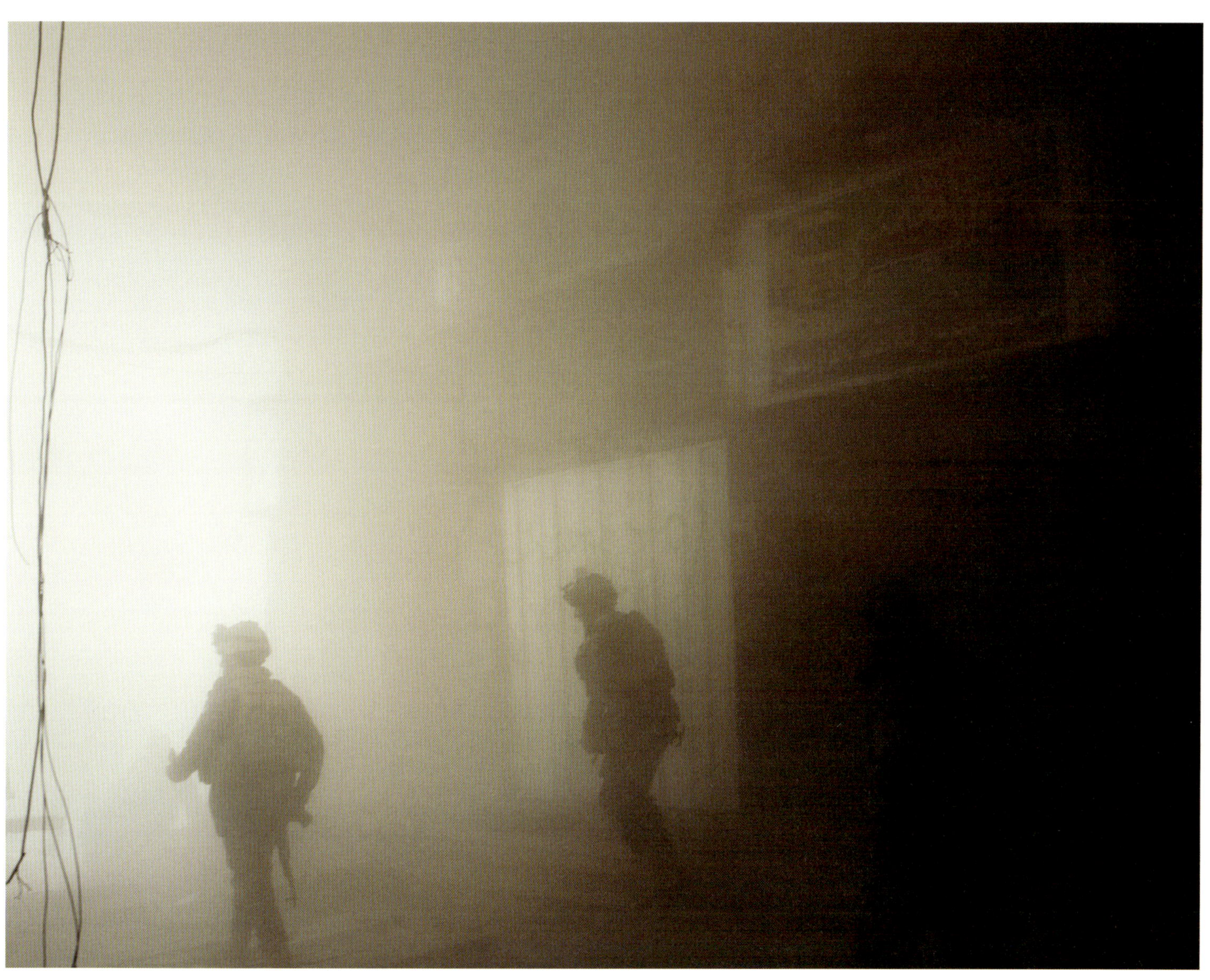

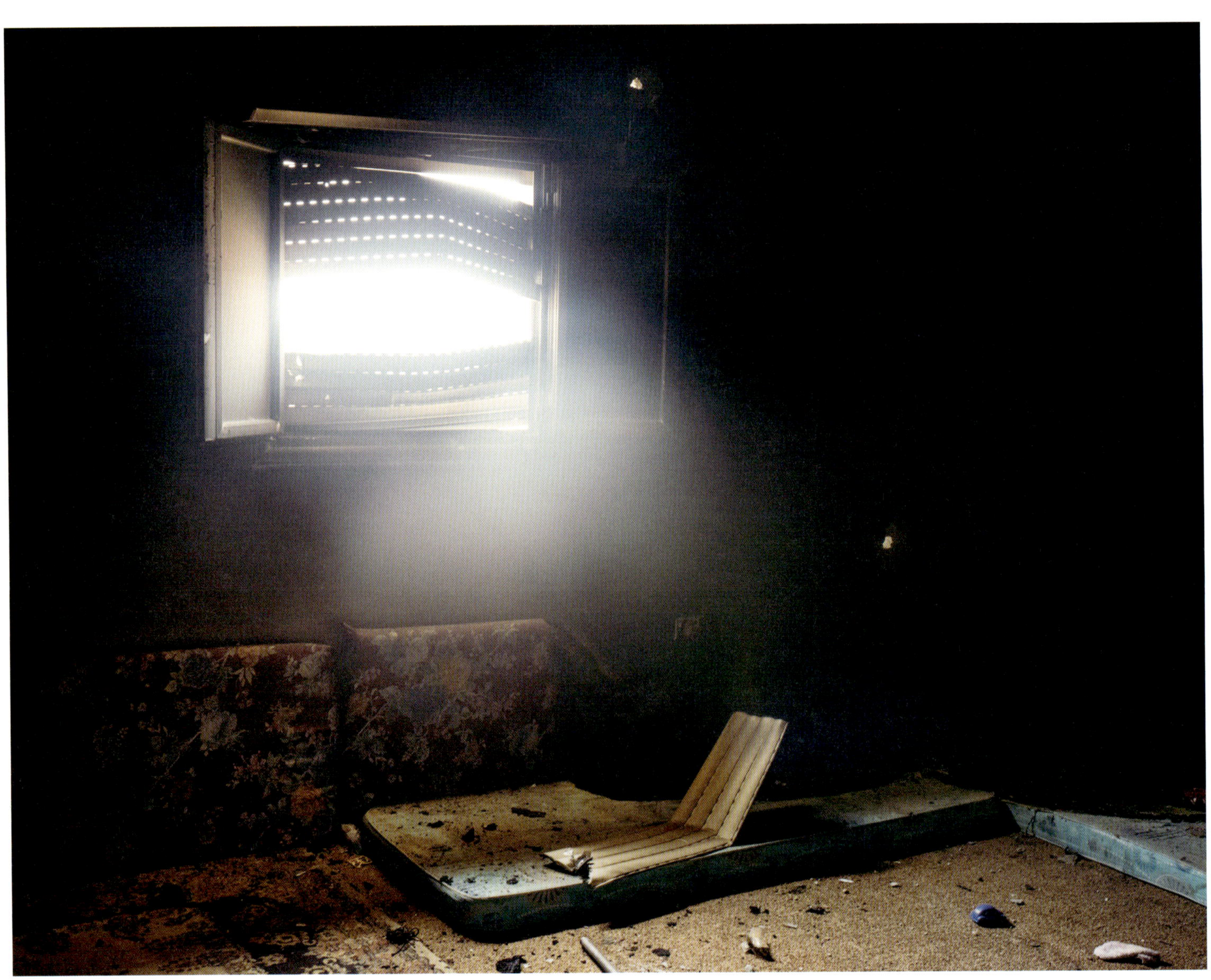

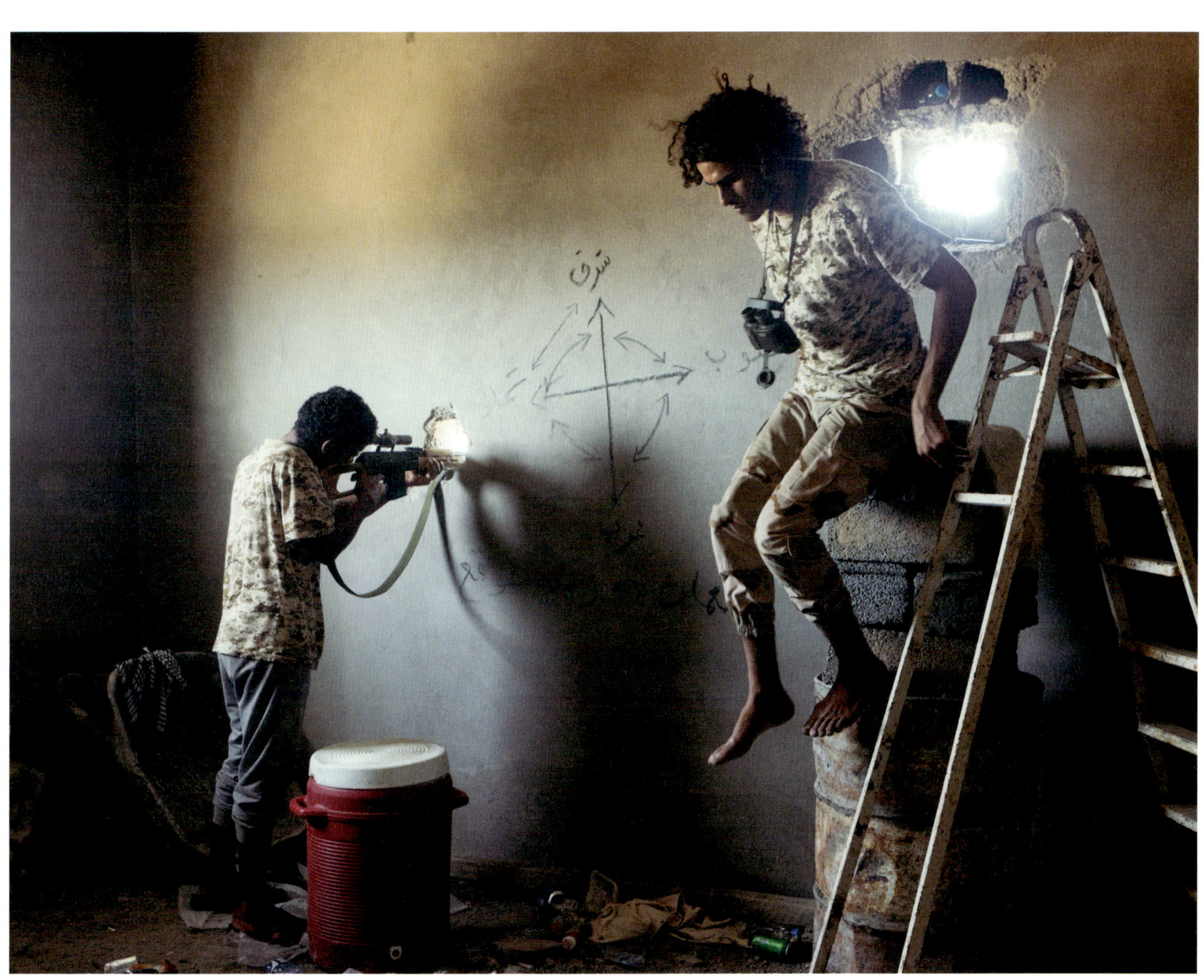

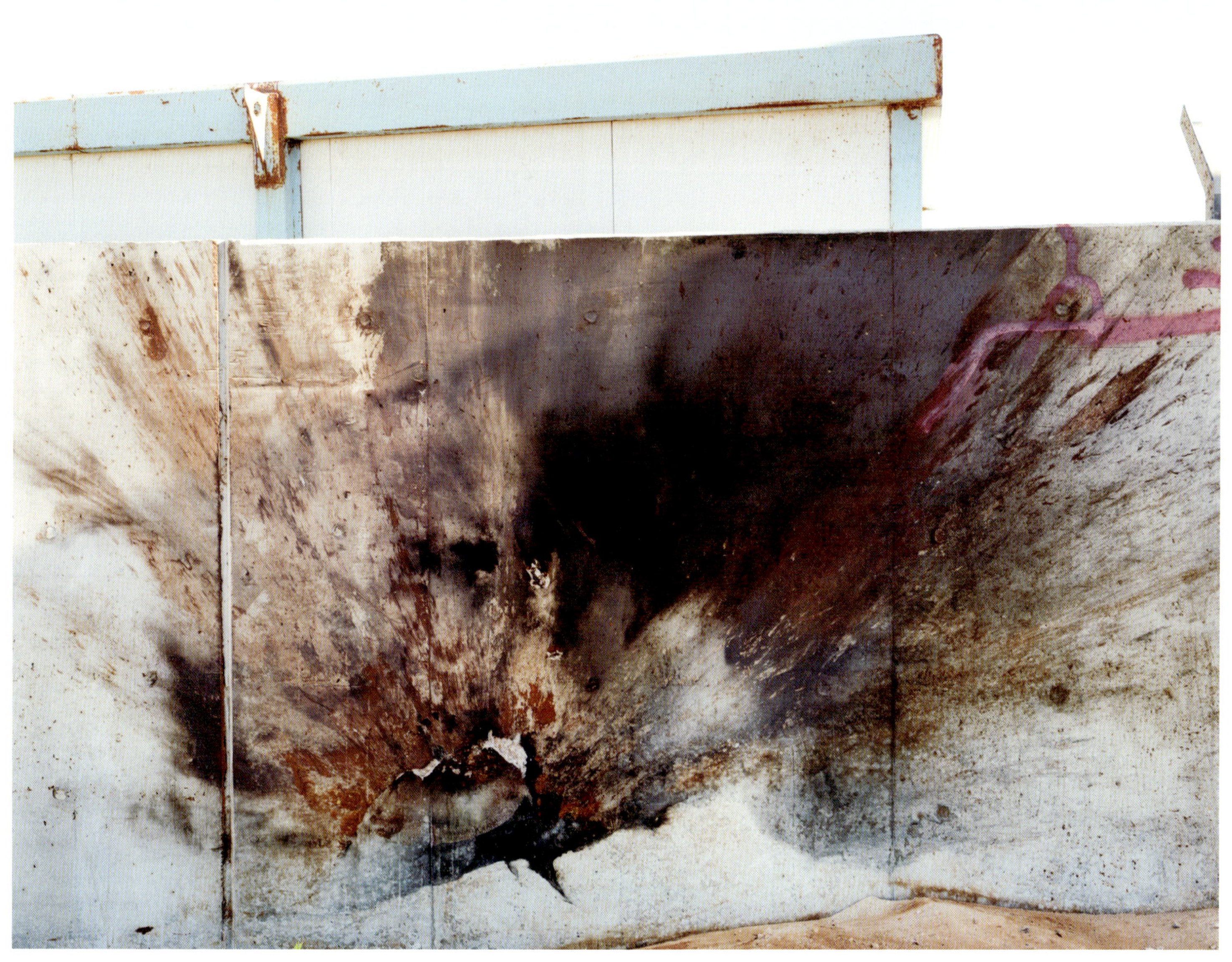

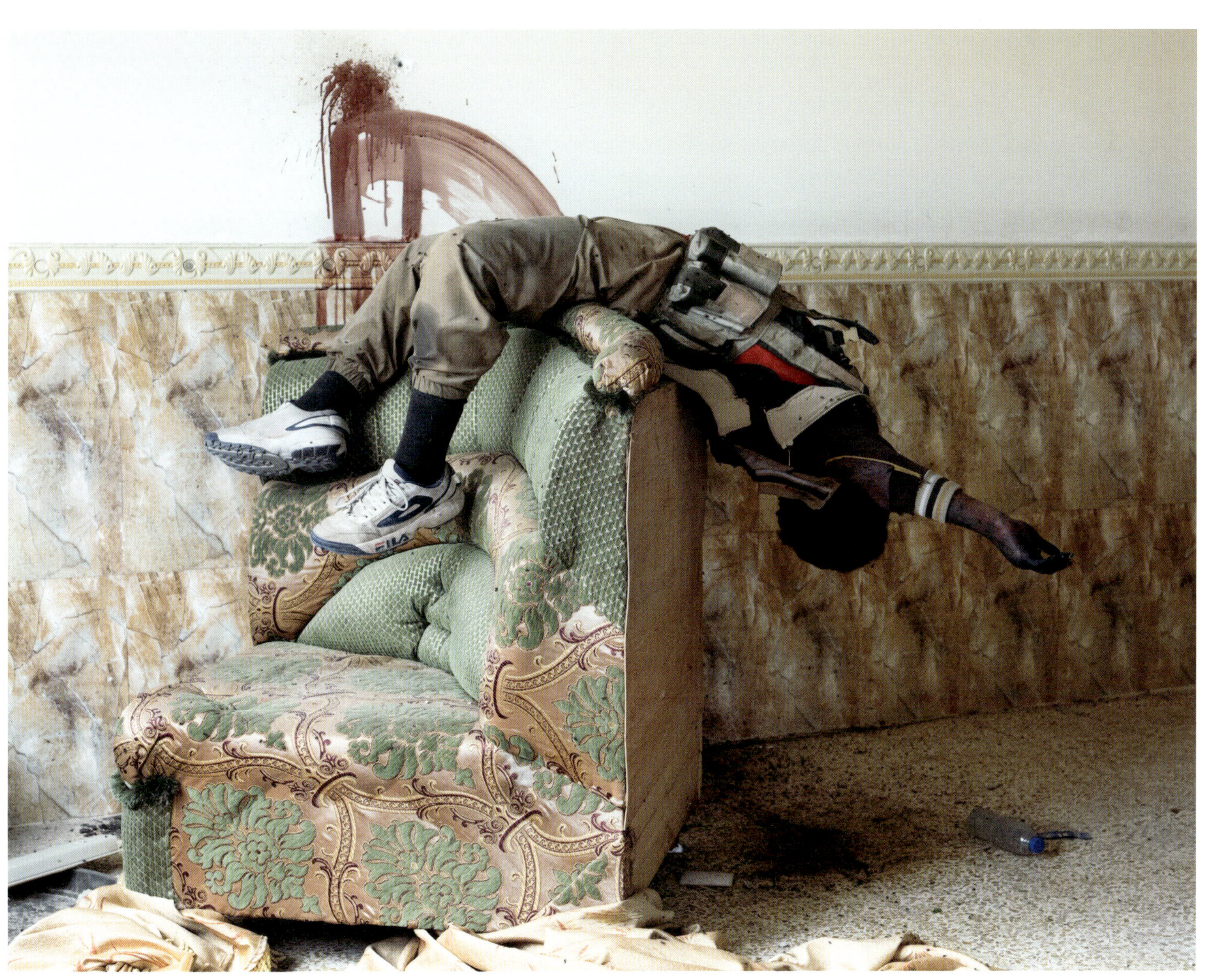
FILA

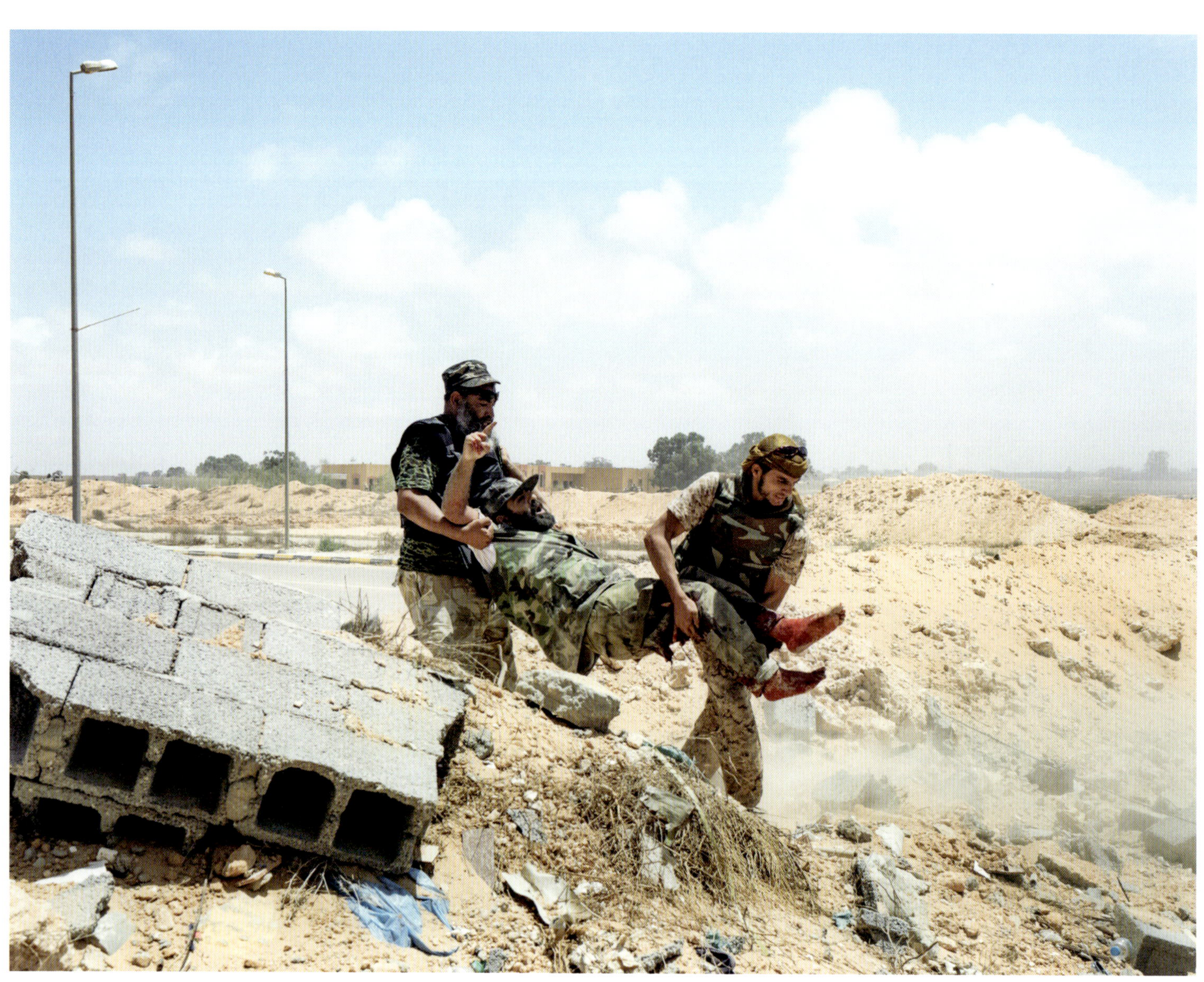

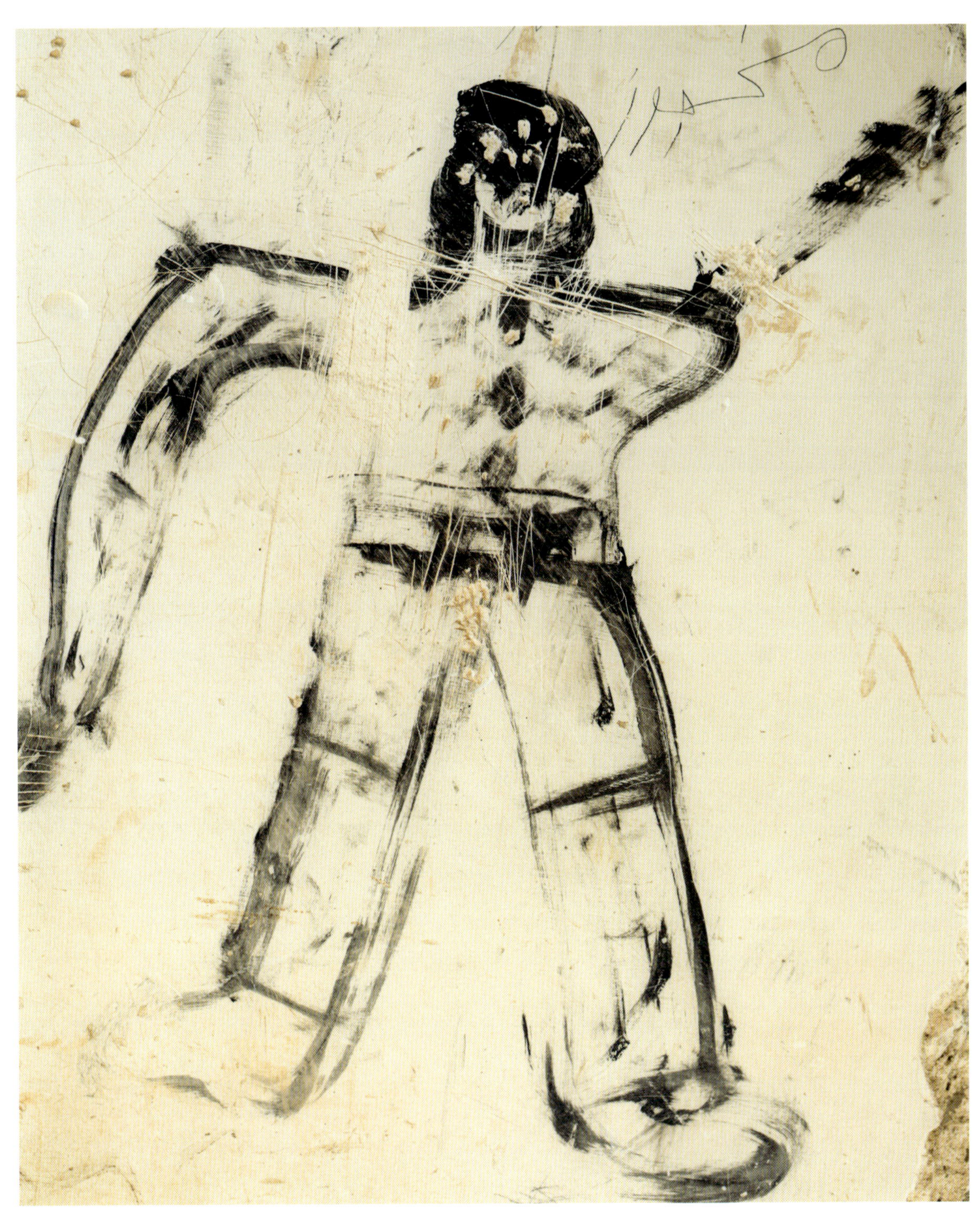

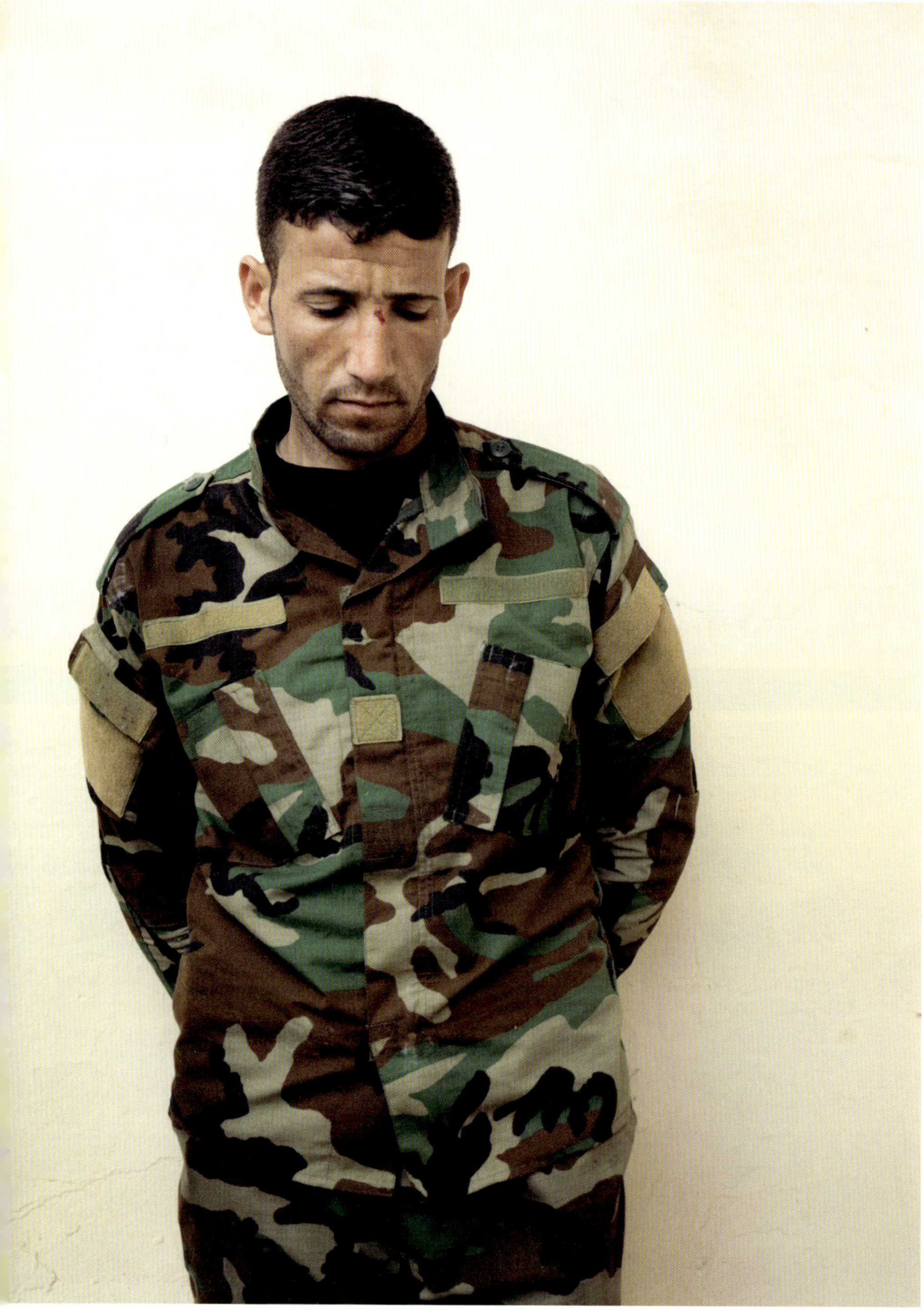

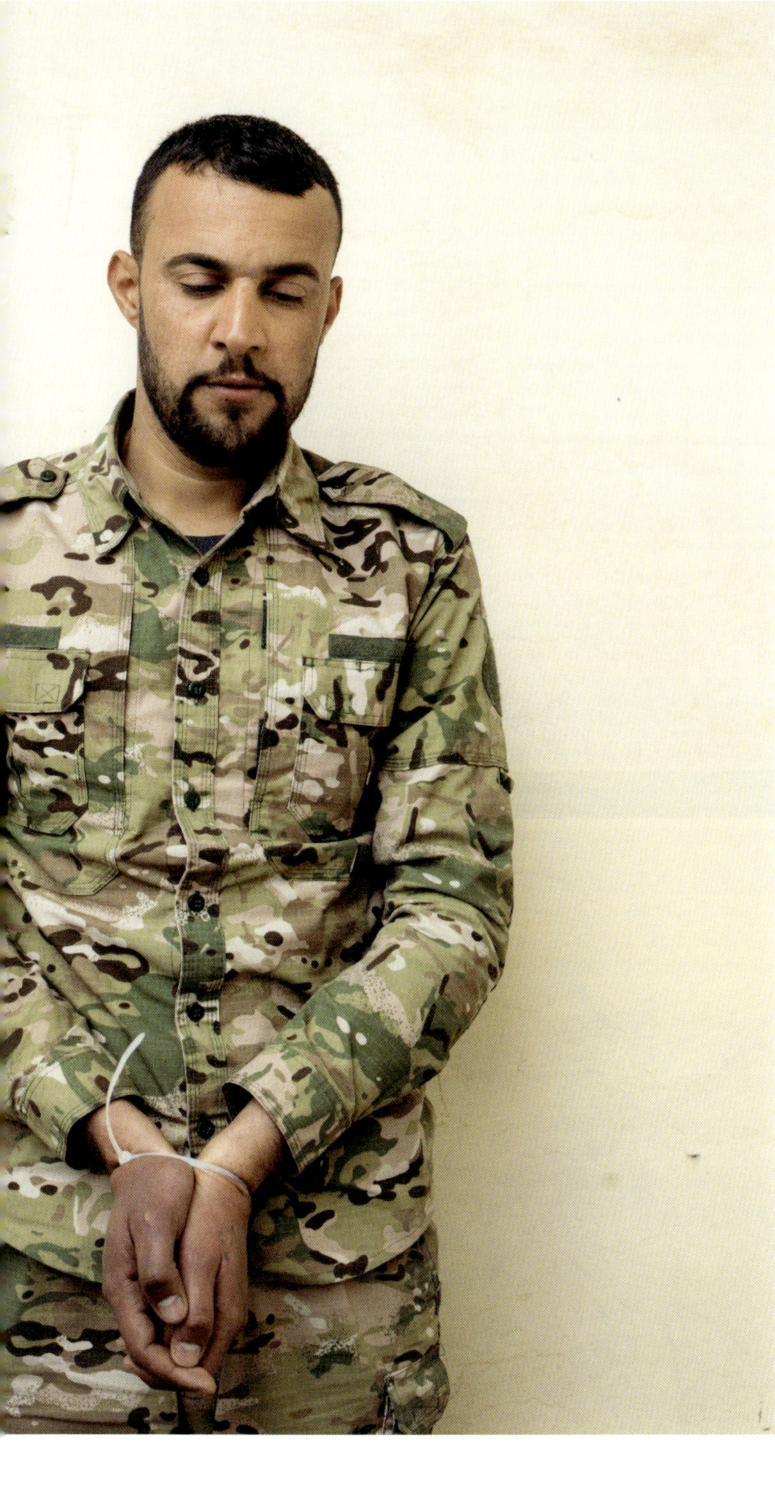

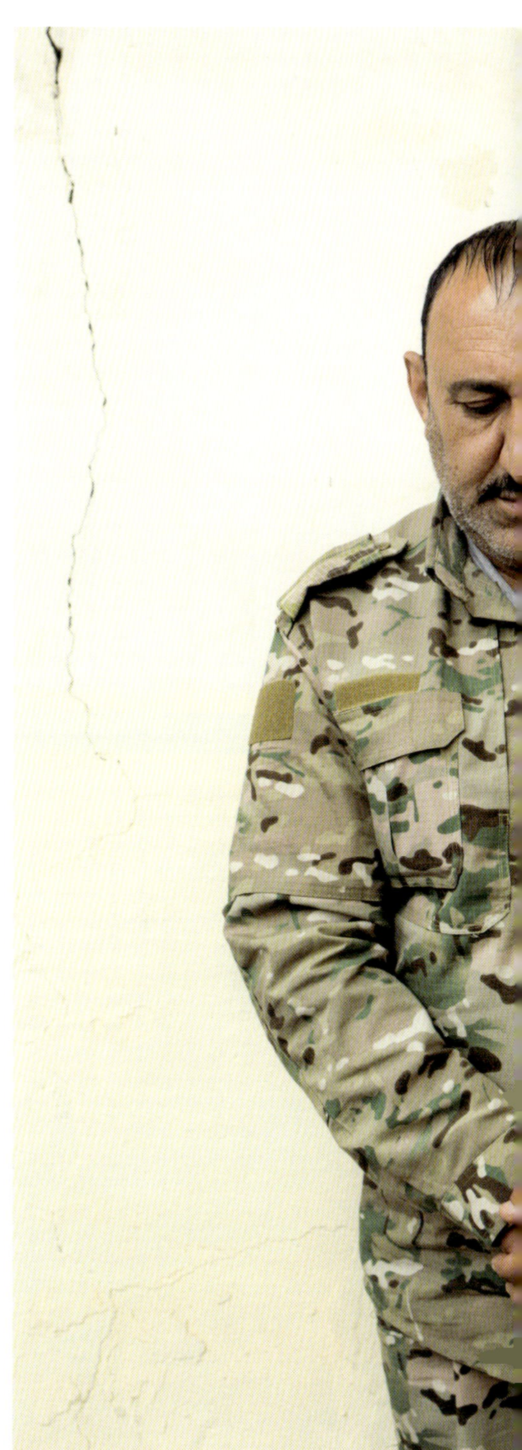

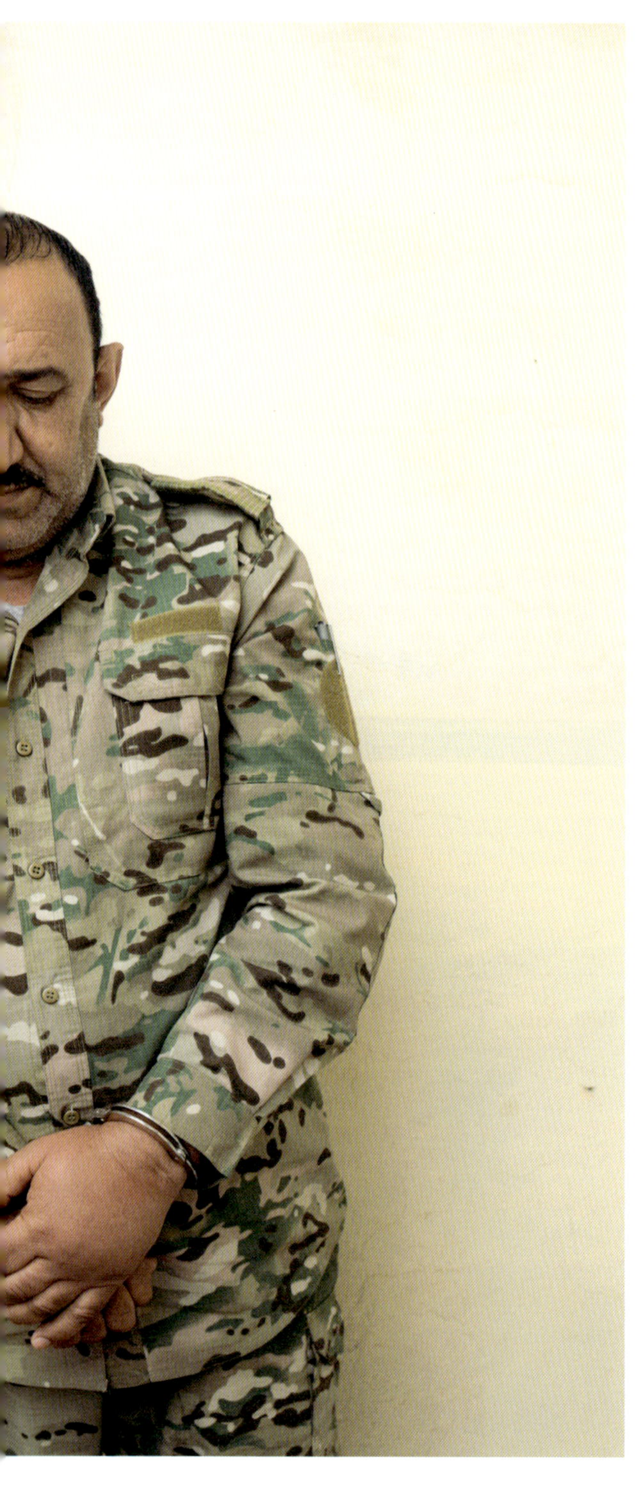

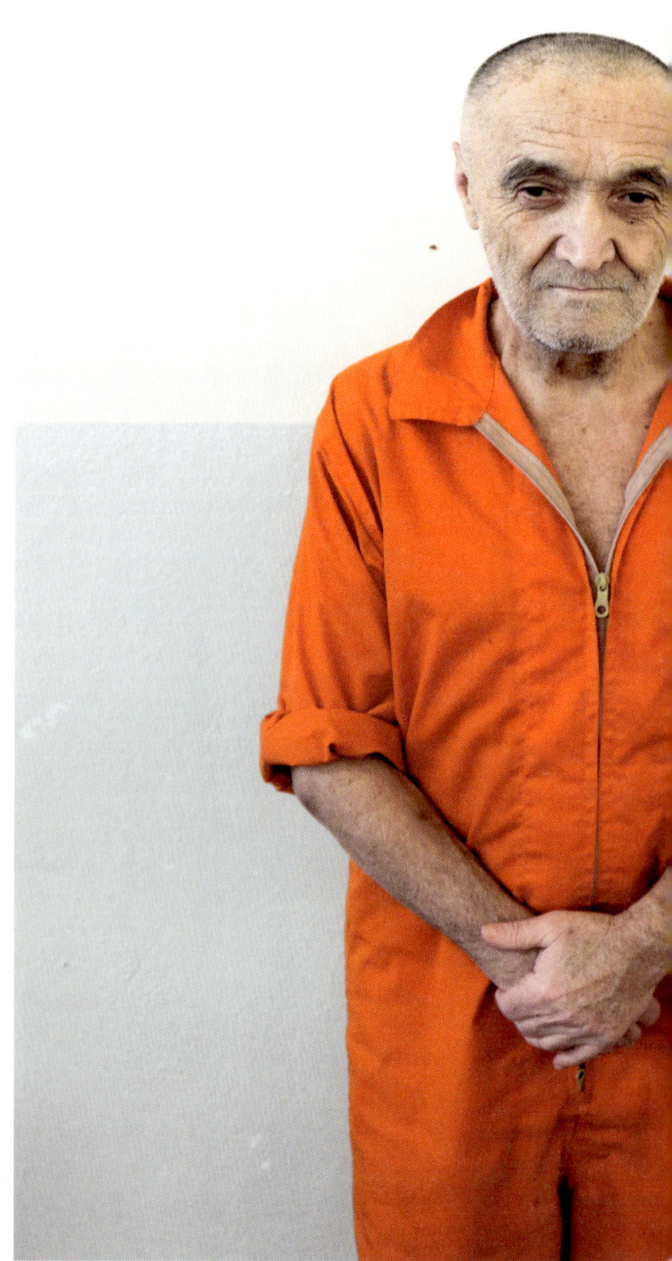

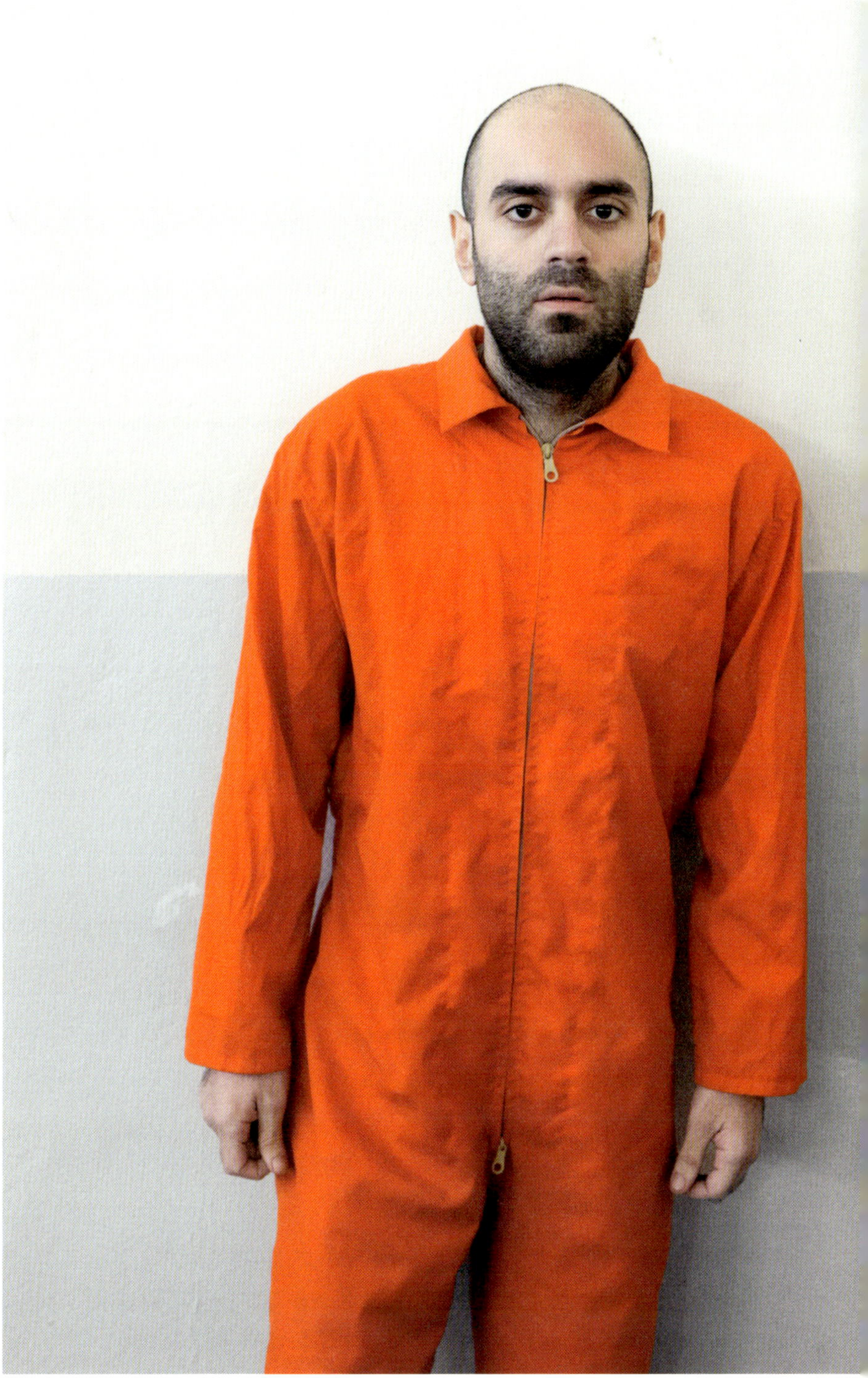

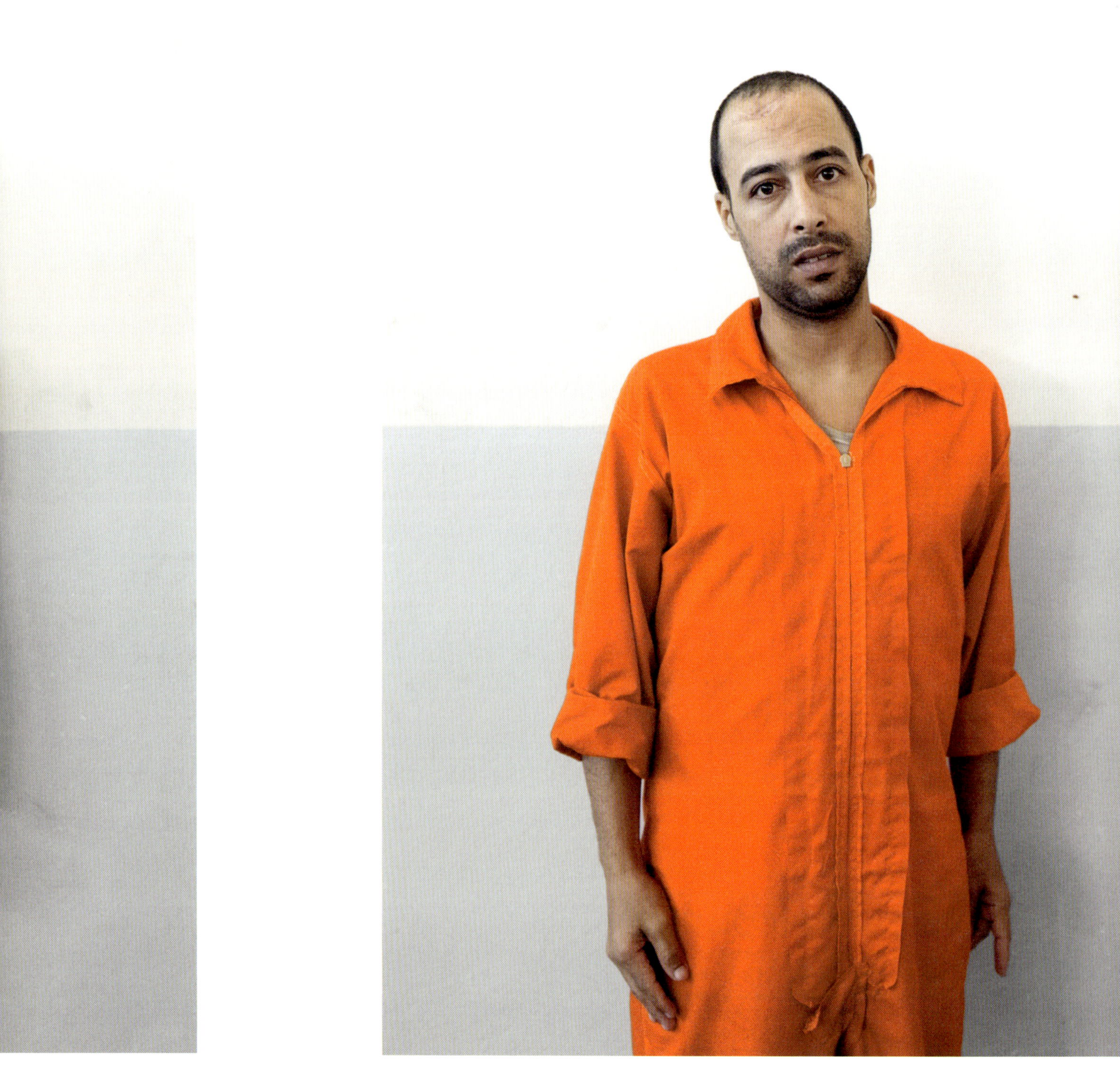

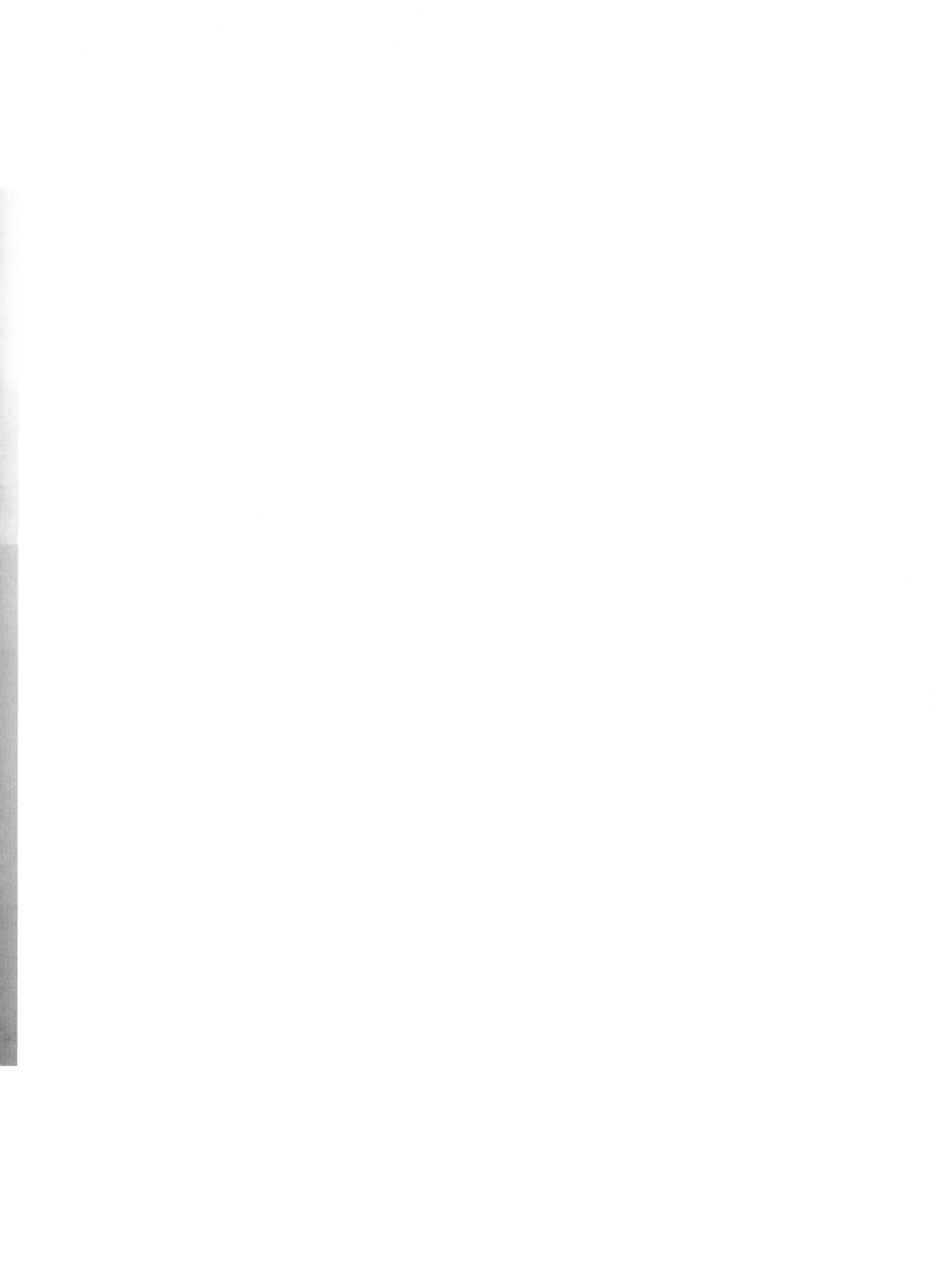

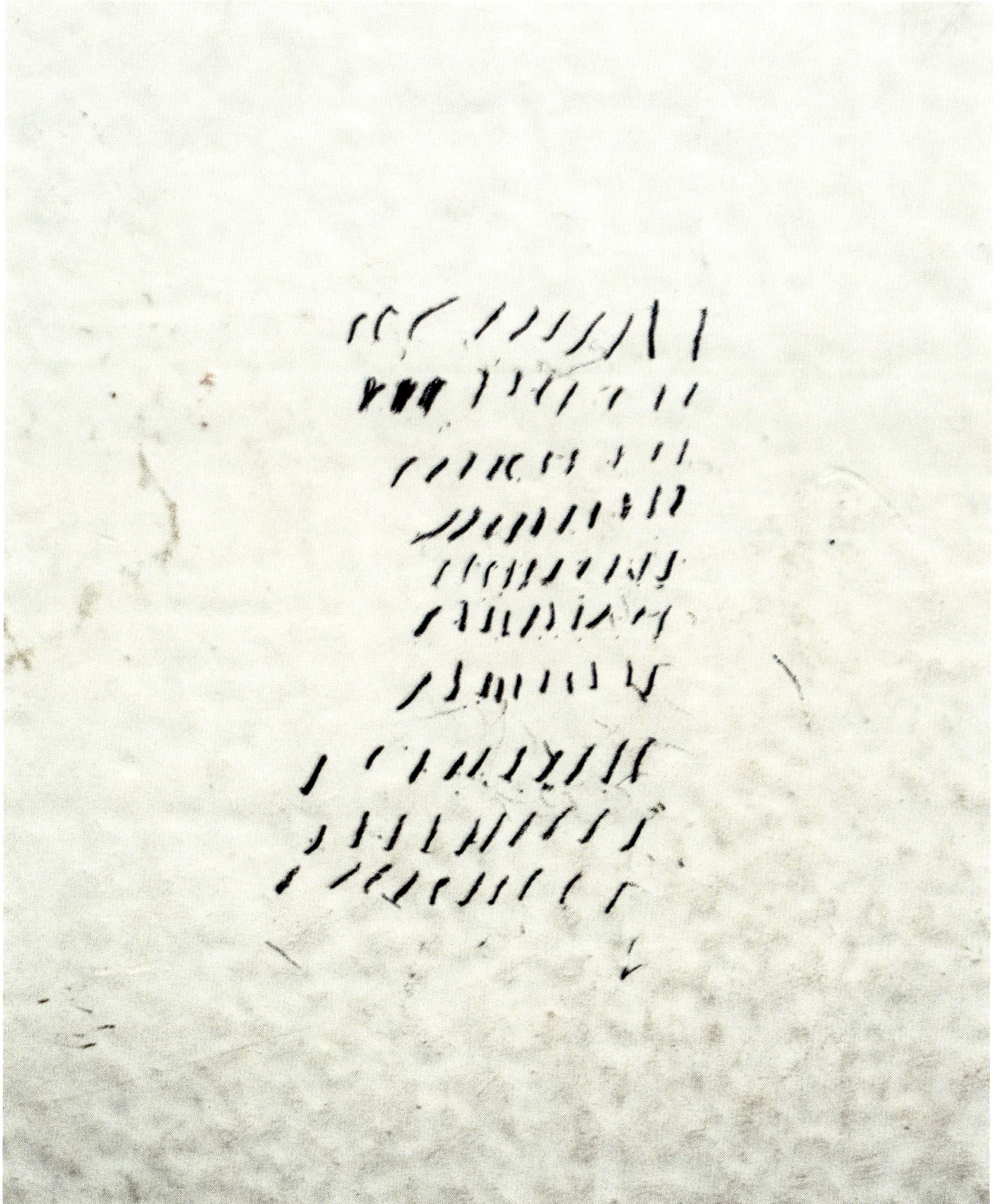

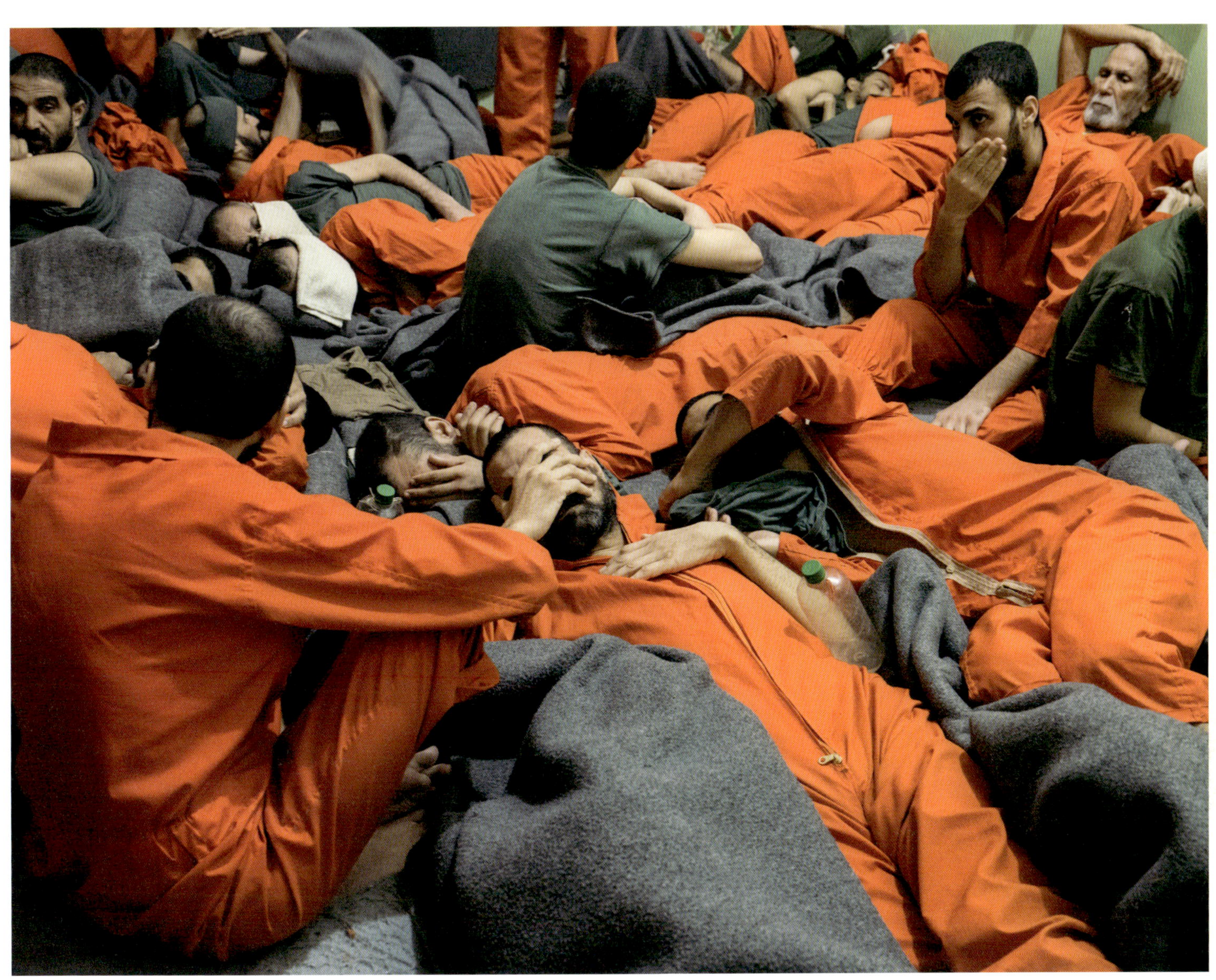

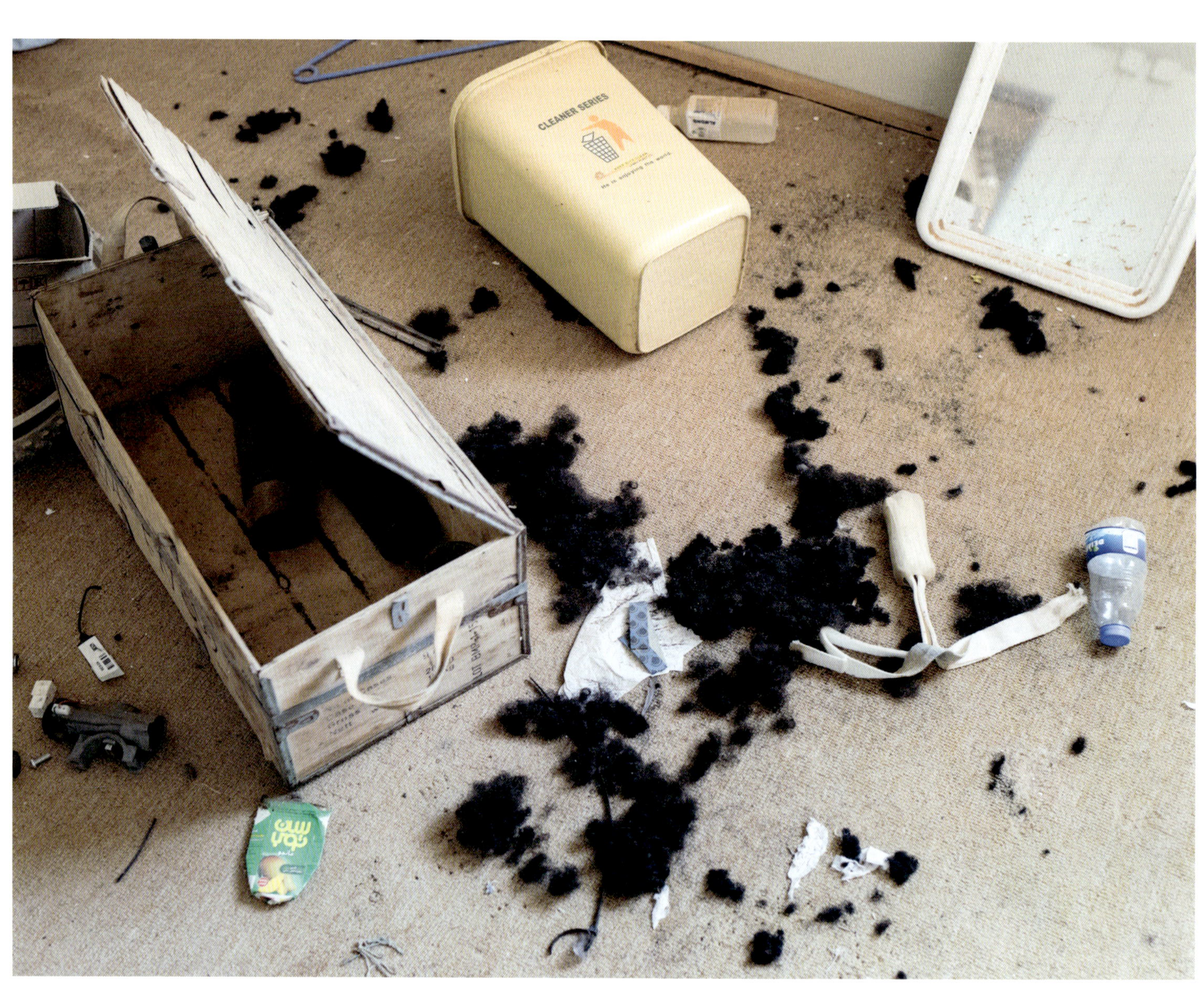
CLEANER SERIES
He is enjoying the world

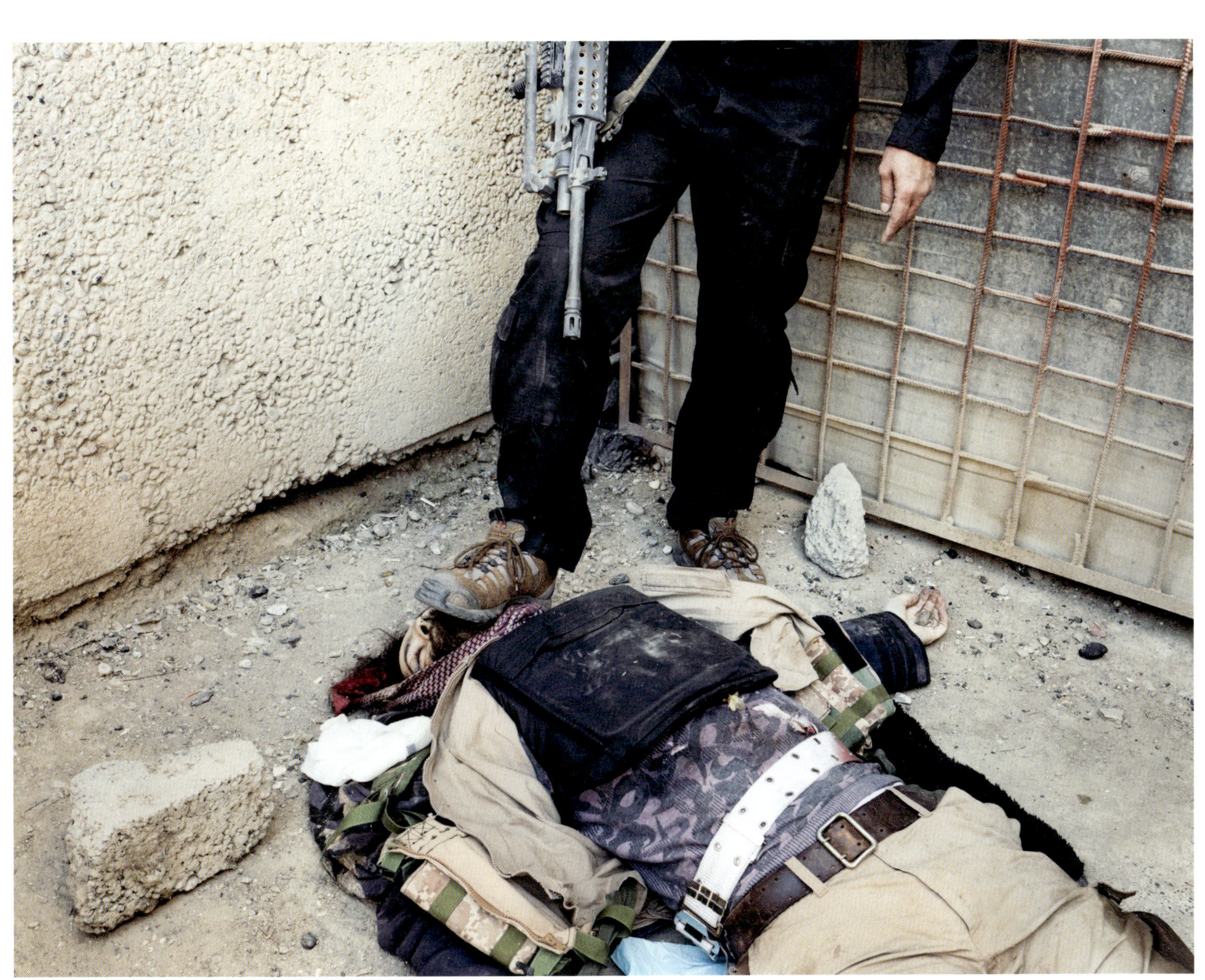

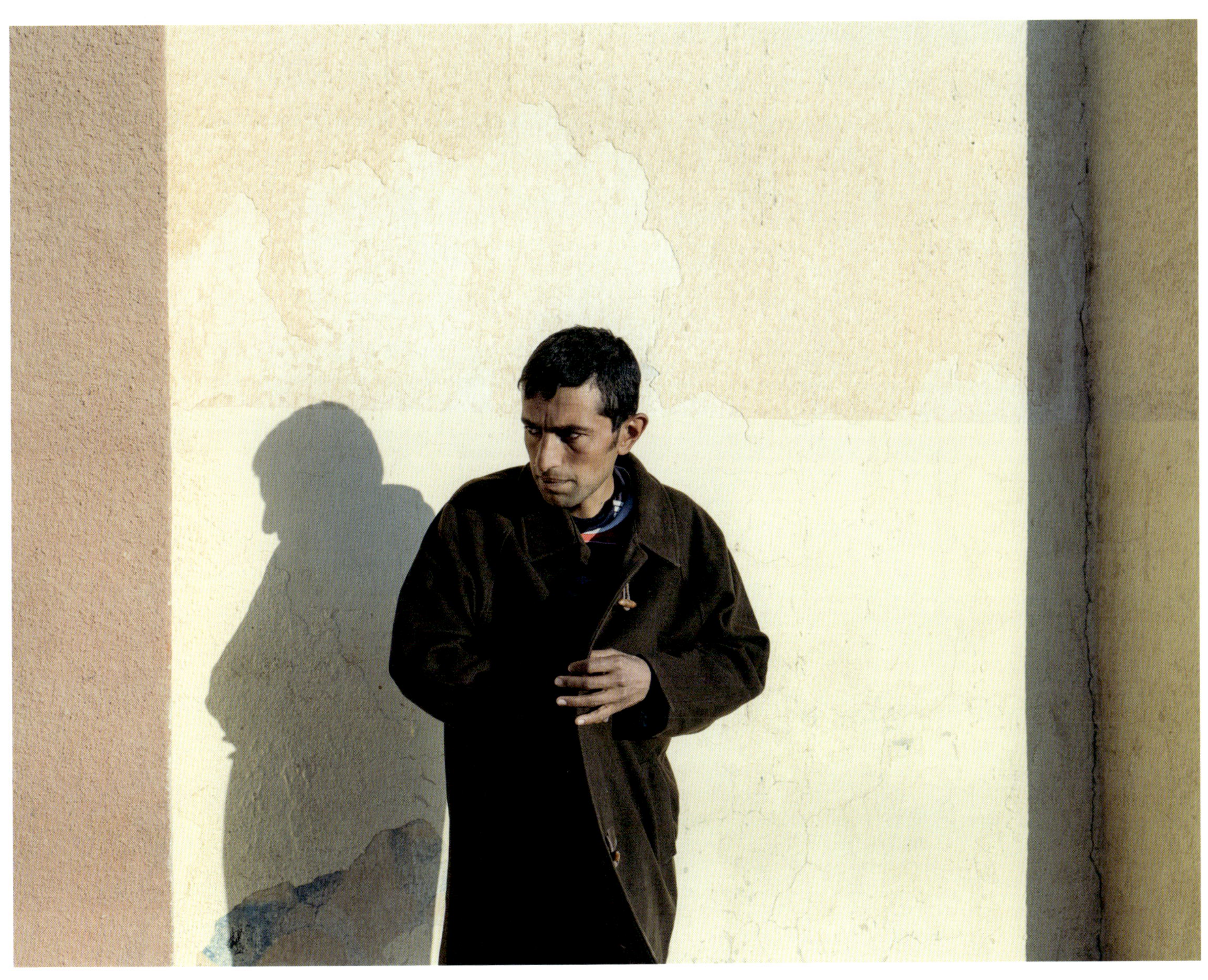

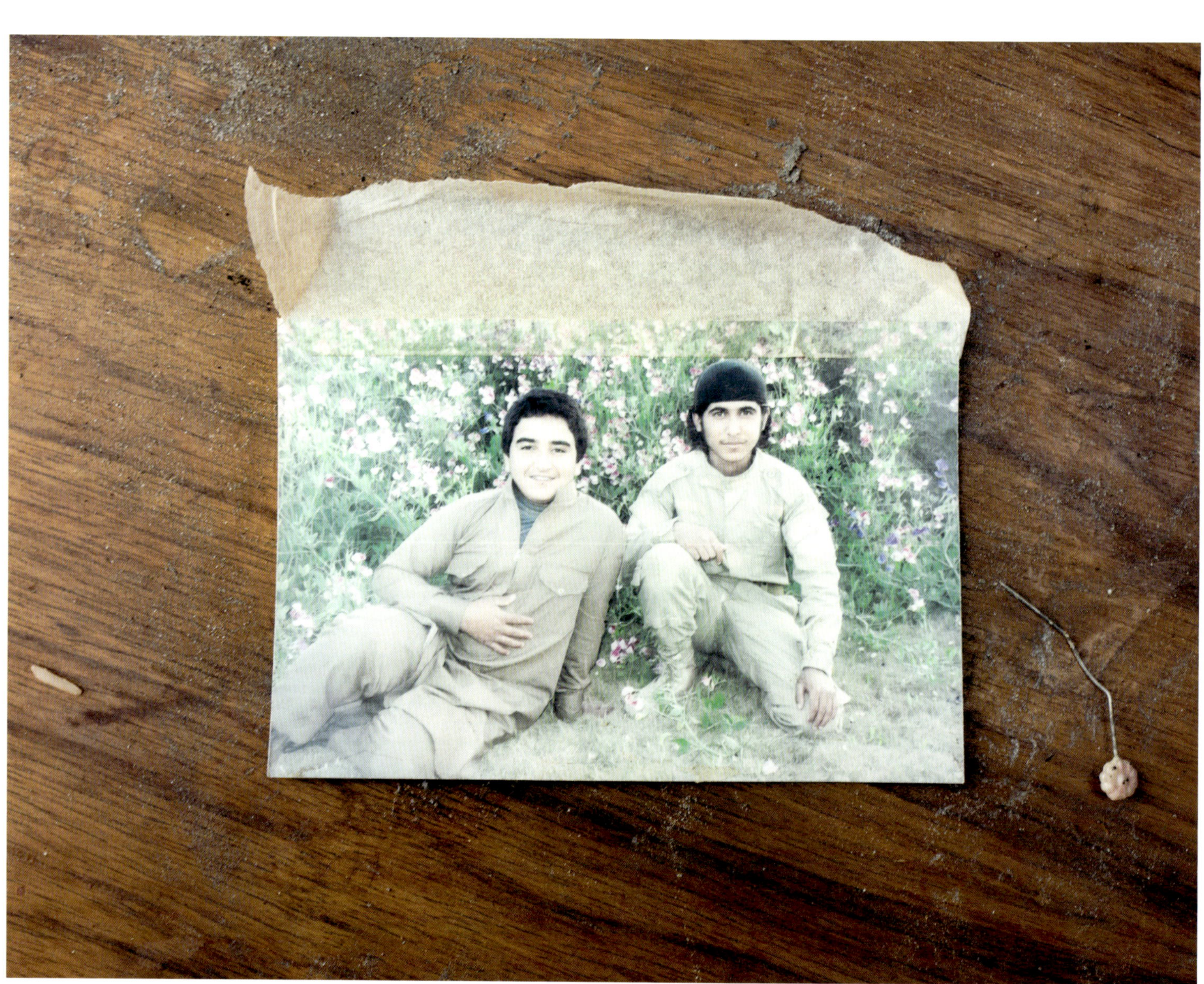

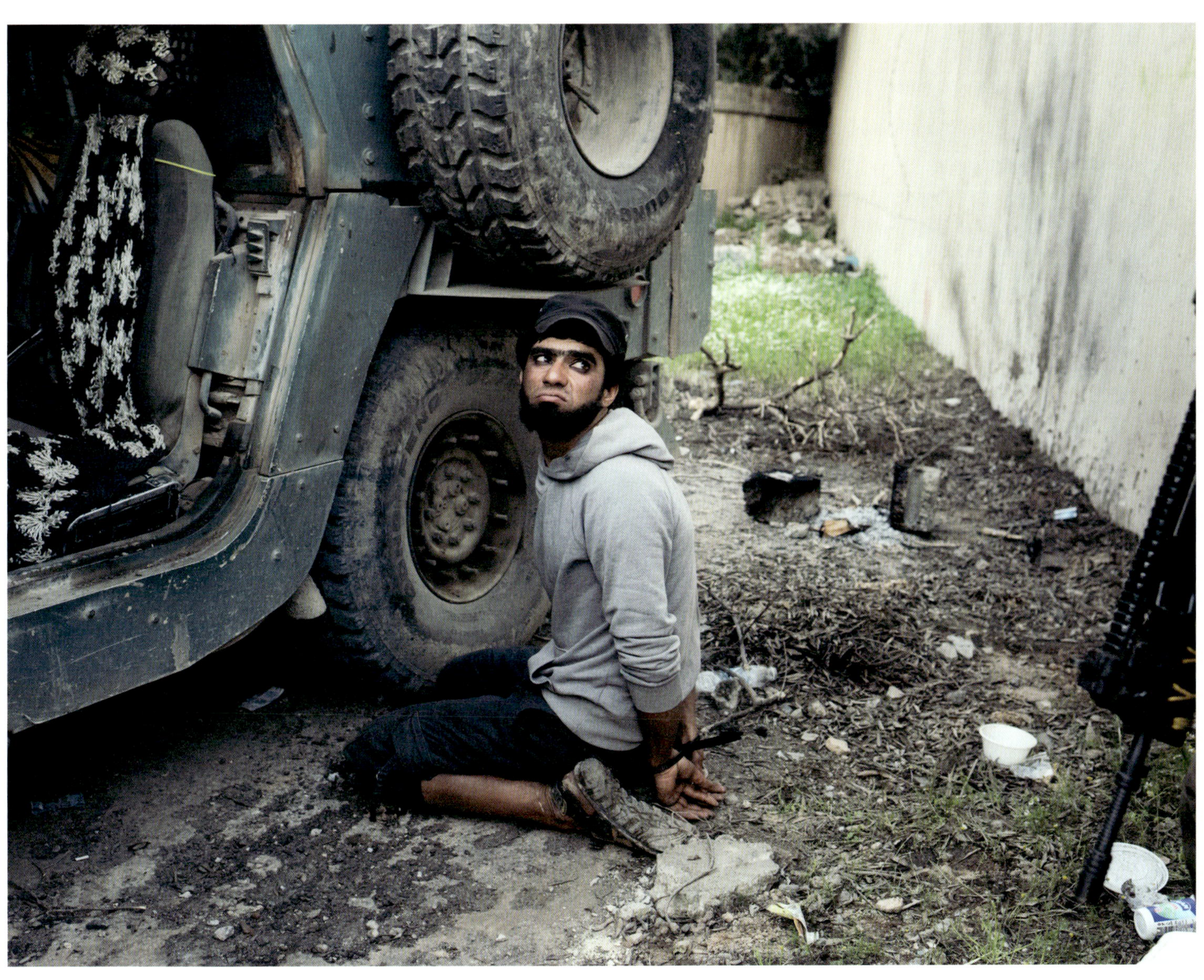

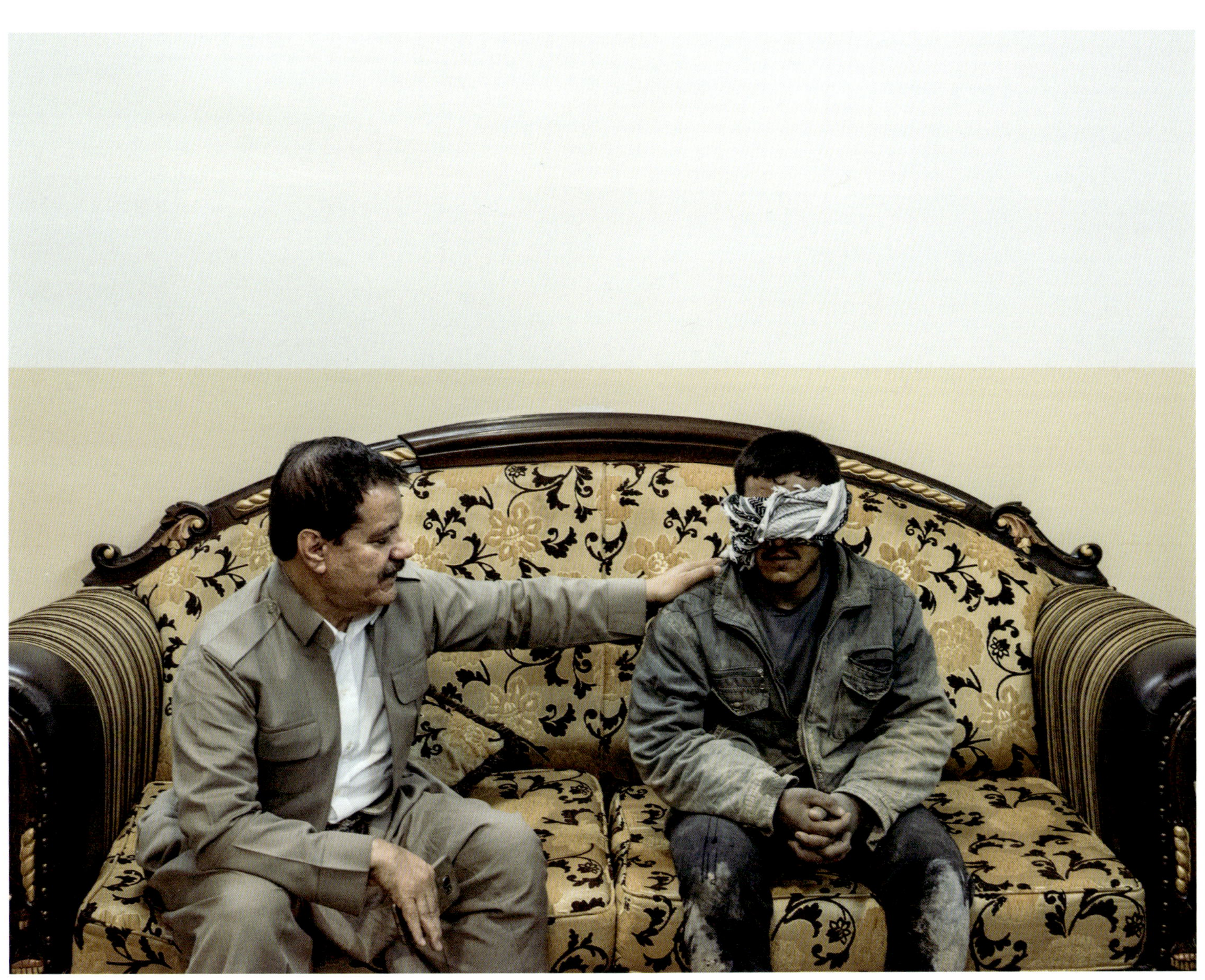

'AND THE PEOPLE SEARCH FOR A SOLUTION IN THE MIRAGE OF THE DESERT OF THE LABYRINTH, WHILE THE SOLUTION IS IN THEIR HANDS...'

To

ABU HAMZA SINIGALI,

QADAMATH.

ASSALAM ALAIKUM (W),

Kaif-a-hal, I had already wrote numerous letters about this issue, so you are familiar with this. This letter is also about requesting to allow me to do Isthishahad.

But this letter was requested of me to write, so I am very happy.

Let me know the procedures to complete the processing for Isthishahad.

Jazakallahu-khair,

Abu Bake Al Hindi,

Qadamath.

عدد ١

٣١٢٥ بوتاسيوم

١٢٧٥ سكر

٦٠٠ جربتول

RECIPE FOR EXPLOSIVE

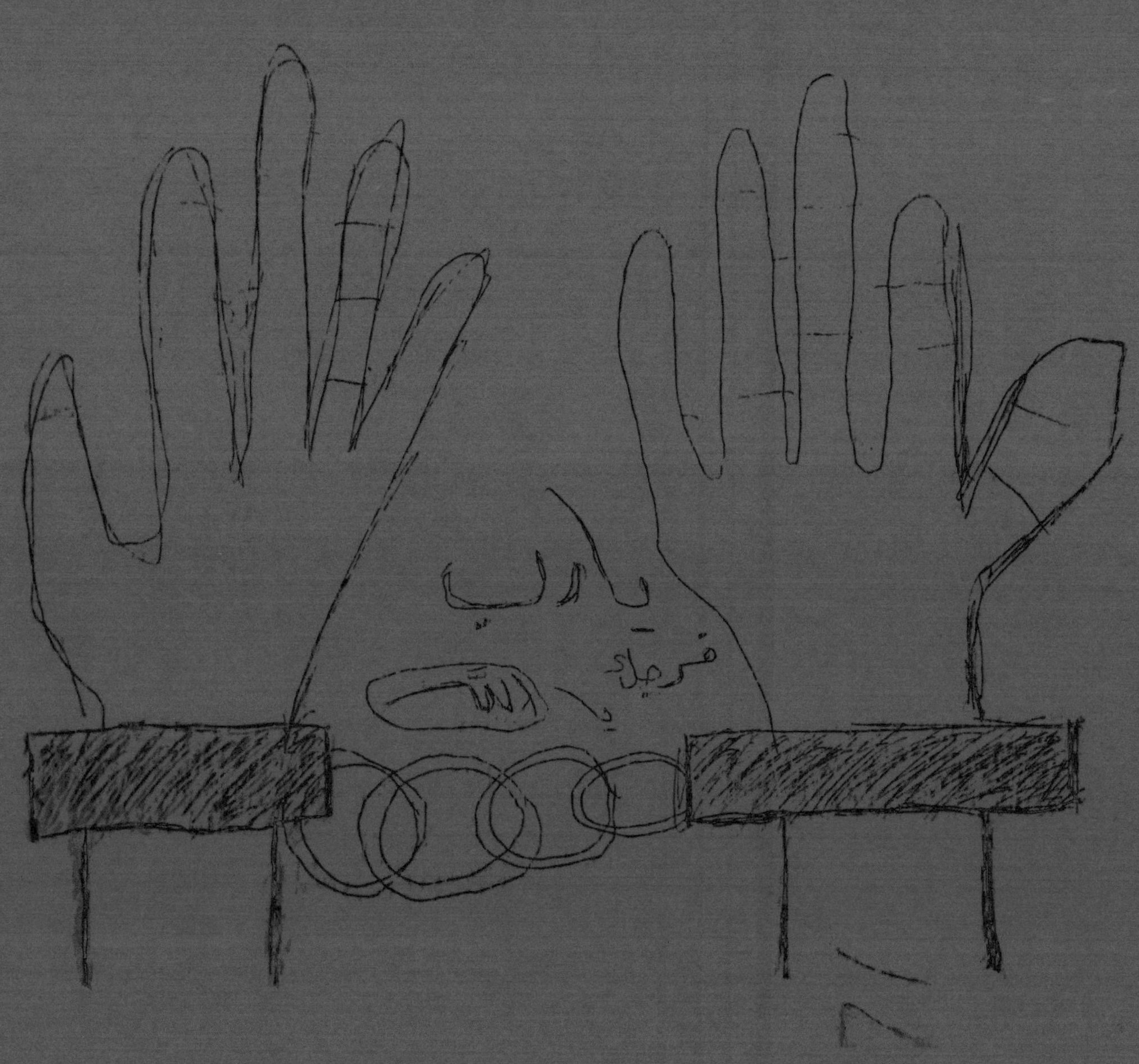
يا رب
فرجك يا الله

'HE DETONATED HIS EXPLOSIVE BELT AT THE CHECKPOINT FOR ONE OF THE PRISON'S ENTRANCES AND SUCCEEDED IN KILLING AND WOUNDING AT LEAST FIFTEEN.'

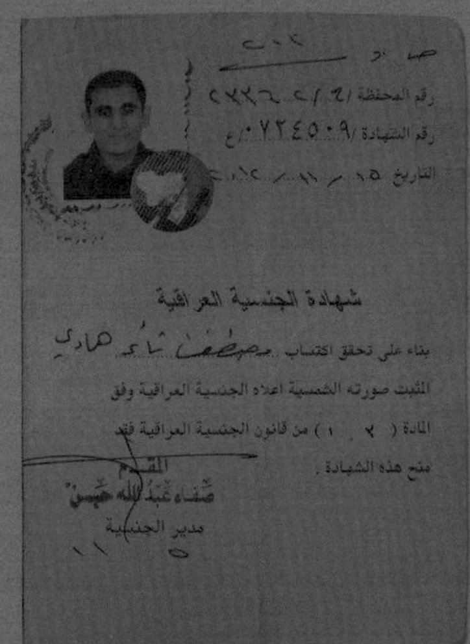

شهادة الجنسية العراقية

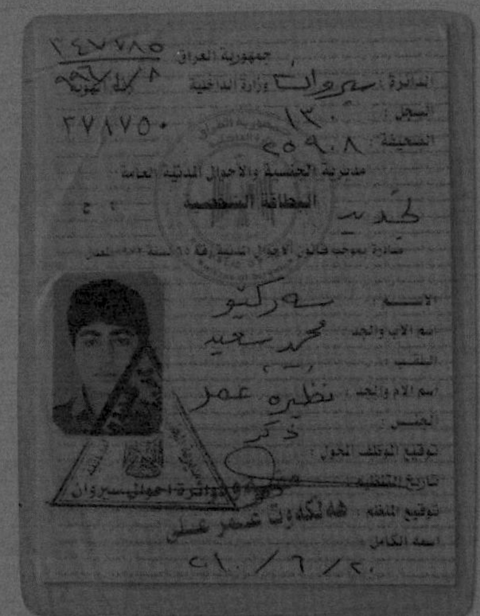

جمهورية العراق
وزارة الداخلية
مديرية الجنسية والاحوال المدنية العامة
البطاقة الشخصية

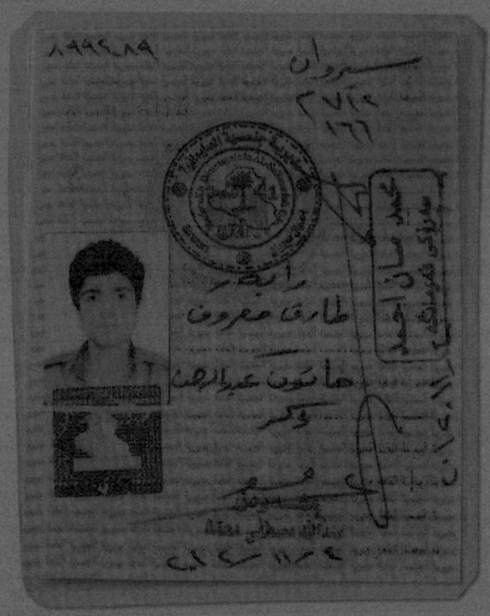

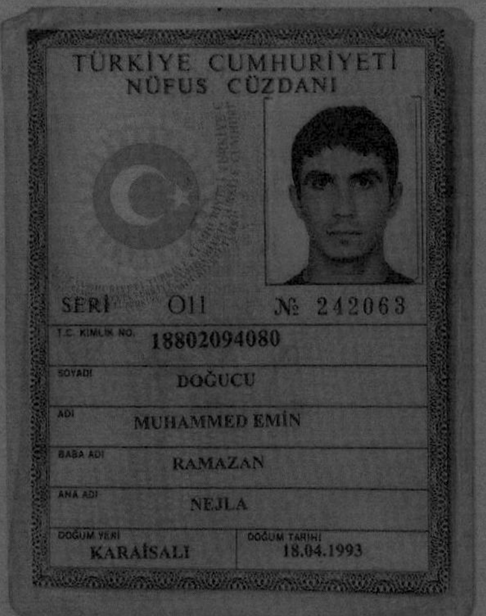

TÜRKİYE CUMHURİYETİ
NÜFUS CÜZDANI
SERİ O11 № 242063
T.C. KİMLİK NO. 18802094080
SOYADI DOĞUCU
ADI MUHAMMED EMİN
BABA ADI RAMAZAN
ANA ADI NEJLA
DOĞUM YERİ KARAİSALI
DOĞUM TARİHİ 18.04.1993

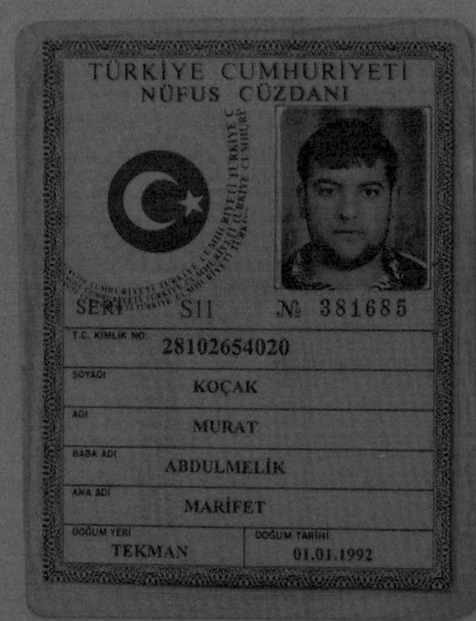

TÜRKİYE CUMHURİYETİ
NÜFUS CÜZDANI
SERİ S11 № 381685
T.C. KİMLİK NO. 28102654020
SOYADI KOÇAK
ADI MURAT
BABA ADI ABDULMELİK
ANA ADI MARİFET
DOĞUM YERİ TEKMAN
DOĞUM TARİHİ 01.01.1992

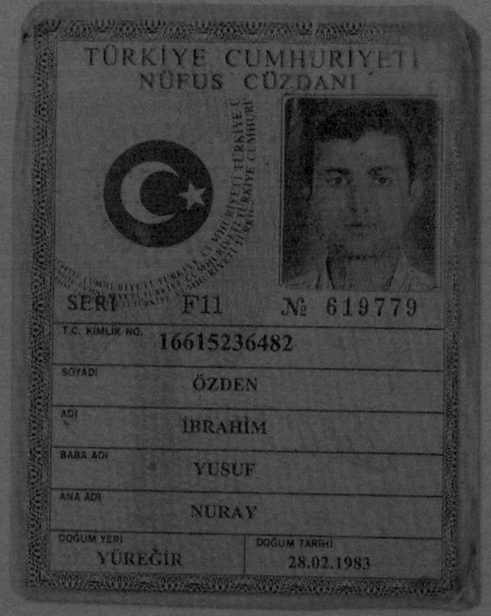

TÜRKİYE CUMHURİYETİ
NÜFUS CÜZDANI
SERİ F11 № 619779
T.C. KİMLİK NO. 16615236482
SOYADI ÖZDEN
ADI İBRAHİM
BABA ADI YUSUF
ANA ADI NURAY
DOĞUM YERİ YÜREĞİR
DOĞUM TARİHİ 28.02.1983

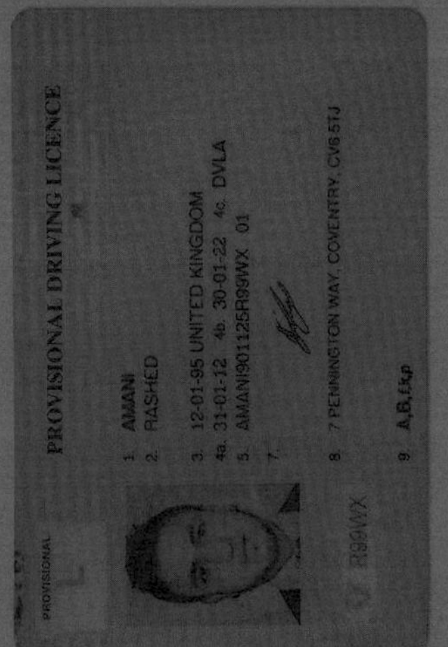

PROVISIONAL DRIVING LICENCE
1 AMANI
2 RASHED
3 12-01-95 UNITED KINGDOM
4a 31-01-12 4b 30-01-22 4c DVLA
5 AMANI901125R99WX 01
8 7 PENNINGTON WAY, COVENTRY, CV6 5TJ
9 A,B,f,k,p

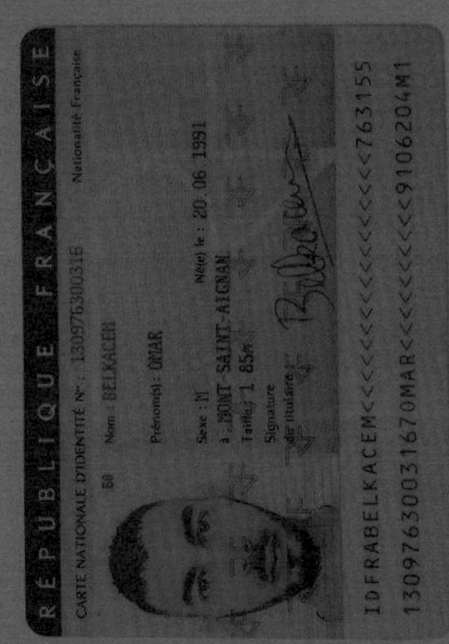

RÉPUBLIQUE FRANÇAISE
CARTE NATIONALE D'IDENTITÉ N°: 130976300316
Nationalité Française
Nom: BELKACEM
Prénom(s): OMAR
Sexe: M
Né(e) le: 20 06 1991
Taille: 1,85m
Signature du titulaire

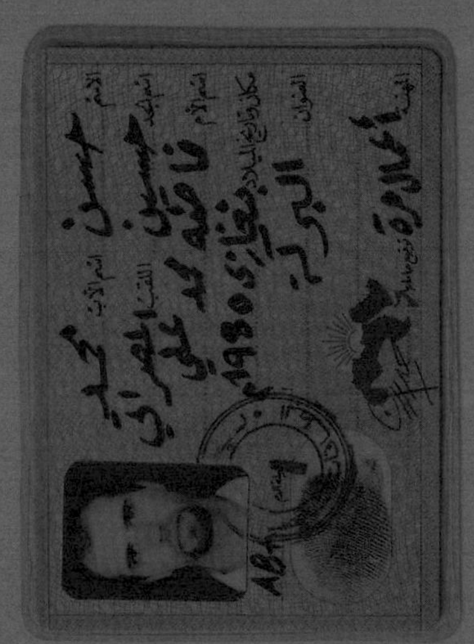

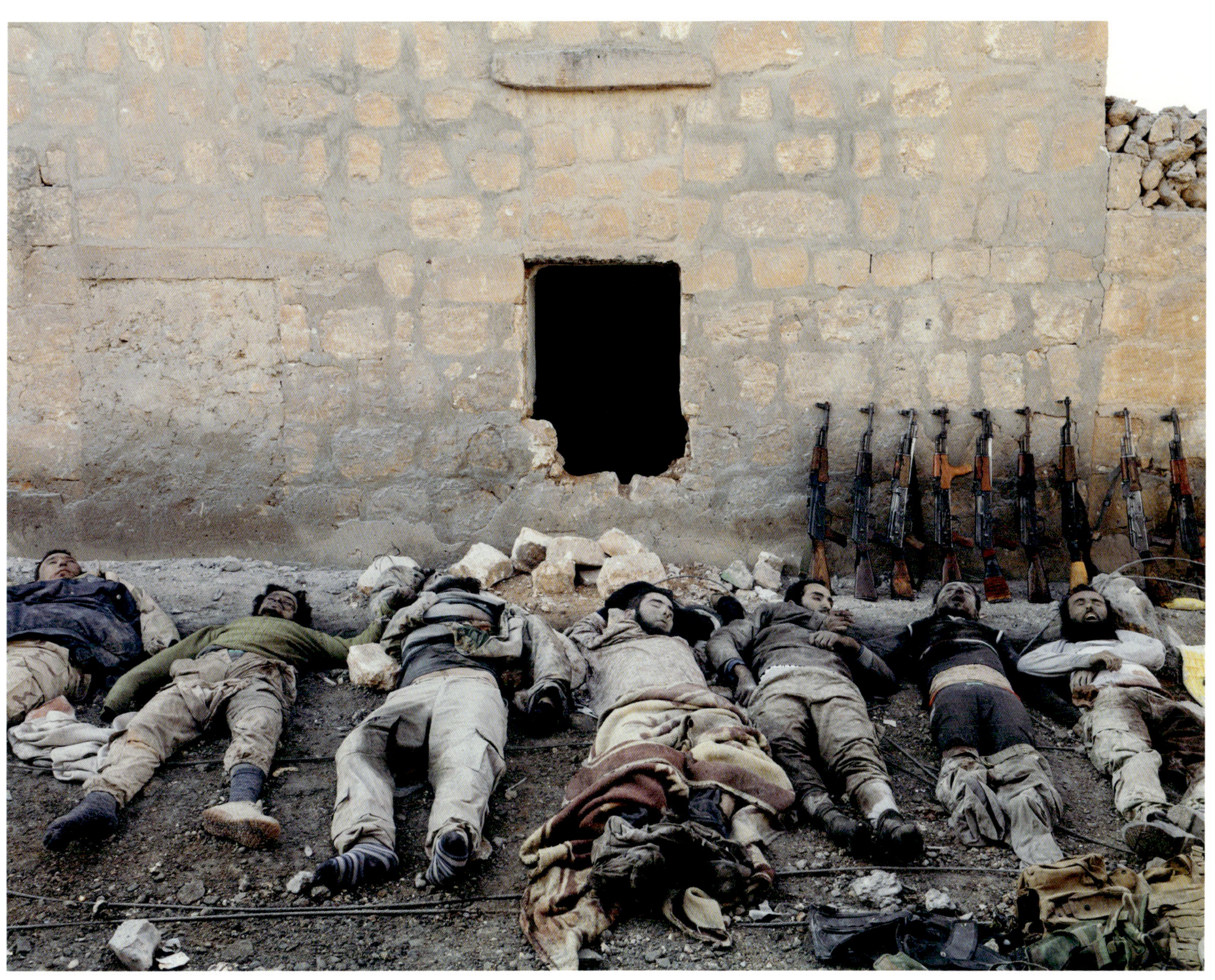

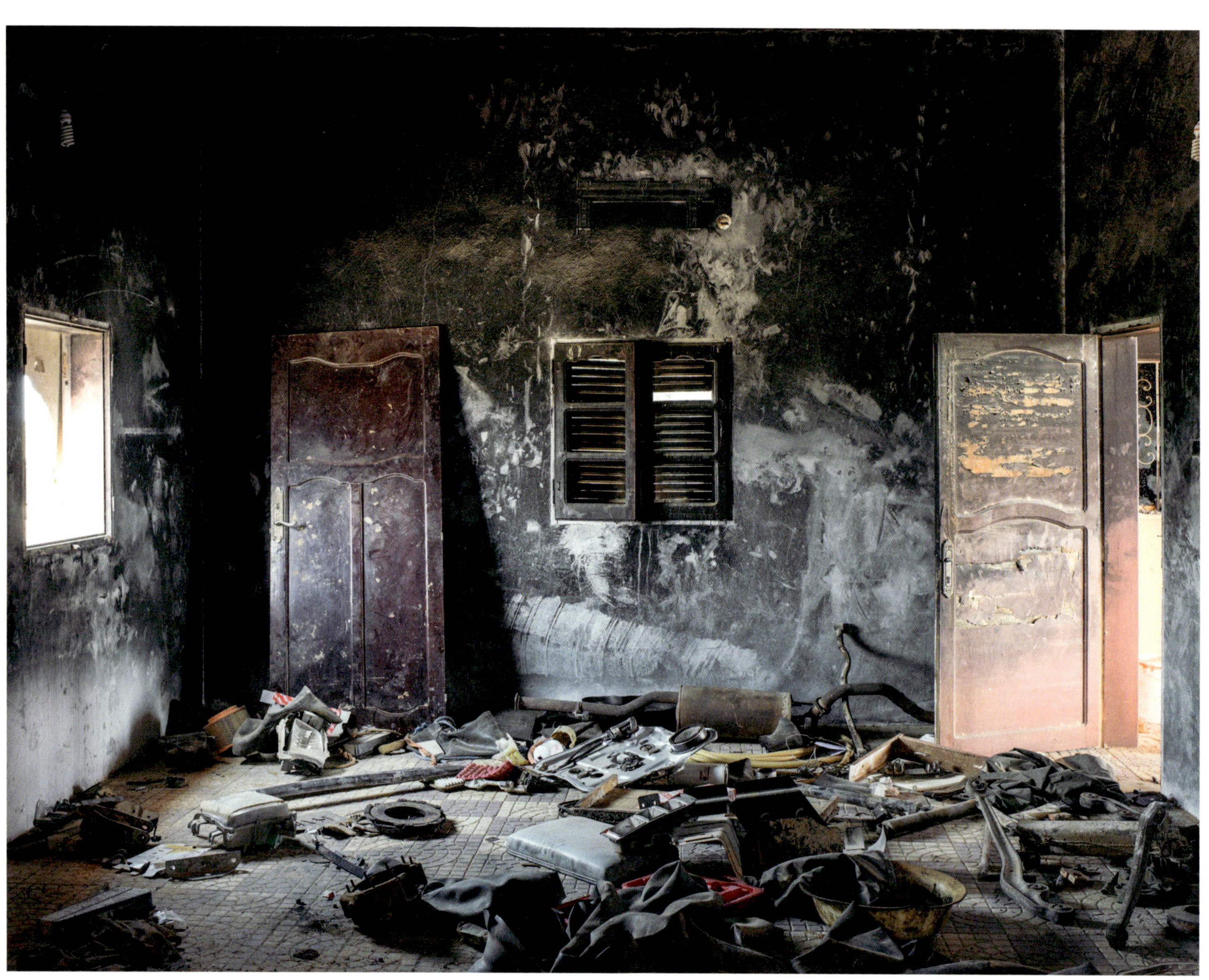

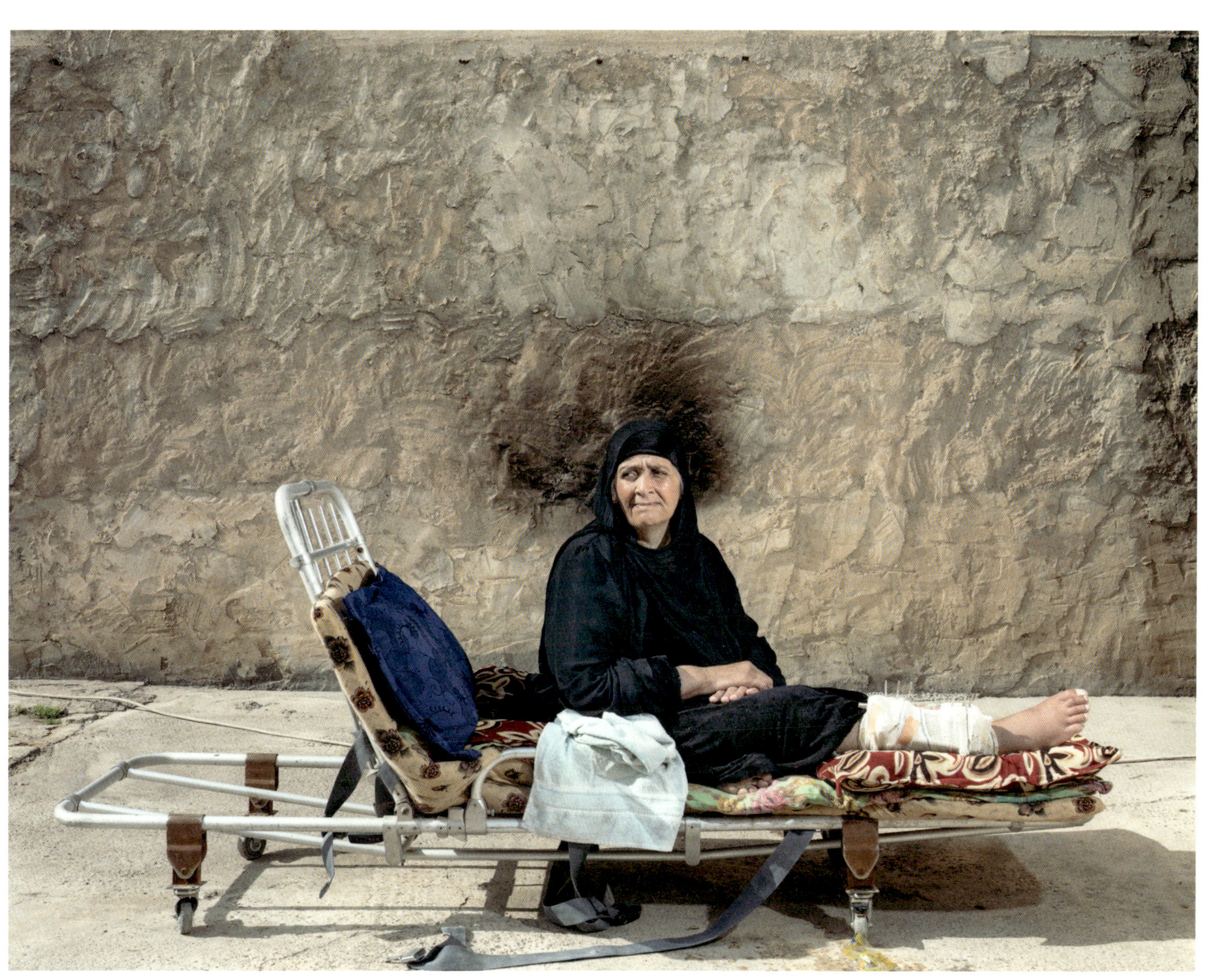

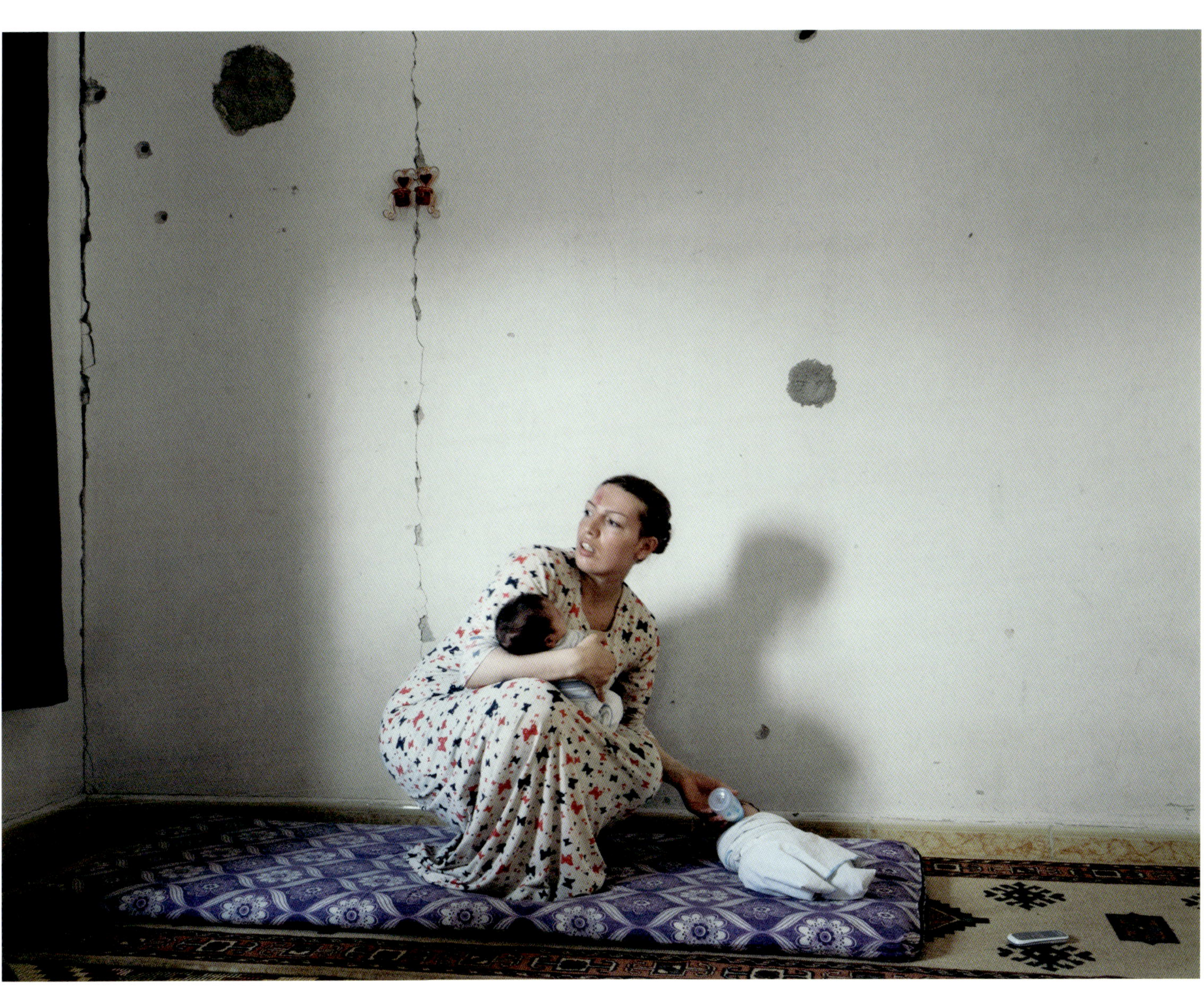

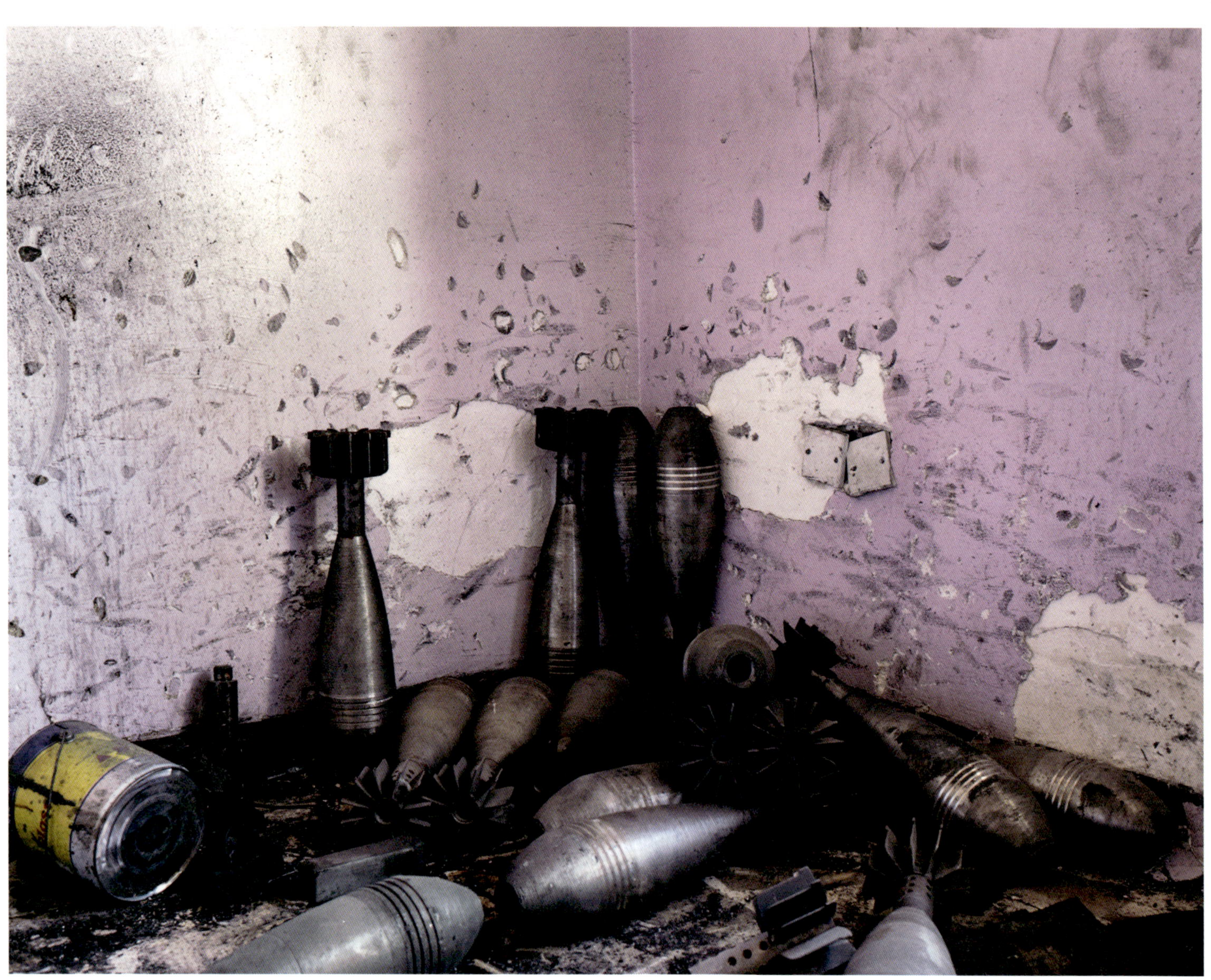

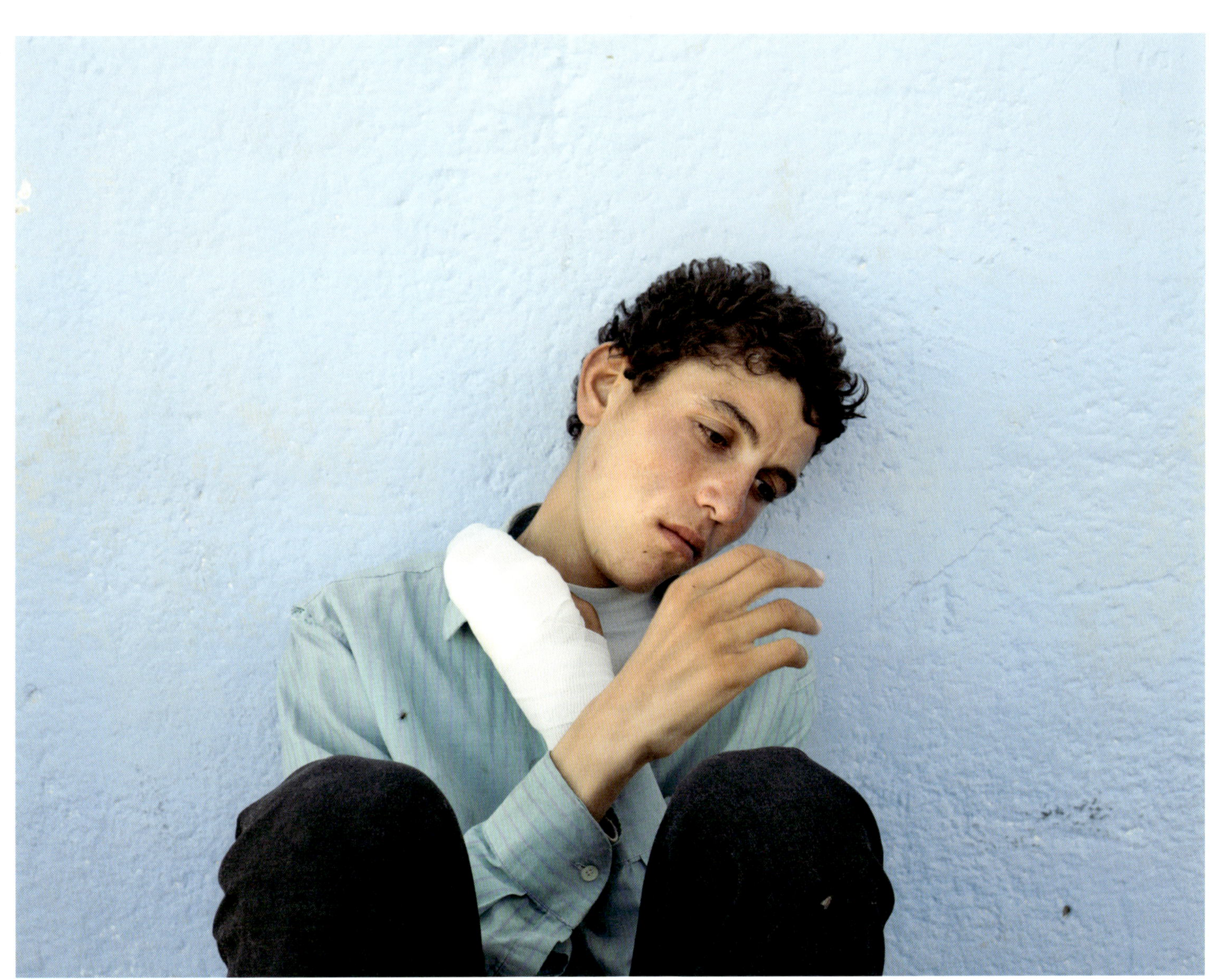

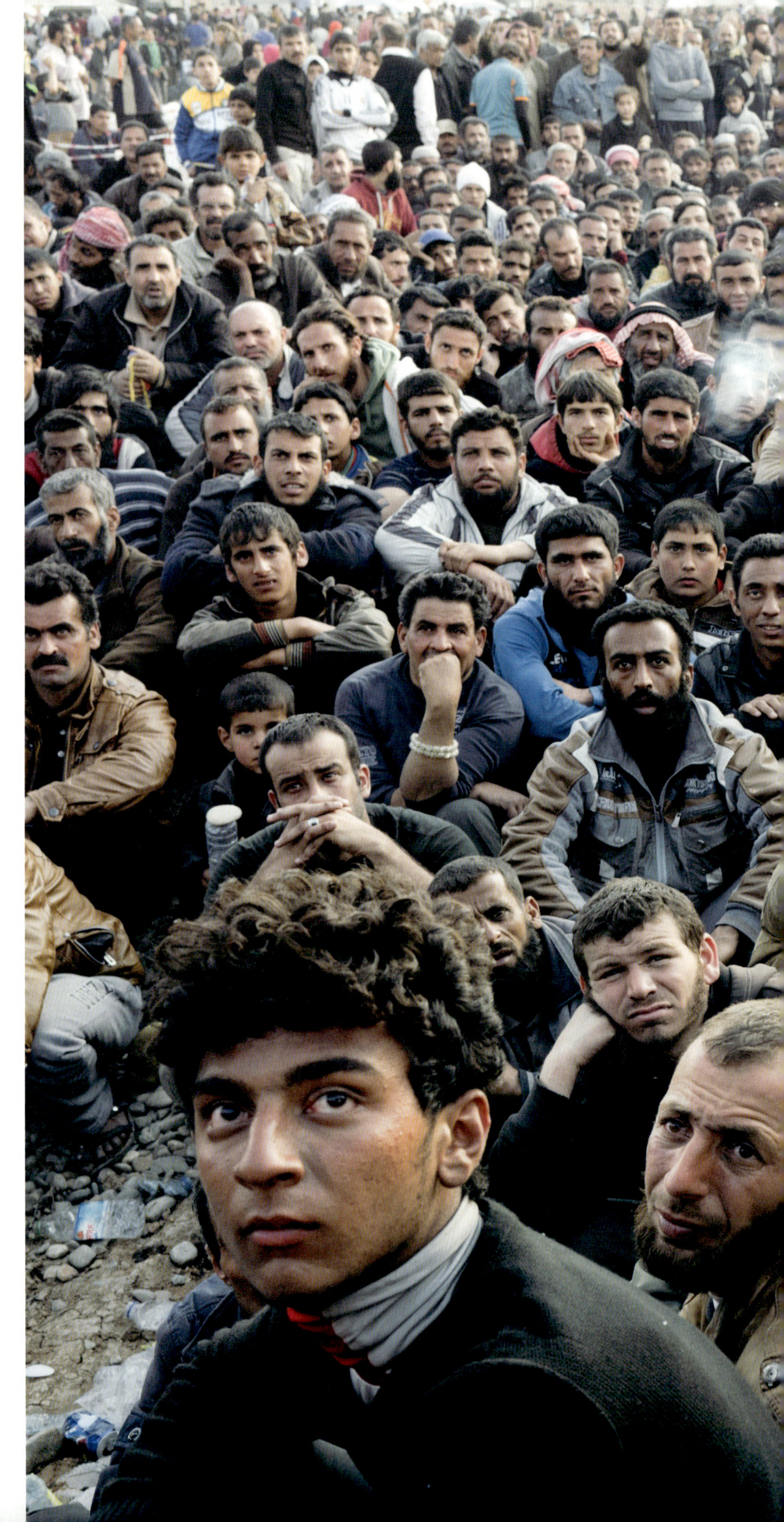

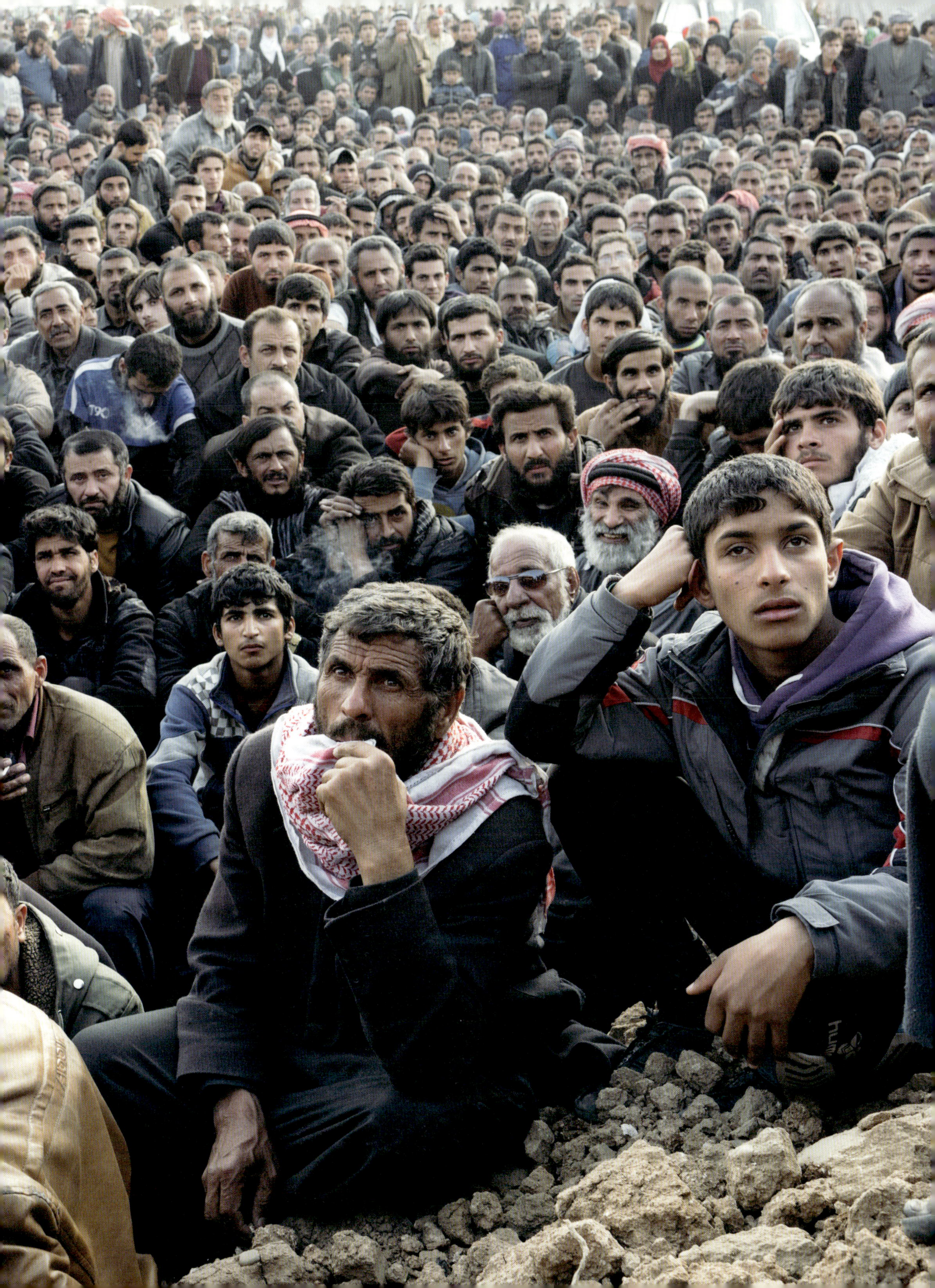

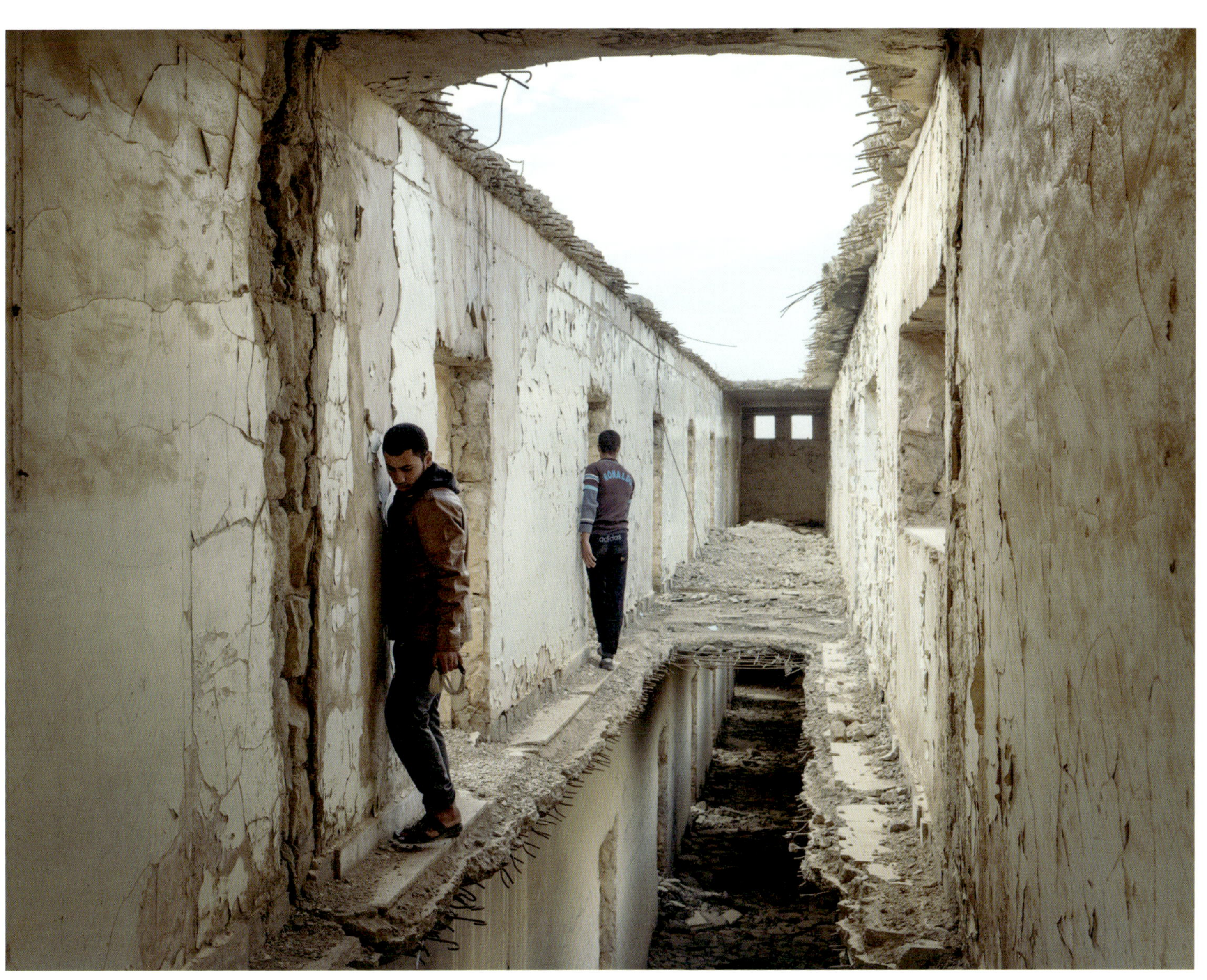
RONALDO
adidas

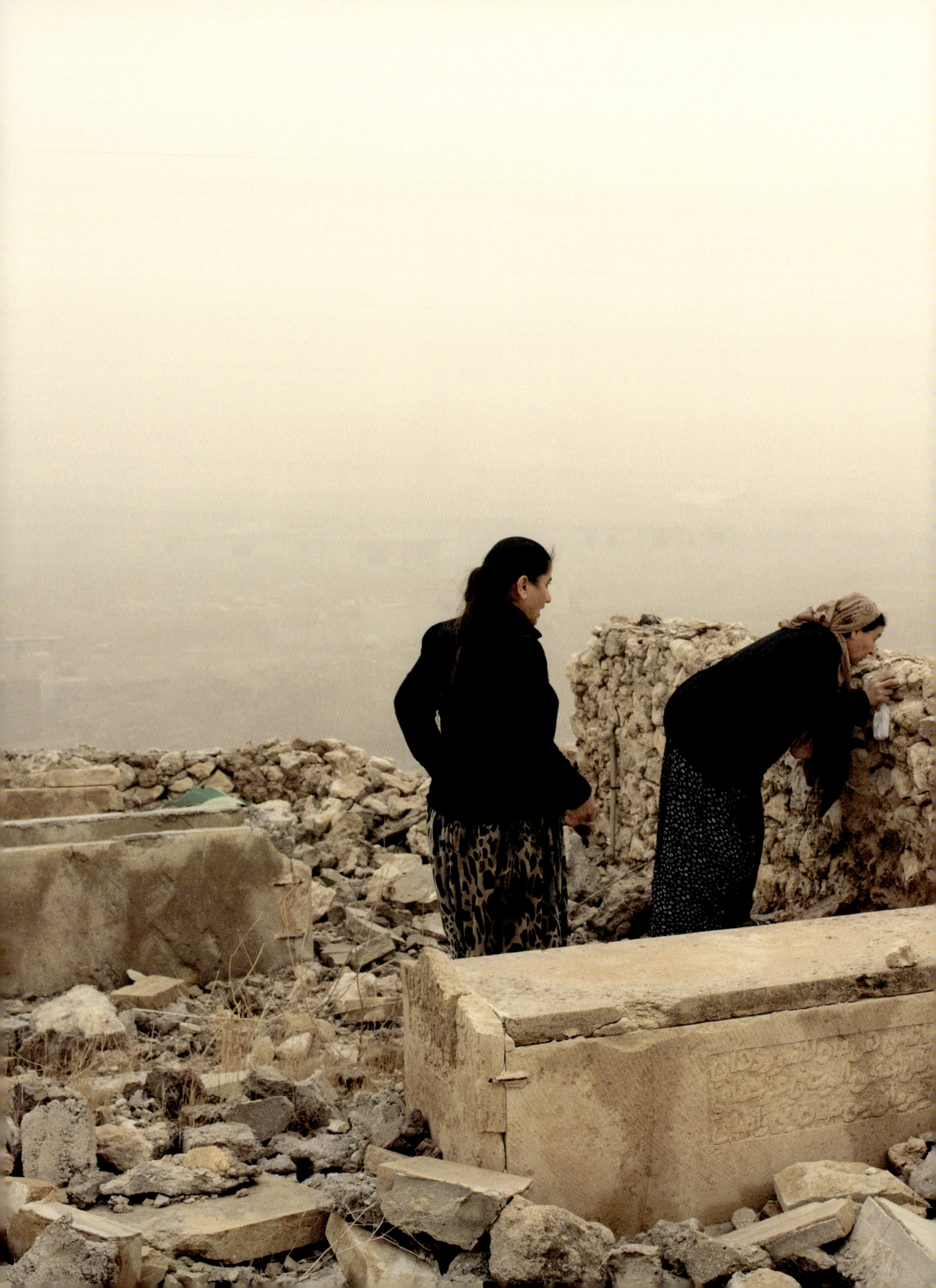

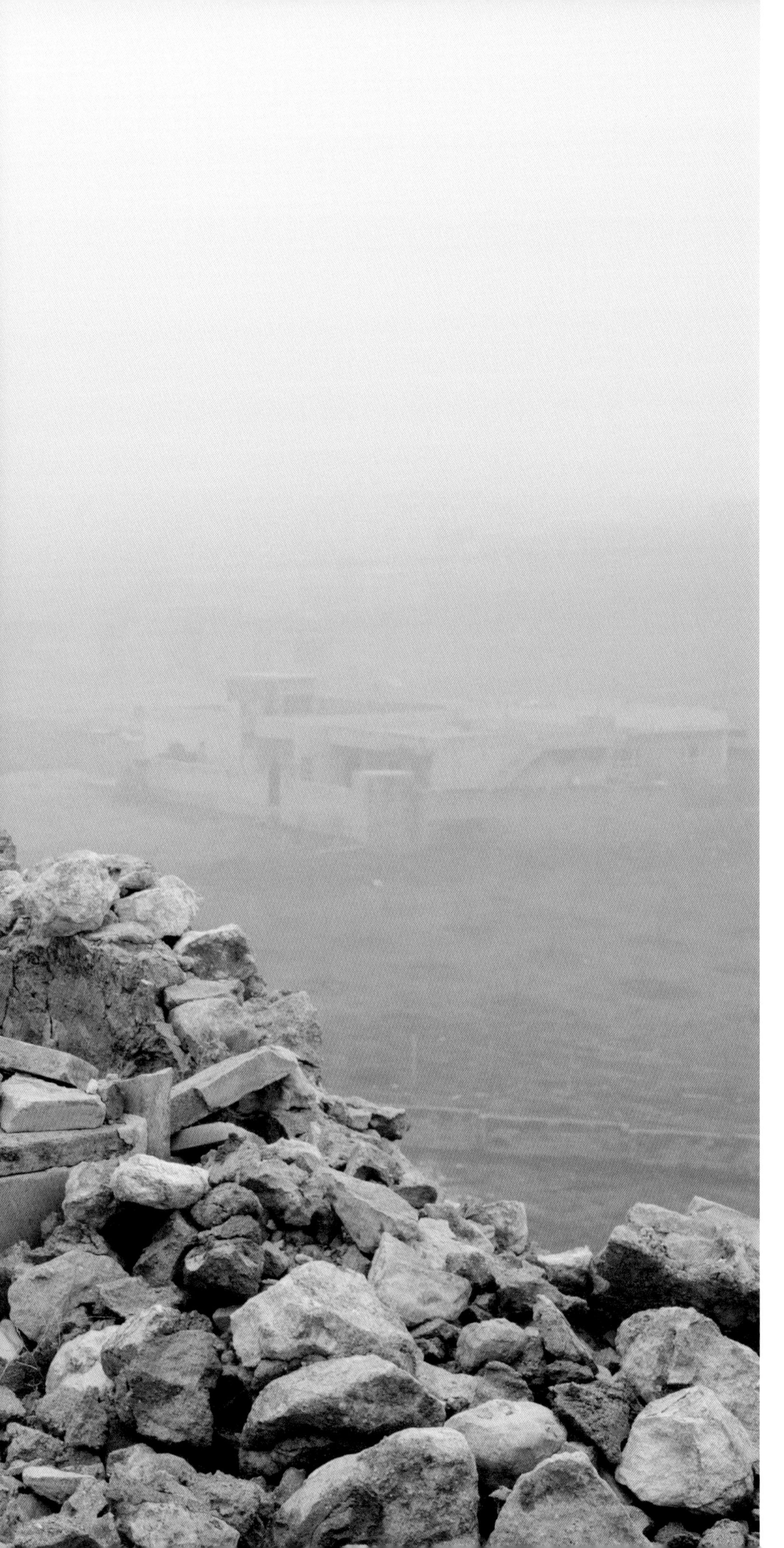

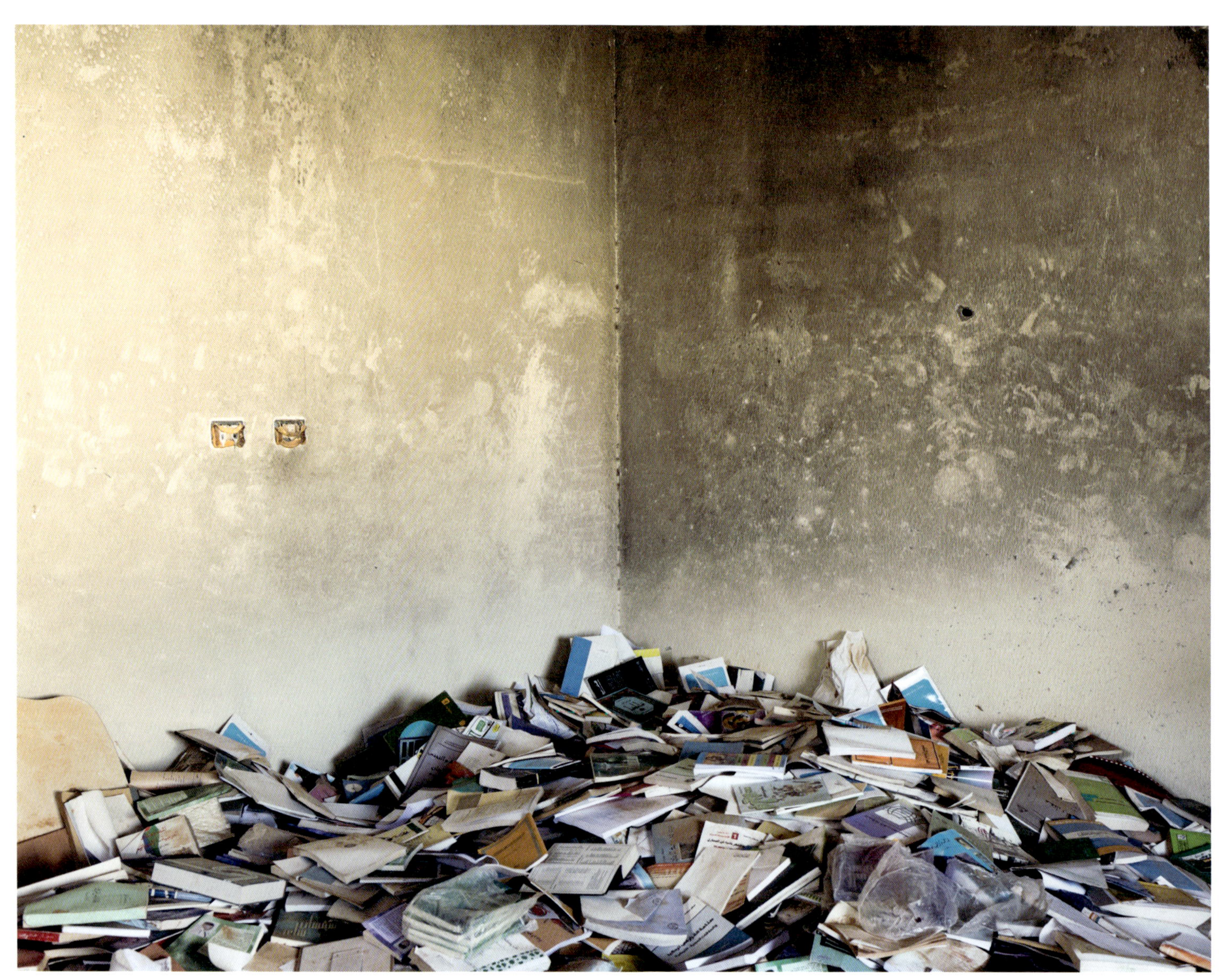

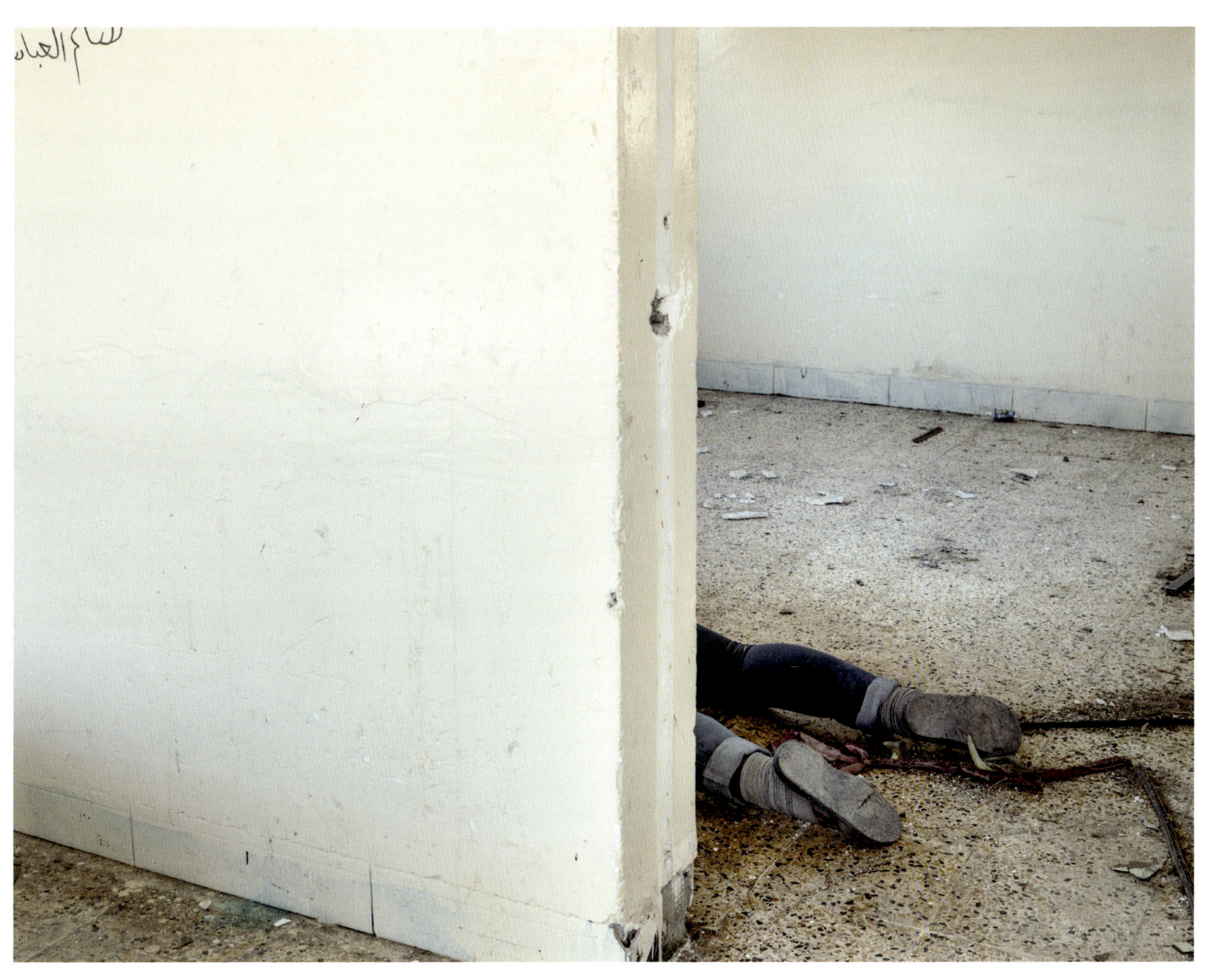

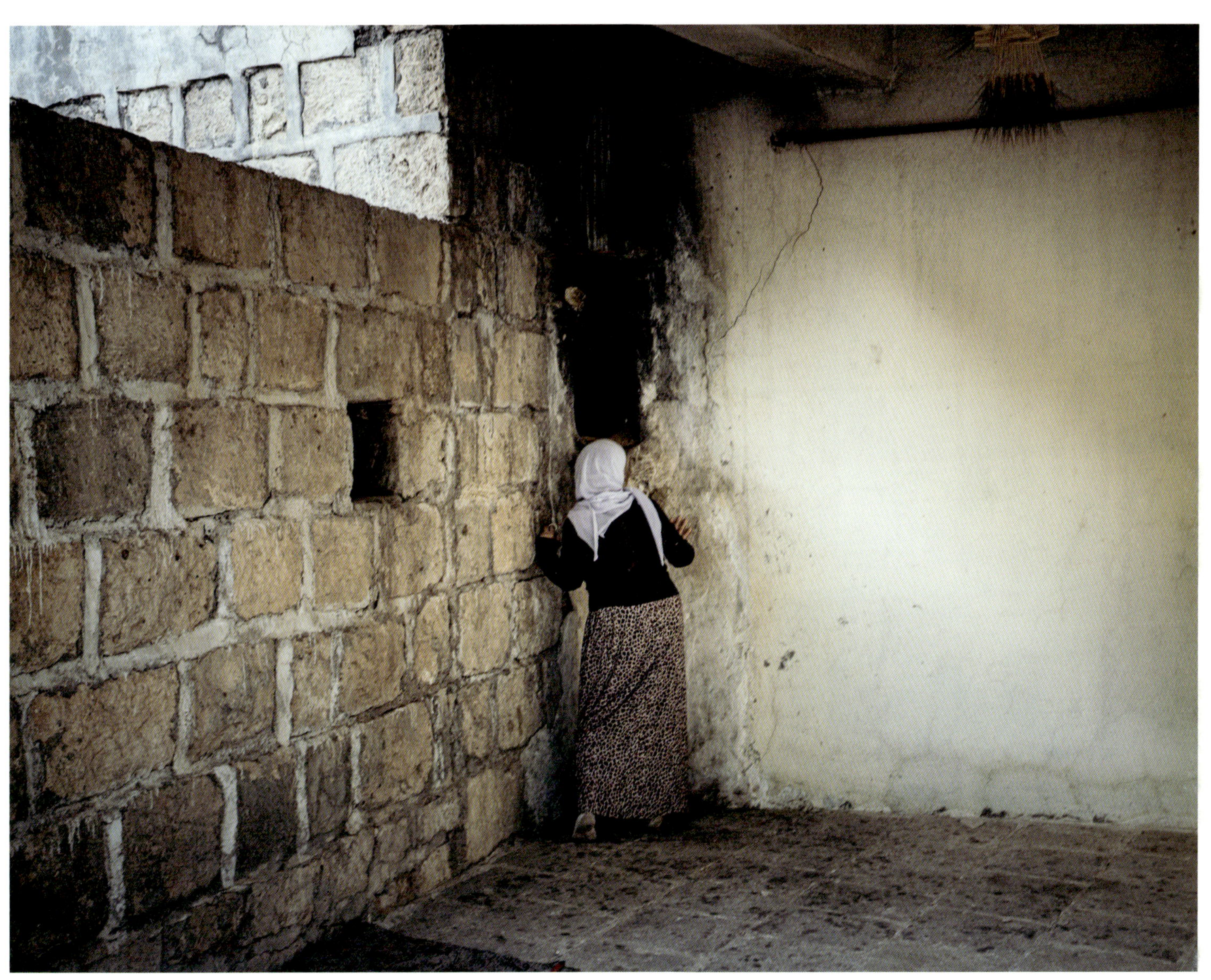

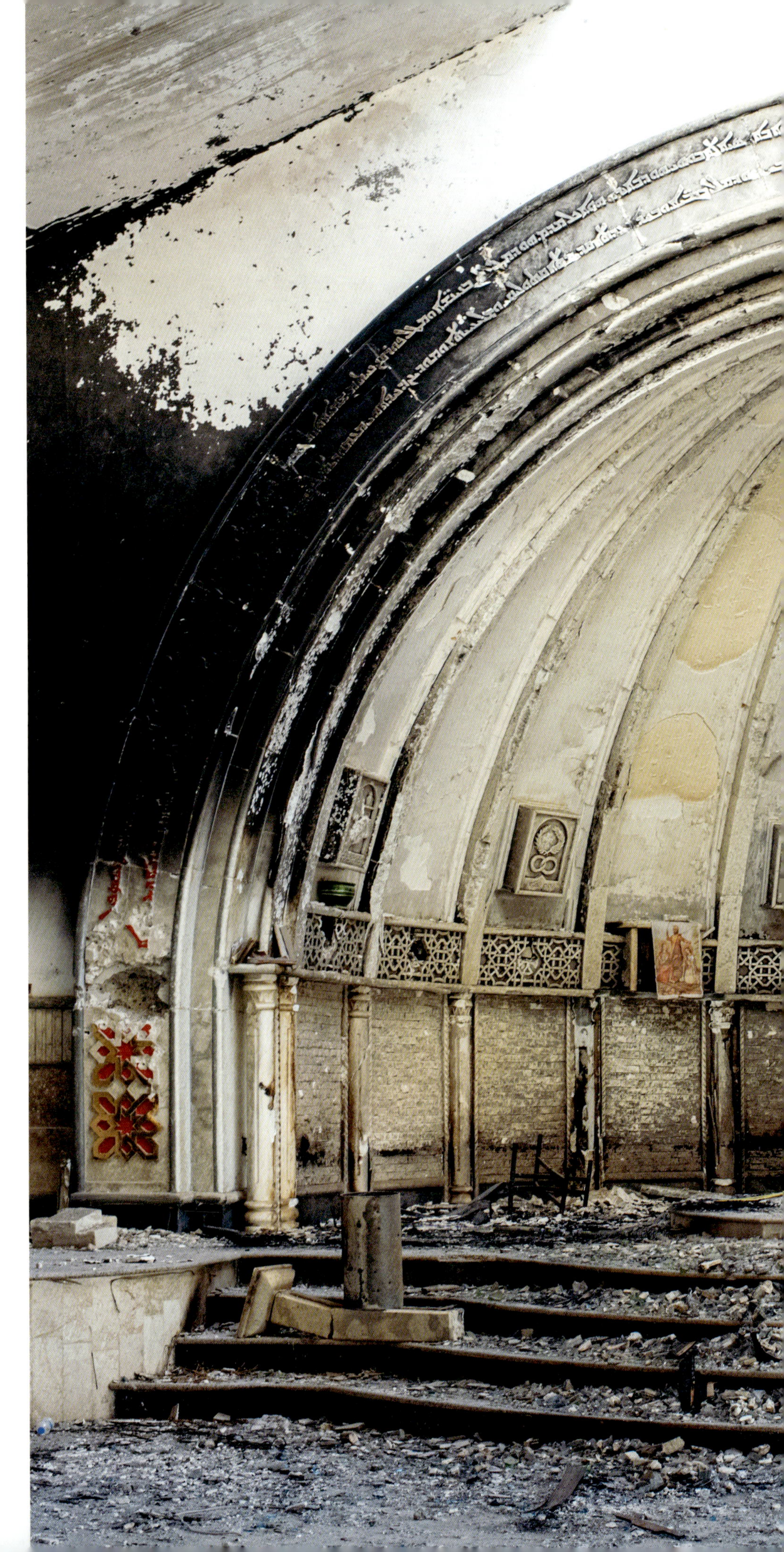

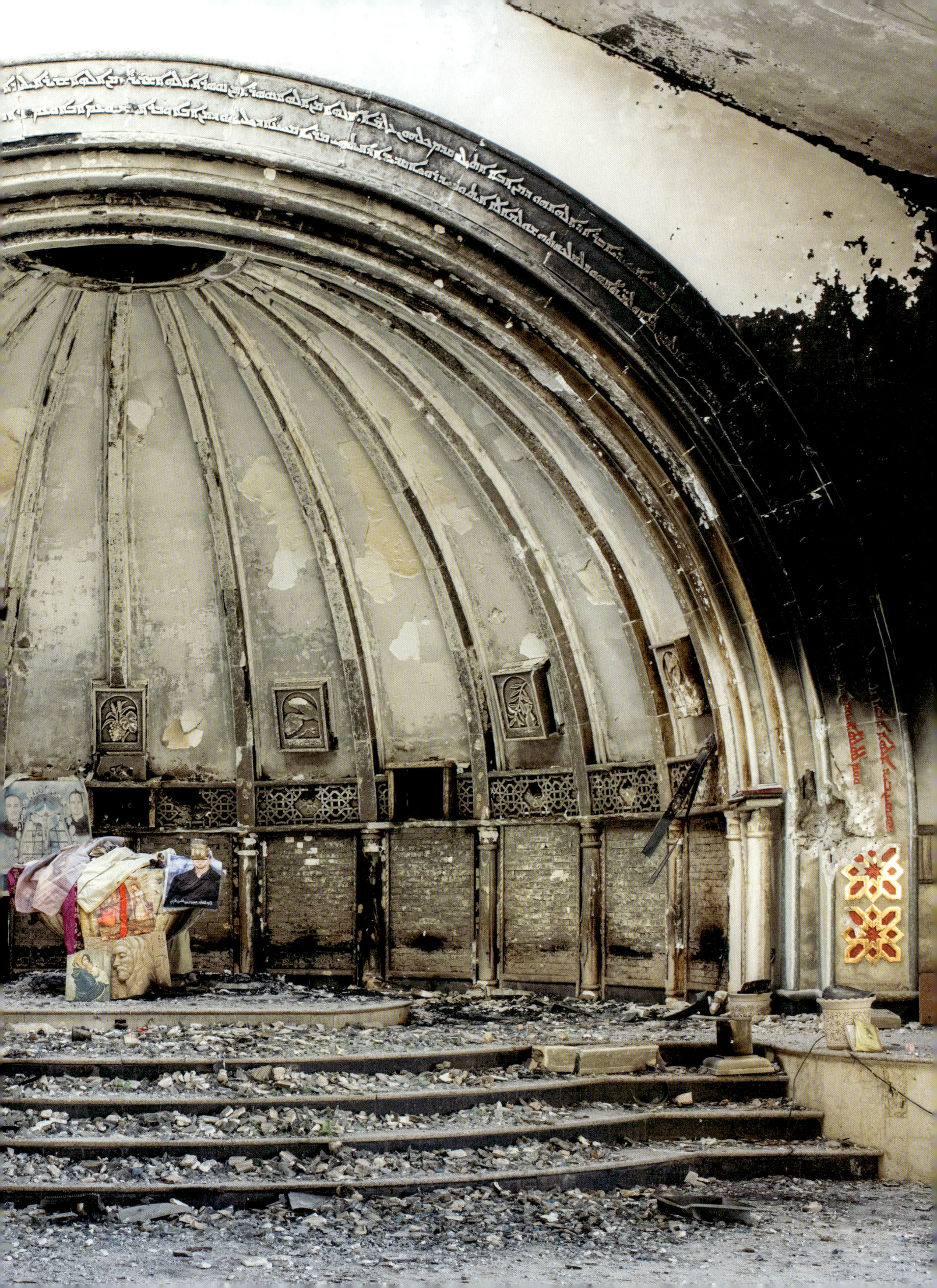

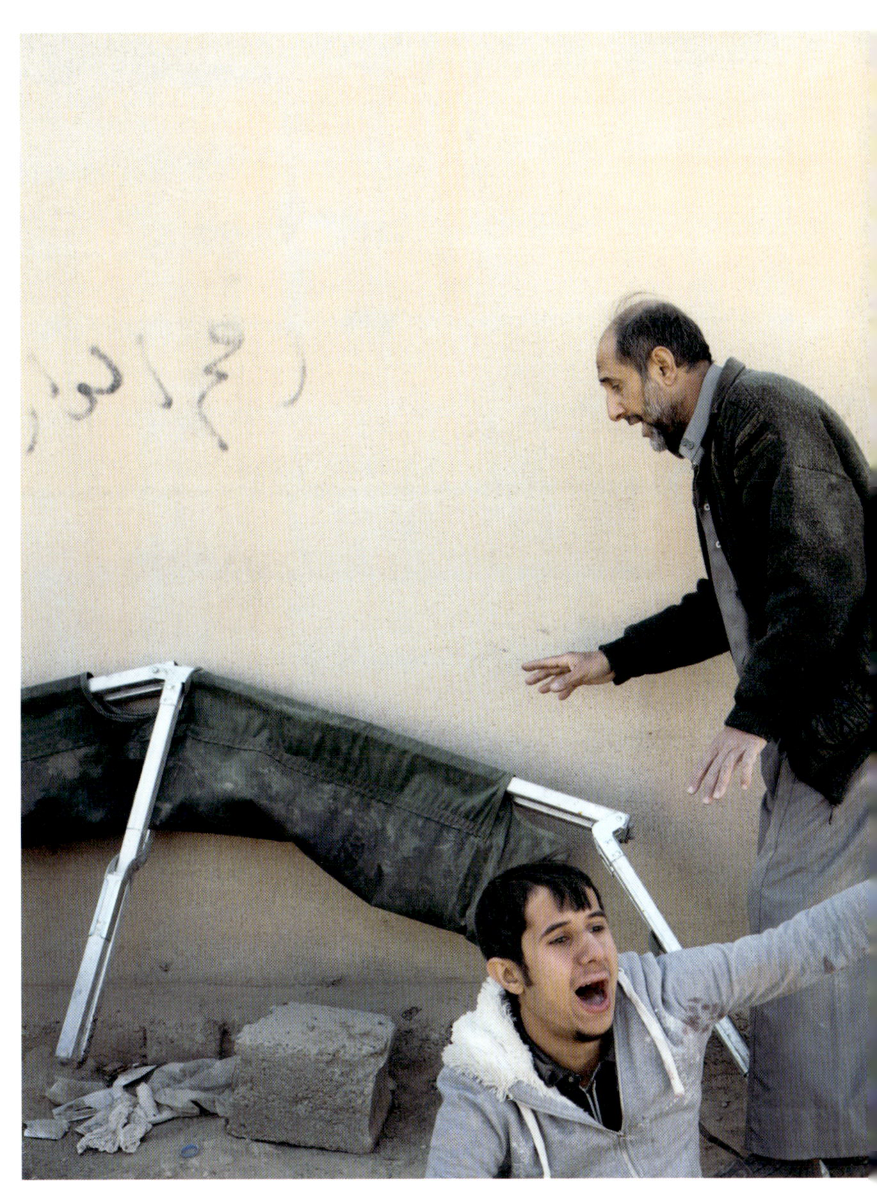

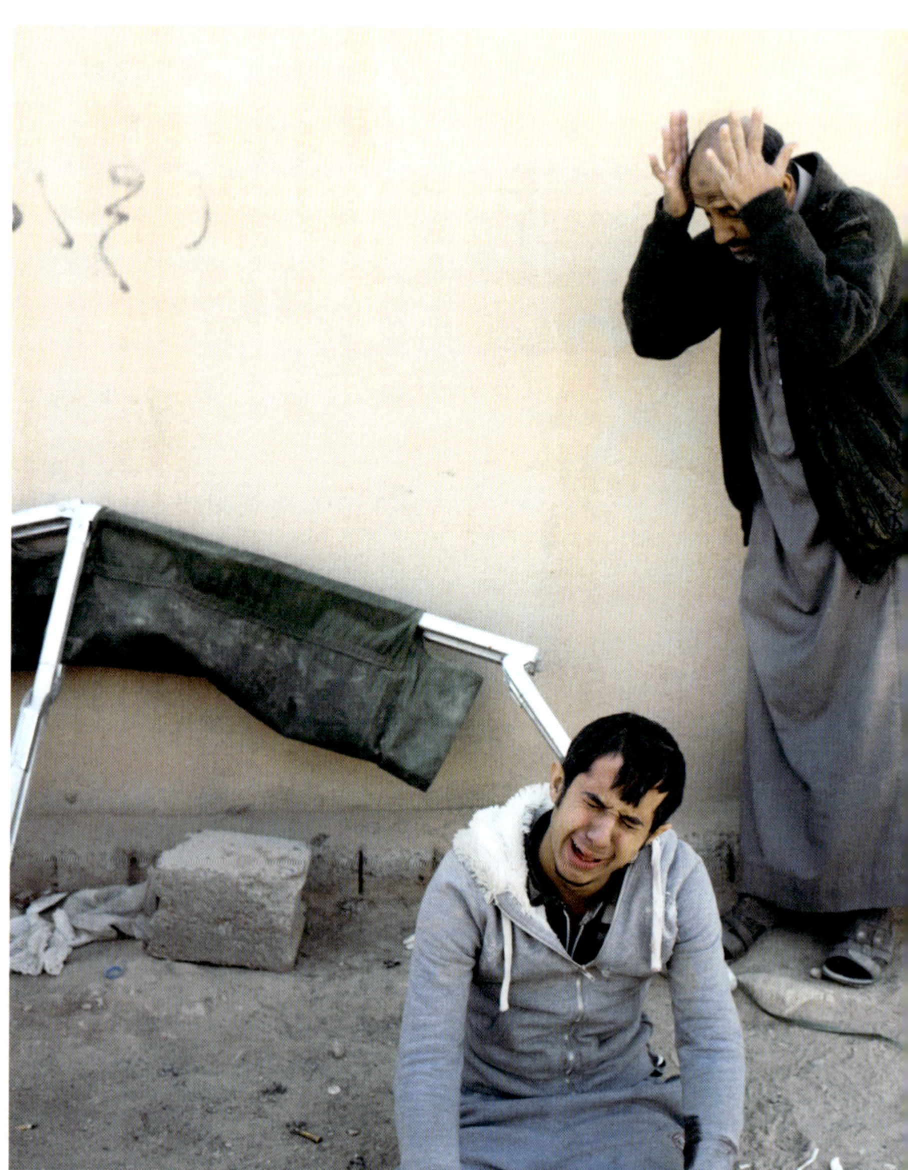

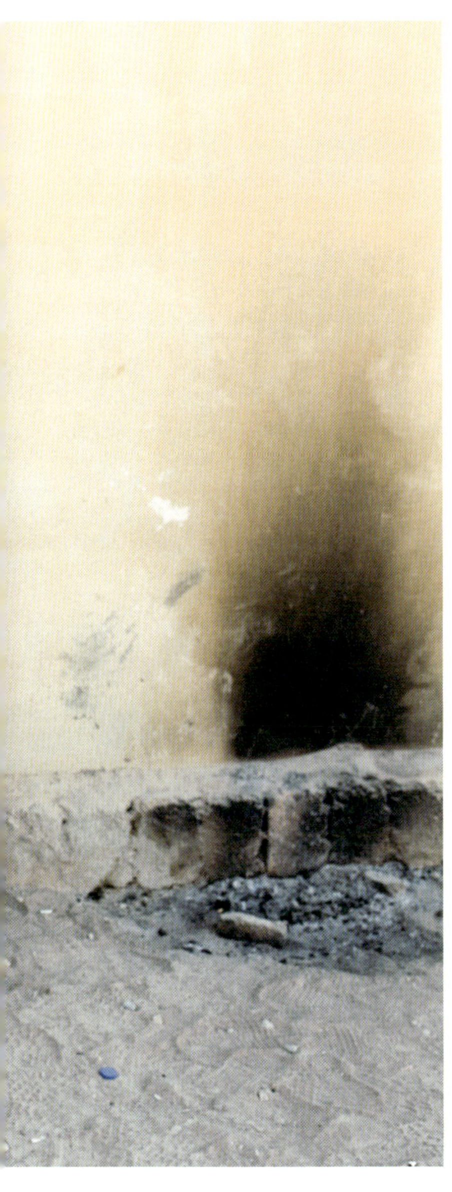

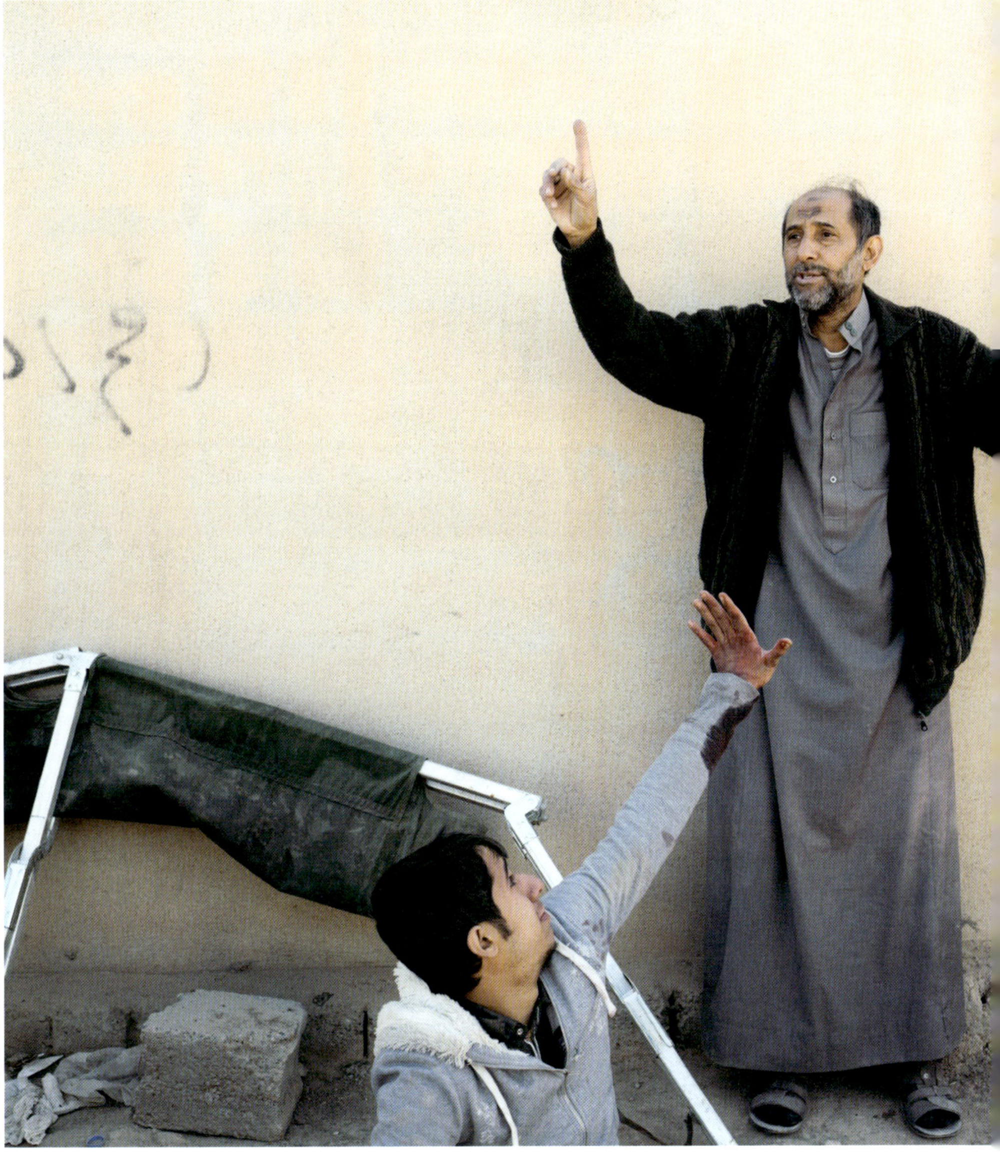

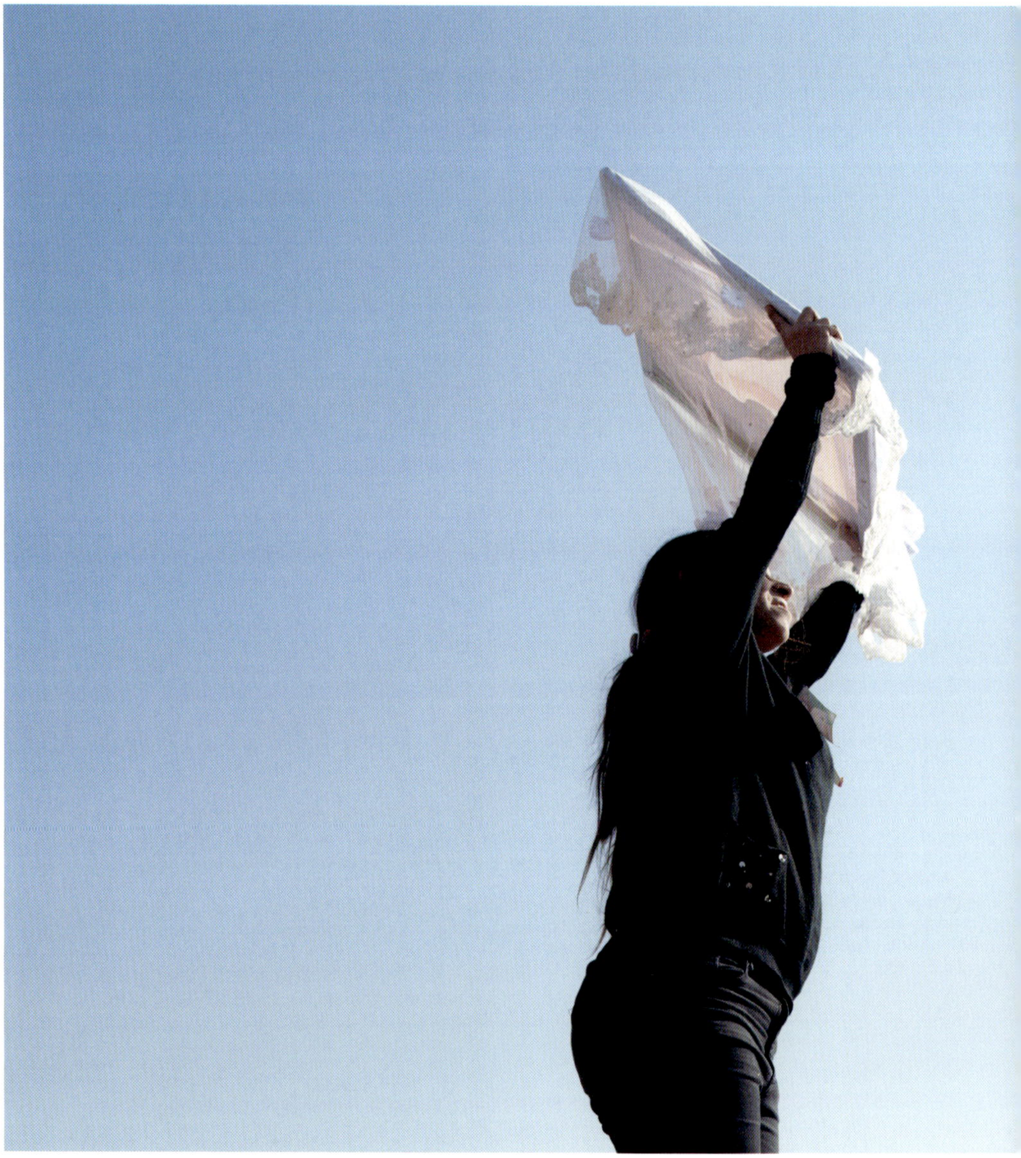

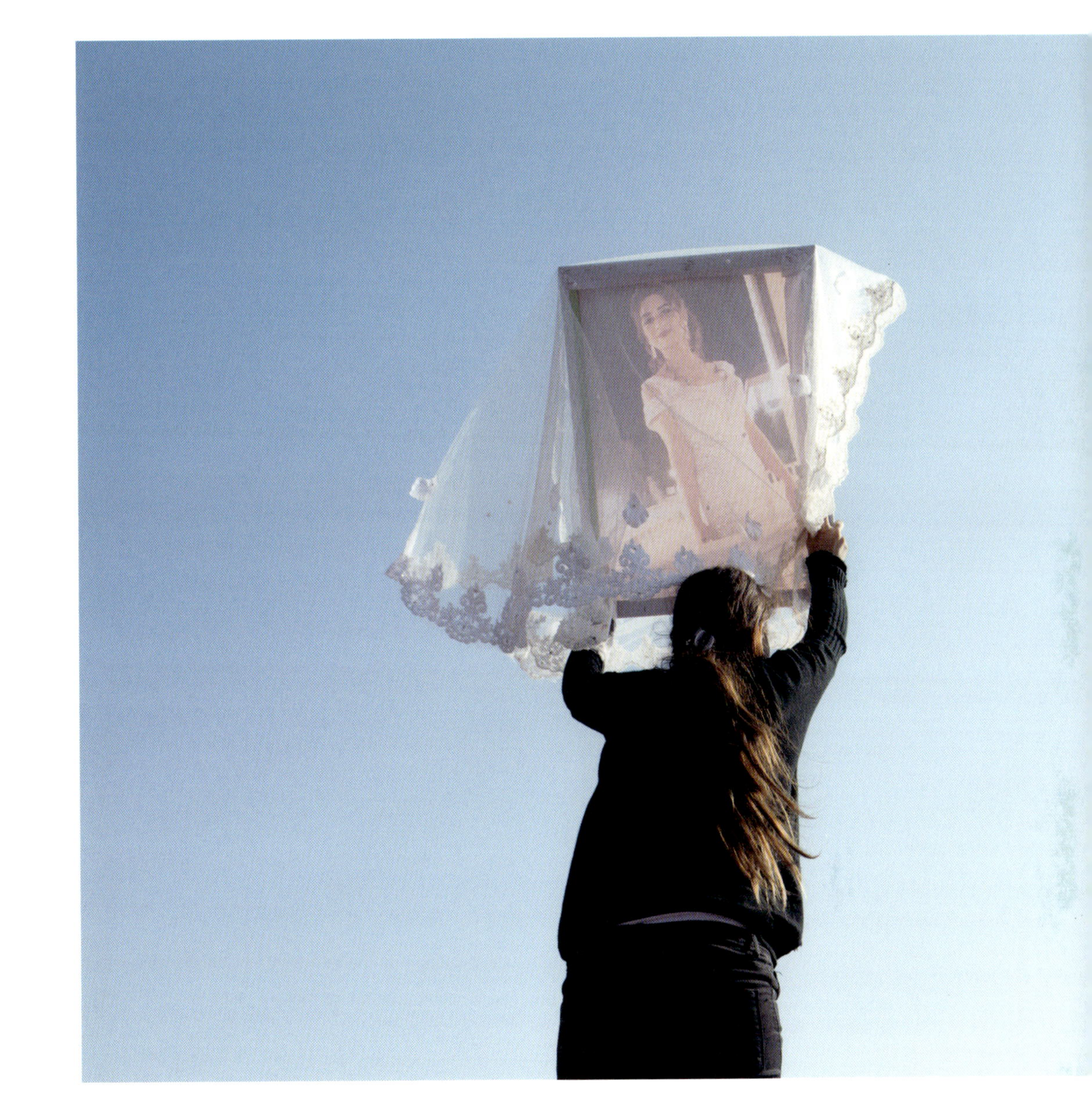

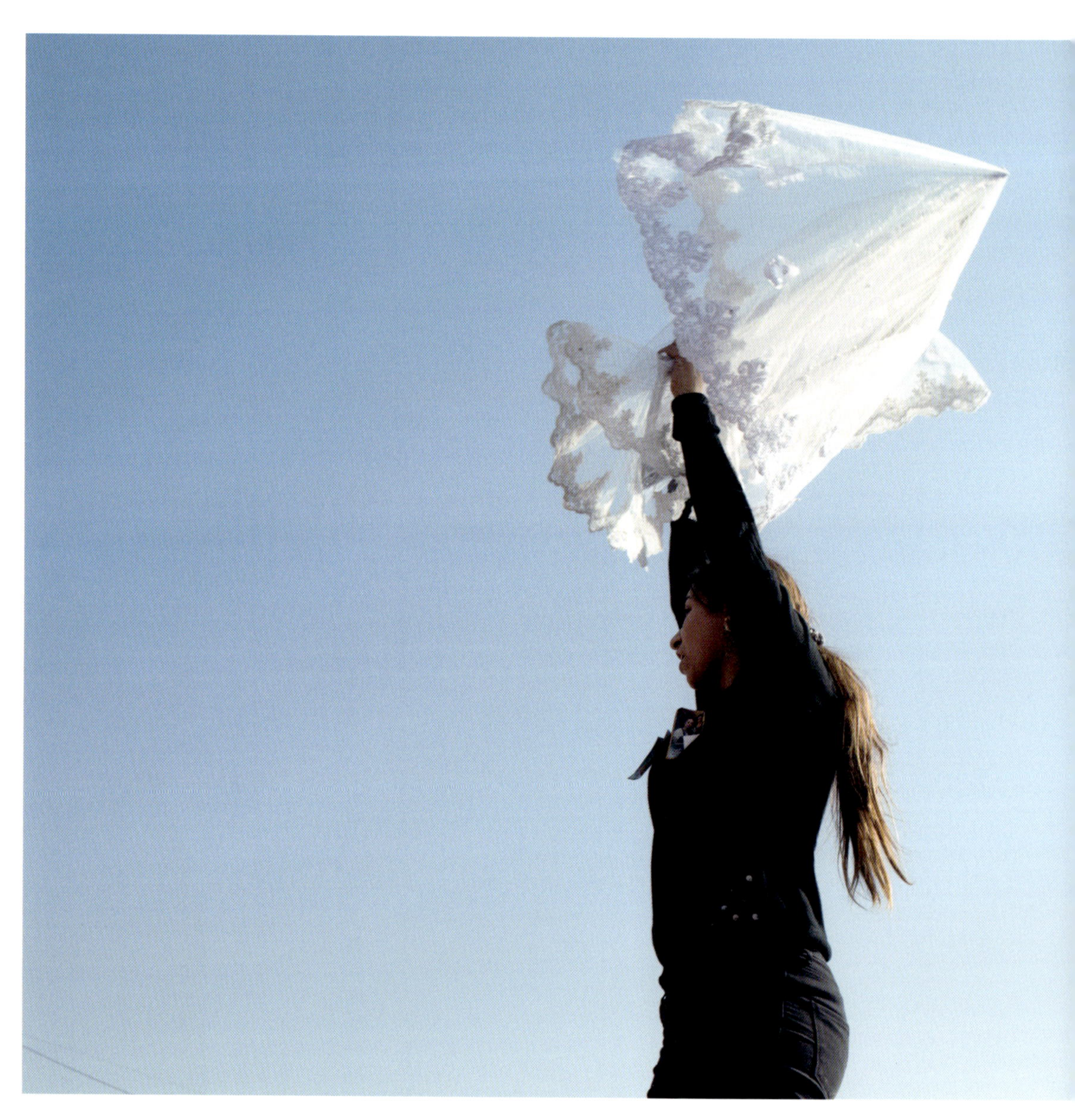

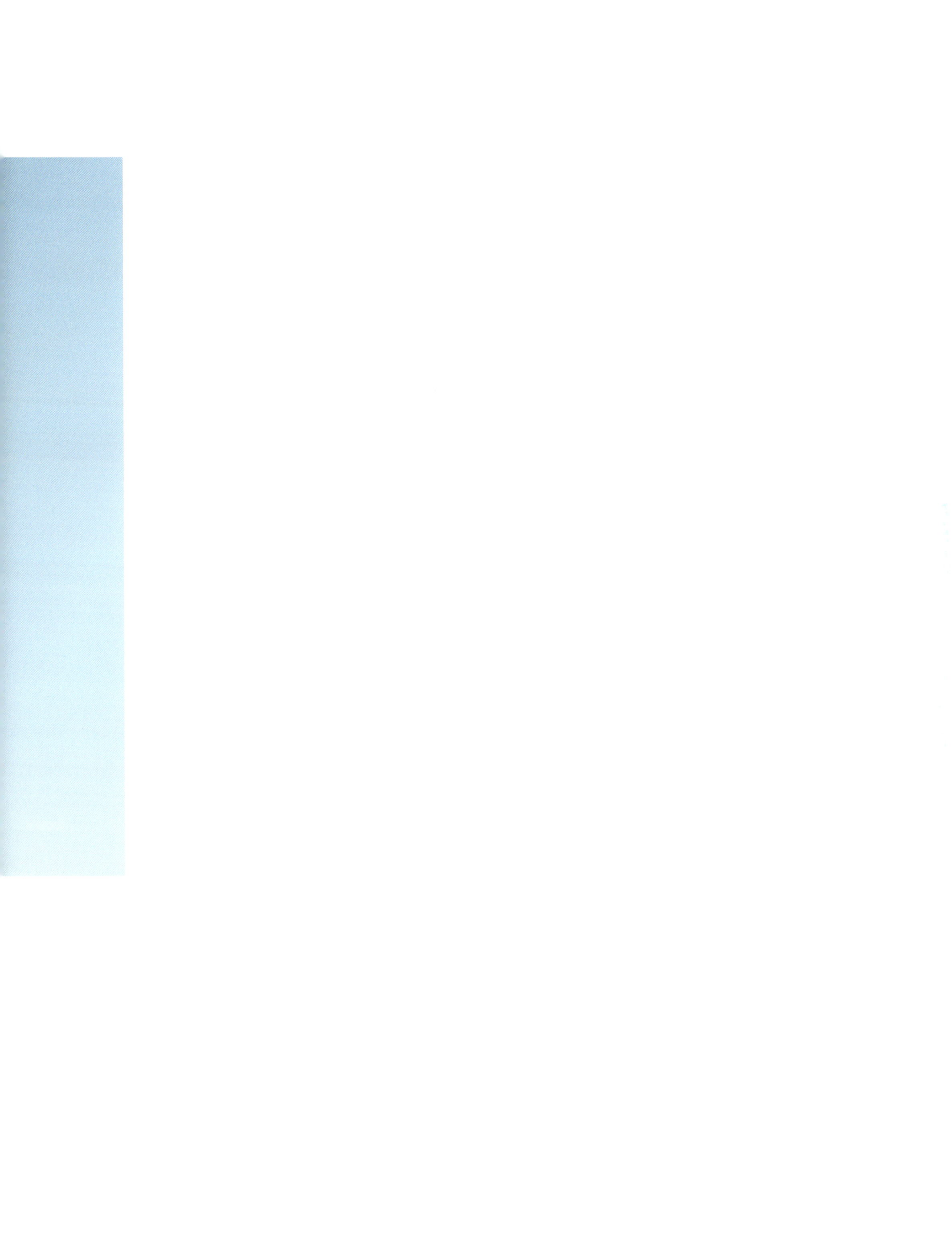

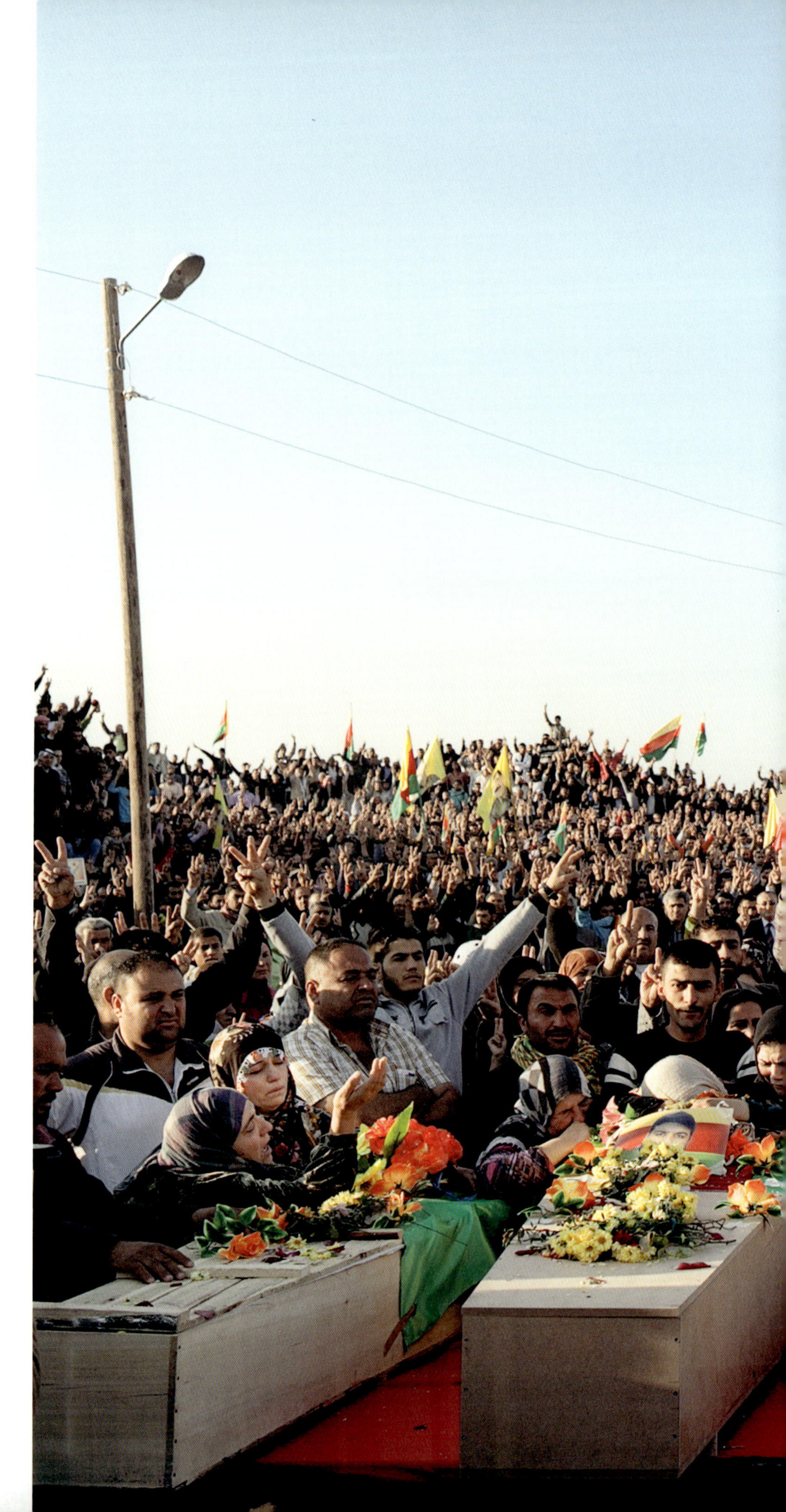

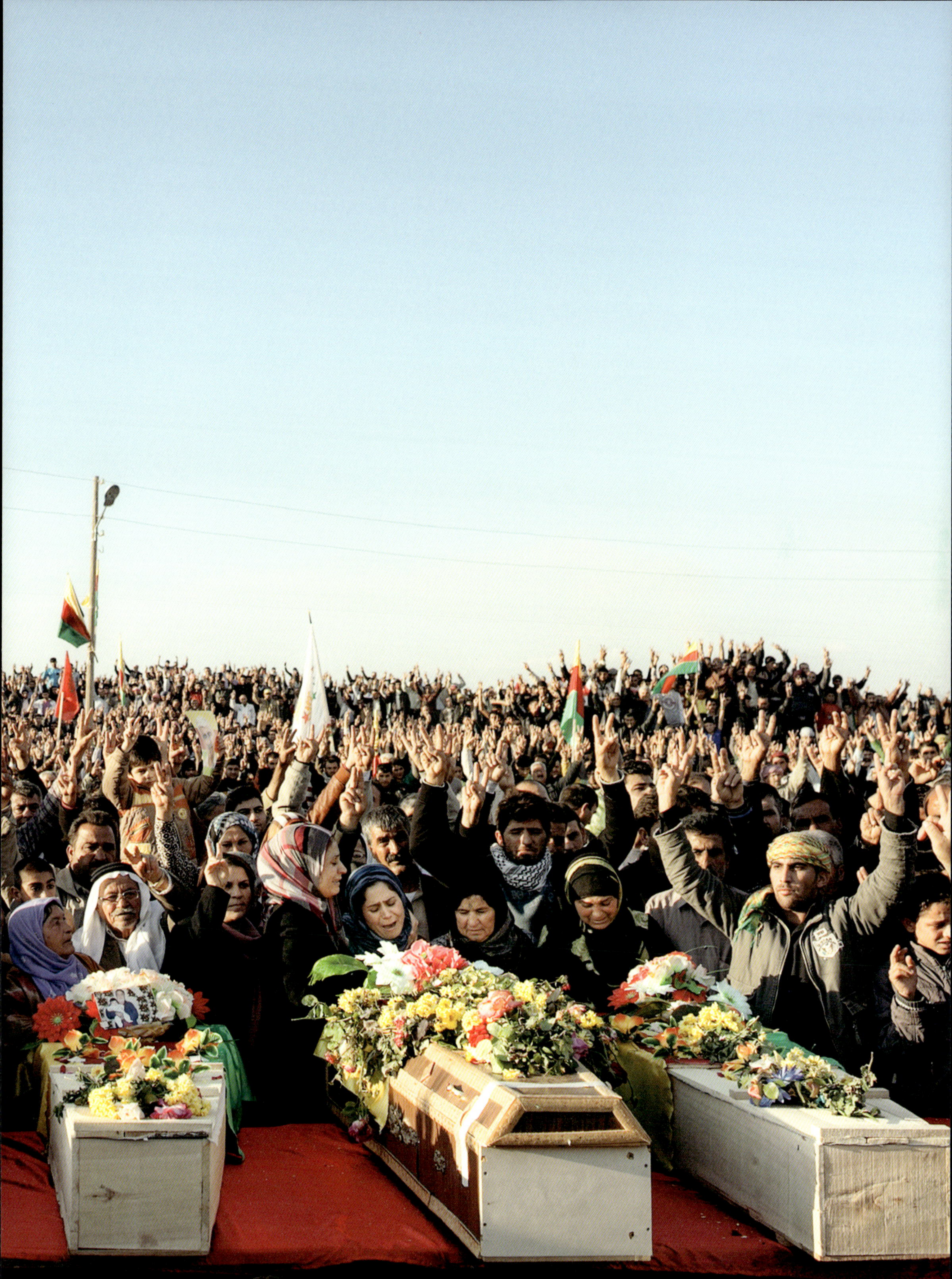

'DURING TIMES OF WAR, TRIBULATIONS, AND HARDSHIP, WORRIES ABOUND AND HEARTS REACH THE THROATS.'

'AS MUCH AS SOME LIBERAL JOURNALIST WOULD LIKE YOU TO BELIEVE THAT WE DO WHAT WE DO BECAUSE WE'RE SIMPLY MONSTERS WITH NO LOGIC BEHIND OUR COURSE OF ACTION, THE FACT IS THAT WE CONTINUE TO WAGE AND ESCALATE A CALCULATED WAR.'

صحيفة أسبوعية تصدر عن ديوان الإعلام المركزي | الخميس ١١ جمادى الأولى
العـدد ٦٧

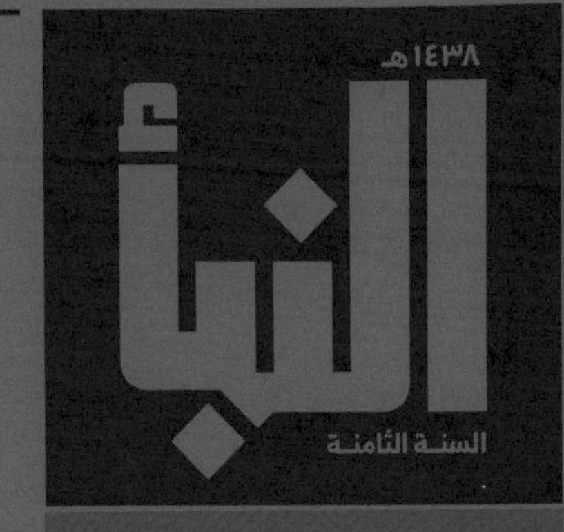

أمير ديوان الصحة: أنشأنا مؤسسات صحية متميزة وجامعاتنا الطبية تخرّج الكوادر المؤهلة

٨

معارك مستمرة على أطراف الباب وخسائر للنصيرية شرق خناصر

١٠

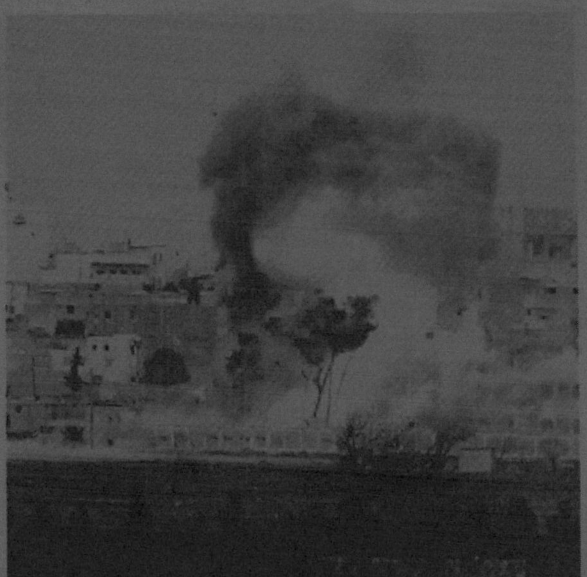

تدور مواجهات محتدمة بين جيش الدولة الإسلامية من جهة والجيش التركي المرتد وفصائل الصحوات من جهة أخرى على محوري مدينة الباب وبلدة بزاعة، في الوقت الذي أحبط فيه المجاهدون جميع محاولات الجيش النصيري للتقدم شرق بلدة خناصر، وقتلوا ٨٠ مرتدا من عناصره.

فقد شن الجيش التركي المرتد وفصائل الصحوات الأربعاء (١٠/ جمادى الأولى)، هجوما هو الأعنف على مدينة الباب، واندلعت مواجهات محتدمة بينهم وبين المجاهدين دون أن يتمكنوا من دخول أي حي من أحياء المدينة.

فقد حاولت قوات كبيرة من الصحوات والجيش التركي المرتد معززين بعشرات الآليات والمدرعات العسكرية ومئات الجنود المشاة التقدم من أكثر من محور في محيط مدينة الباب وخاصة من الجهة الغربية للمدينة حيث تركز هجومهم، وقد تمكن جنود الدولة الإسلامية -بفضل الله- من إحباط هجوم المرتدين على السكن الشبابي غربي المدينة وقتلوا وأصابوا ...

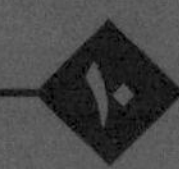

مقتل ٣٢ رافضياً في الدور بعملية انغماسية

٥

٧٥ قتيلاً وجريحاً من الروافض جنوب تلعفر

٦

٥٠ قتيلاً من الجيش النصيري قرب مطار الـ T4

١١

إفشال حملة للجيش المصري وسط سيناء

١٢

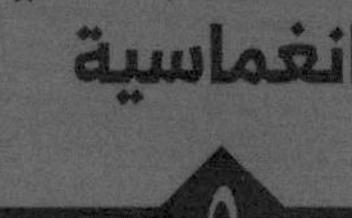
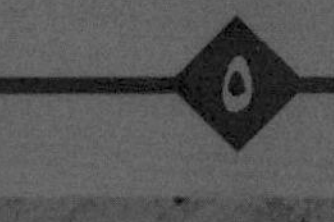
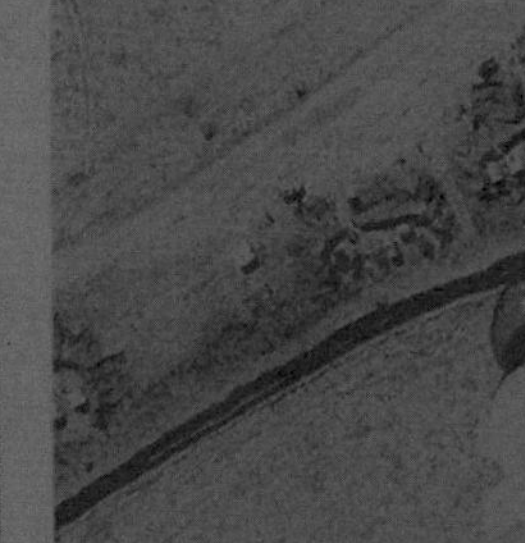

طائرات المجاهدين المسيرة
مصدر رعب جديد للمرتدين

٤

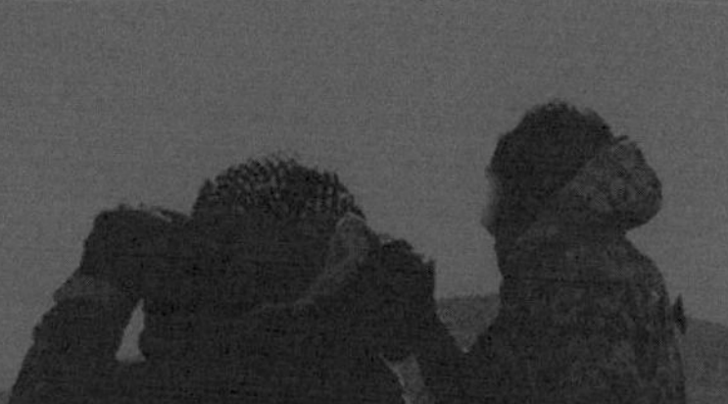

حملة مشتركة للصحوات
والجيش النصيري في القلمون الشرقي

١٣

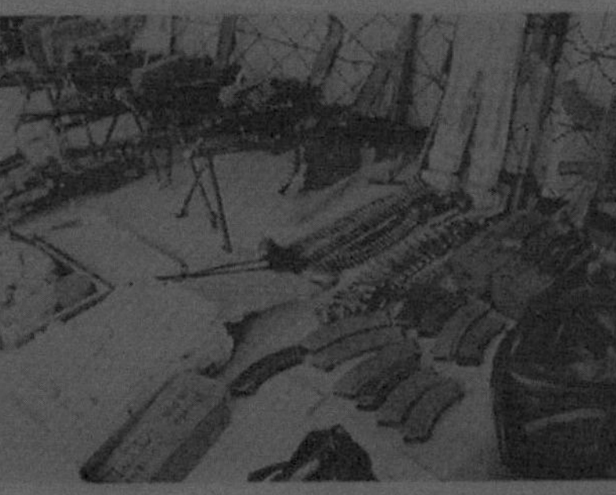

توكلوا على الله لا على عُدَدكم

١٤

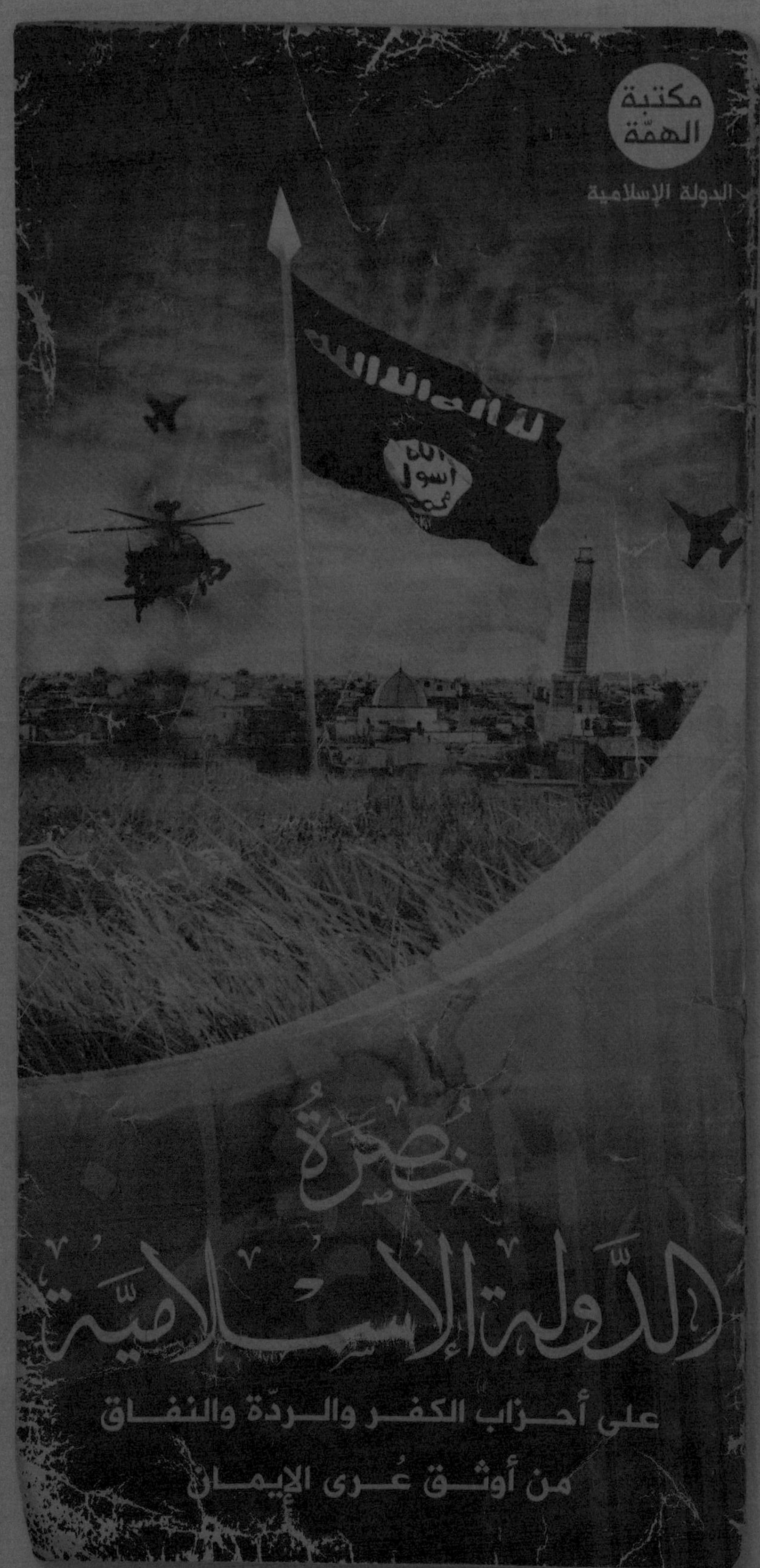
مكتبة
الهمّة
الدولة الإسلامية
نصرة
الدولة الإسلامية
على أحزاب الكفر والردّة والنفاق
من أوثق عُرى الإيمان

'THE HISTORICAL ORIGIN OF THE "ARAB SPRING" BANNERS—IS A FLAG DESIGNED BY THE BRITISH CRUSADER MARK SYKES. YES, MARK SYKES OF THE SYKES-PICOT AGREEMENT, WHICH DIVIDED THE MUSLIMS' LANDS INTO NATIONALIST STATES.'

الدَّوْلَةُ الإِسْلَامِيَّةُ

خِلَافَةٌ عَلَى مِنْهَاجِ النُّبُوَّةِ

دِيـوَانُ الحِسْبَـةِ

وِلَايَةُ نِينَـوَى

لا إله إلا الله
الله رسول محمد

التاريخ : ١٤ / ربيع الأول / ١٤٣٦هـ

الموافق : ٥ / ١ / ٢٠١٥ م

بِسْمِ اللهِ الرَّحْمَنِ الرَّحِيمِ

(شُرُوطُ الحِجَابِ الشَّرْعِي)

الحَمْدُ لِلهِ، وَالصَّلاةُ وَالسَّلامُ عَلَى رَسُولِ اللهِ، وَعَلَى آلِهِ وَصَحْبِهِ وَمَنْ وَالاهُ، ثُمَّ أَمَّا بَعْدُ: فَإِنَّ الشَّرِيعَةَ الإِسْلامِيَّةَ حَدَّدَتْ خُرُوجَ المَرْأَةِ المُسْلِمَةِ مِنْ بَيْتِهَا وِفْقَ ضَوَابِطَ مُعَيَّنَةٍ، وَمِنْ أَبْرَزِ وَأَهَمِّ هَذِهِ الضَّوَابِطِ مَا هُوَ مُتَعَلِّقٌ بِمَلْبَسِ المَرْأَةِ حَالَ خُرُوجِهَا، وَحَتَّى يَكُونَ لِبَاسُ المَرْأَةِ إِذَا كَانَتْ بِحُضُورِ أَجَانِبَ أَوْ عِنْدَ خُرُوجِهَا مِنَ البَيْتِ لِبَاساً شَرْعِيّاً يَجِبُ أَنْ يَسْتَوْفِيَ الشُّرُوطَ التَّالِيَةَ:

١- أَنْ يَكُونَ سَاتِراً لِجَمِيعِ البَدَنِ: فَيُمْنَعُ ارْتِدَاءُ المَلابِسِ القَصِيرَةِ الَّتِي تَصِلُ إِلَى أَنْصَافِ السَّاقَيْنِ، أَوْ فَتْحُ أَزْرَارِ العَبَاءَاتِ مِنَ الأَسْفَلِ، وَيُمْنَعُ ارْتِدَاءُ الخِمَارِ القَصِيرِ الَّذِي لا يَكَادُ يُغَطِّي الوَجْهَ أَحْيَاناً، وَيَكْشِفُ عَمَّا تَحْتَهُ، وَيَلْزَمُ ارْتِدَاءُ الخِمَارِ الطَّوِيلِ الَّذِي يَصِلُ إِلَى الرُّكْبَةِ، عَلَى أَنْ يَكُونَ وَاسِعاً، وَكَذَلِكَ يَلْزَمُ ارْتِدَاءُ الكَفَّيْنِ وَالجَوْرَبَيْنِ، وَتَغْطِيَةُ العَيْنَيْنِ.

٢- أَنْ يَكُونَ ثَخِيناً لا يَشِفُّ عَمَّا تَحْتَهُ: فَيُمْنَعُ ارْتِدَاءُ الخِمَارِ الَّذِي يَكُونُ قُمَاشُهُ خَفِيفاً يَشِفُّ عَمَّا تَحْتَهُ، لِأَنَّهُ سَيَتَبَيَّنُ مِنْ خِلالِهِ الوَجْهُ، وَفِي حَالَةِ كَوْنِهِ طَوِيلاً خَفِيفاً سَيَتَبَيَّنُ وَجْهُ المَرْأَةِ وَكَذَلِكَ شَيْءٌ مِنْ مَلْبَسِهَا.

٣- أَنْ يَكُونَ فَضْفَاضاً غَيْرَ ضَيِّقٍ: فَيُمْنَعُ مِنَ المَلْبَسِ ارْتِدَاءُ مَا هُوَ ضَيِّقٌ وَيَكْشِفُ عَنْ مَفَاتِنِ المَرْأَةِ، كَالتَّنُّورَةِ لِوَحْدِهَا، أَوِ العَبَاءَةِ أَوِ الجُبَّةِ الضَّيِّقَةِ، وَيُمْنَعُ مِنَ الخِمَارِ ارْتِدَاءُ الخِمَارِ الضَّيِّقِ الَّذِي يَكُونُ عَلَى شَكْلِ عُصْبَةٍ مَشْدُودَةٍ وَاضِحٍ ضِيقُهَا.

٤- أَنْ لا يَكُونَ زِينَةً فِي نَفْسِهِ: فَيُمْنَعُ ارْتِدَاءُ العَبَاءَاتِ الَّتِي فِيهَا زِينَةٌ تَلْفِتُ النَّاظِرَ إِلَيْهَا فَتَكُونُ هَذِهِ العَبَاءَةُ بِحَدِّ ذَاتِهَا فِتْنَةً، وَيُمْنَعُ ارْتِدَاءُ الخِمَارِ المُزَرْكَشِ.

٥- أَنْ لا يَكُونَ مُطَيَّباً وَلا مُبَخَّراً: فَيُمْنَعُ تَطْيِيبُ المَلْبَسِ وَالخِمَارِ عِنْدَ الخُرُوجِ مِنَ البَيْتِ، لِعُمُومِ قَوْلِهِ ﷺ: (أَيُّمَا امْرَأَةٍ خَرَجَتْ مِنْ بَيْتِهَا مُتَطَيِّبَةً تُرِيدُ المَسْجِدَ لَمْ يَقْبَلِ اللهُ عَزَّ وَجَلَّ لَهَا صَلاةً حَتَّى تَرْجِعَ فَتَغْتَسِلَ مِنْهُ غُسْلَهَا مِنَ الجَنَابَةِ). رَوَاهُ أَحْمَدُ.

٦- أَنْ لا يُشْبِهَ لِبَاسَ الرِّجَالِ: فَيُمْنَعُ ارْتِدَاءُ المَرْأَةِ لِأَيِّ لِبَاسٍ يُشْبِهُ لِبَاسَ الرَّجُلِ.

٧- أَنْ لا يُشْبِهَ لِبَاسَ الكَافِرَاتِ: فَيُمْنَعُ ارْتِدَاءُ المَرْأَةِ لِأَيِّ لِبَاسٍ يُشْبِهُ لِبَاسَ الكَافِرَاتِ، لِأَنَّهُ تَشَبُّهٌ بِهِنَّ، قَالَ رَسُولُ اللهِ ﷺ: (مَنْ تَشَبَّهَ بِقَوْمٍ فَهُوَ مِنْهُمْ). رَوَاهُ أَبُو دَاوُد.

مُلاحَظَة: يَكُونُ الالْتِزَامُ بِالمُقَرَّرَاتِ الَّتِي ذُكِرَتْ آنِفاً مُنْذُ تَارِيخِ نَشْرِ البَيَانِ وَلِمُدَّةِ أَرْبَعَةِ أَيَّامٍ، وَبِنَاءً عَلَى هَذَا، فَإِنَّ المُخَالِفَ لِهَذِهِ المُقَرَّرَاتِ الَّتِي رُوعِيَتْ فِيهَا المَصَالِحُ الشَّرْعِيَّةُ المُعْتَبَرَةُ سَيُعَرِّضُ نفسه لِعُقُوبَةٍ تَعْزِيرِيَّةٍ مُنْضَبِطَةٍ وِفْقَ ضَوَابِطِ الشَّرِيعَةِ الغَرَّاءِ.

الدَّوْلَةُ الإِسْلامِيَّةُ

وَصَلَّى اللهُ عَلَى سَيِّدِنَا مُحَمَّدٍ وَعَلَى آلِهِ وَصَحْبِهِ أَجْمَعِينَ

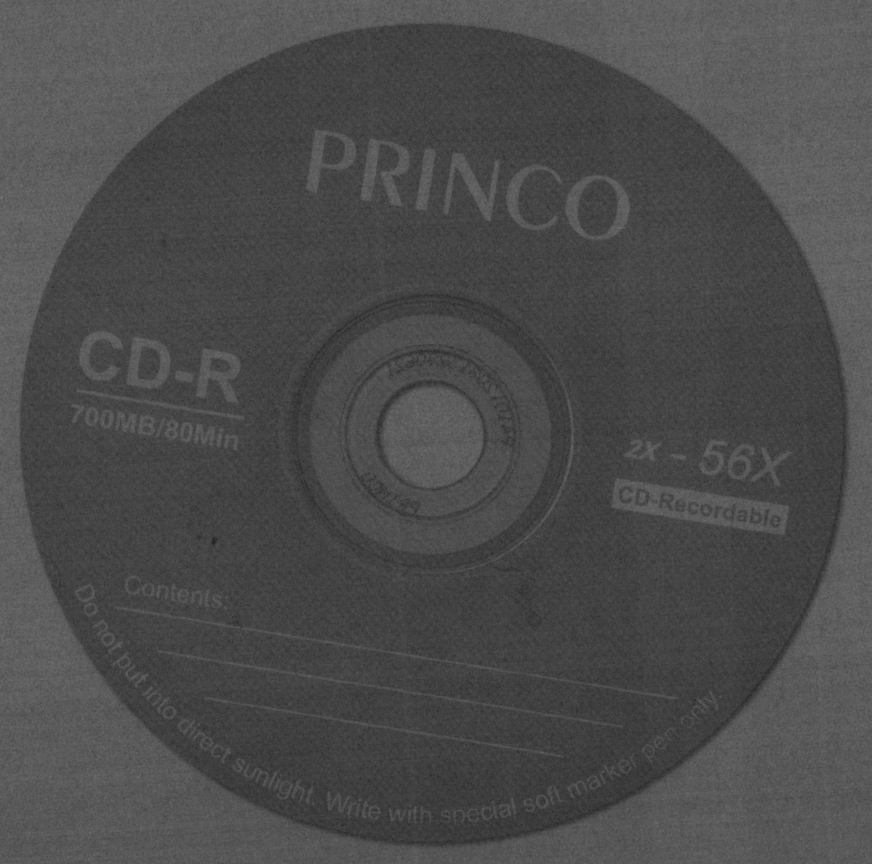

PRINCO
CD-R
700MB/80Min
2x - 56X
CD-Recordable
Contents:
Do not put into direct sunlight. Write with special soft marker pen only.

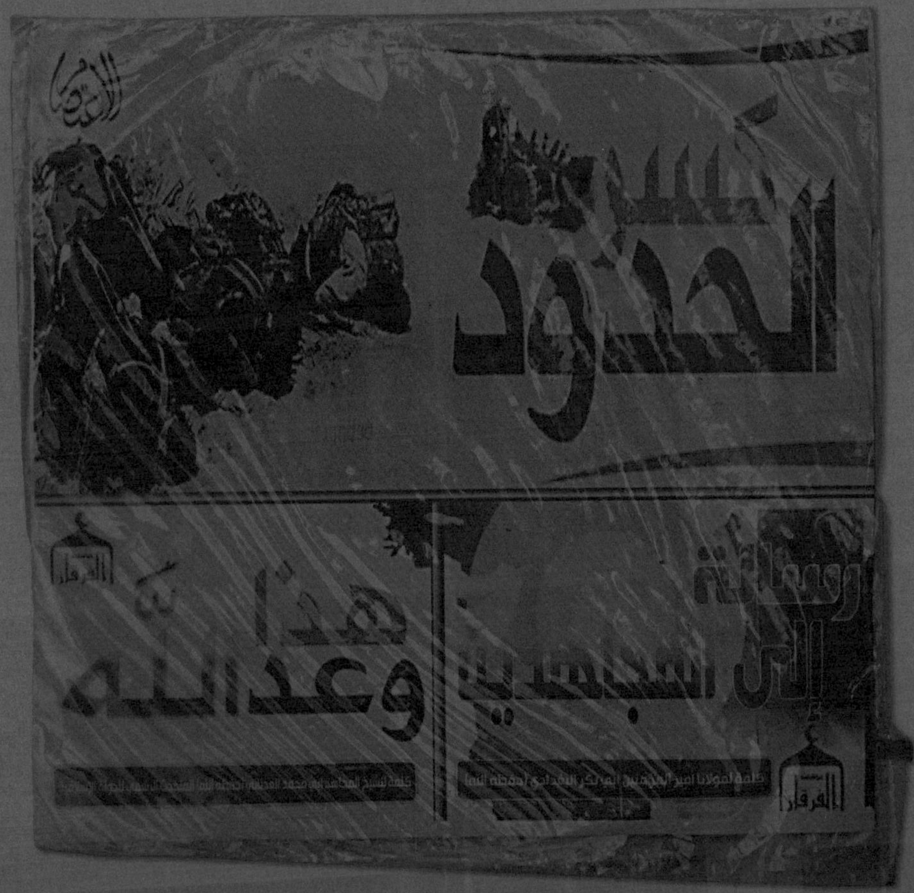

الحدود
هذا
وعد الله

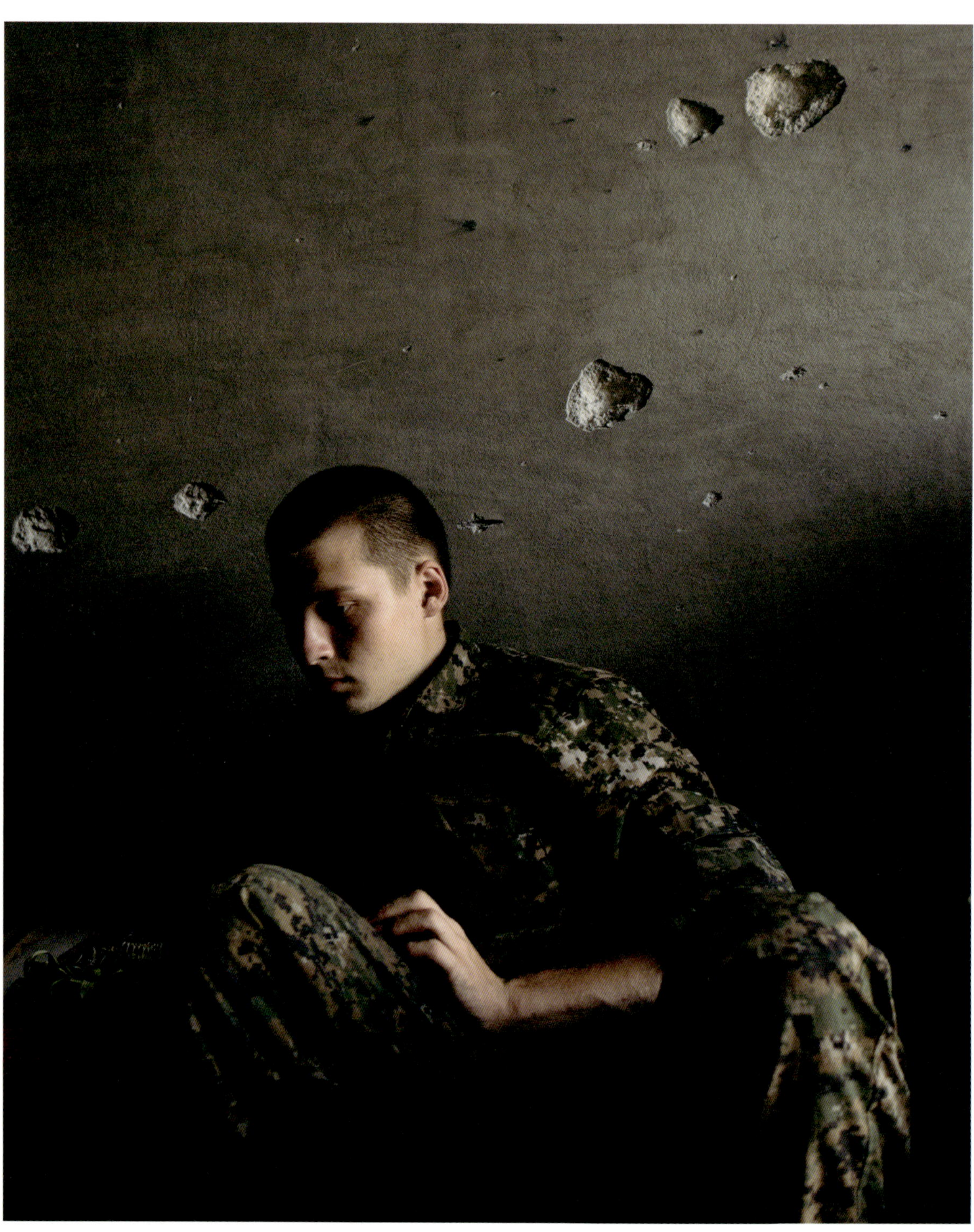

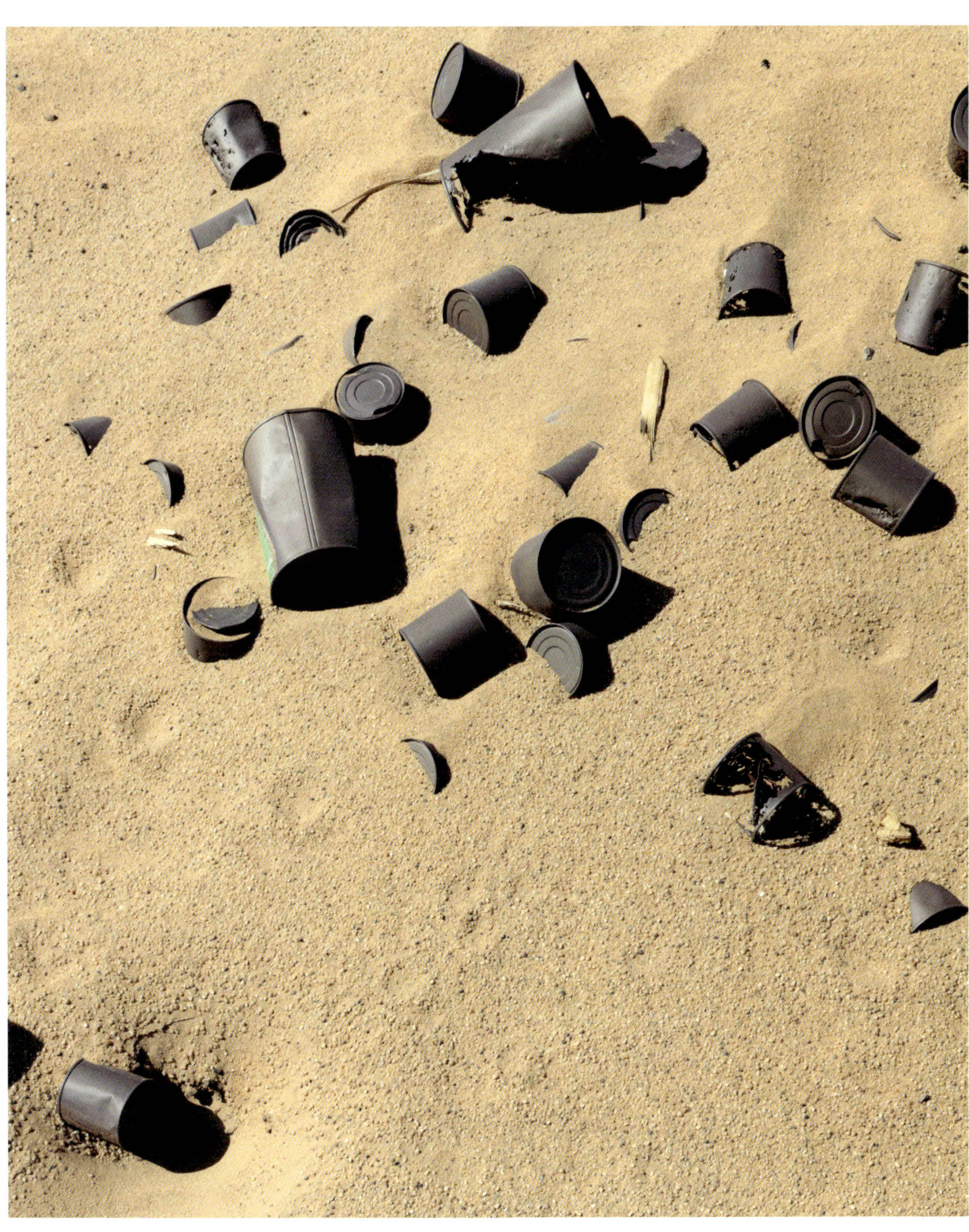

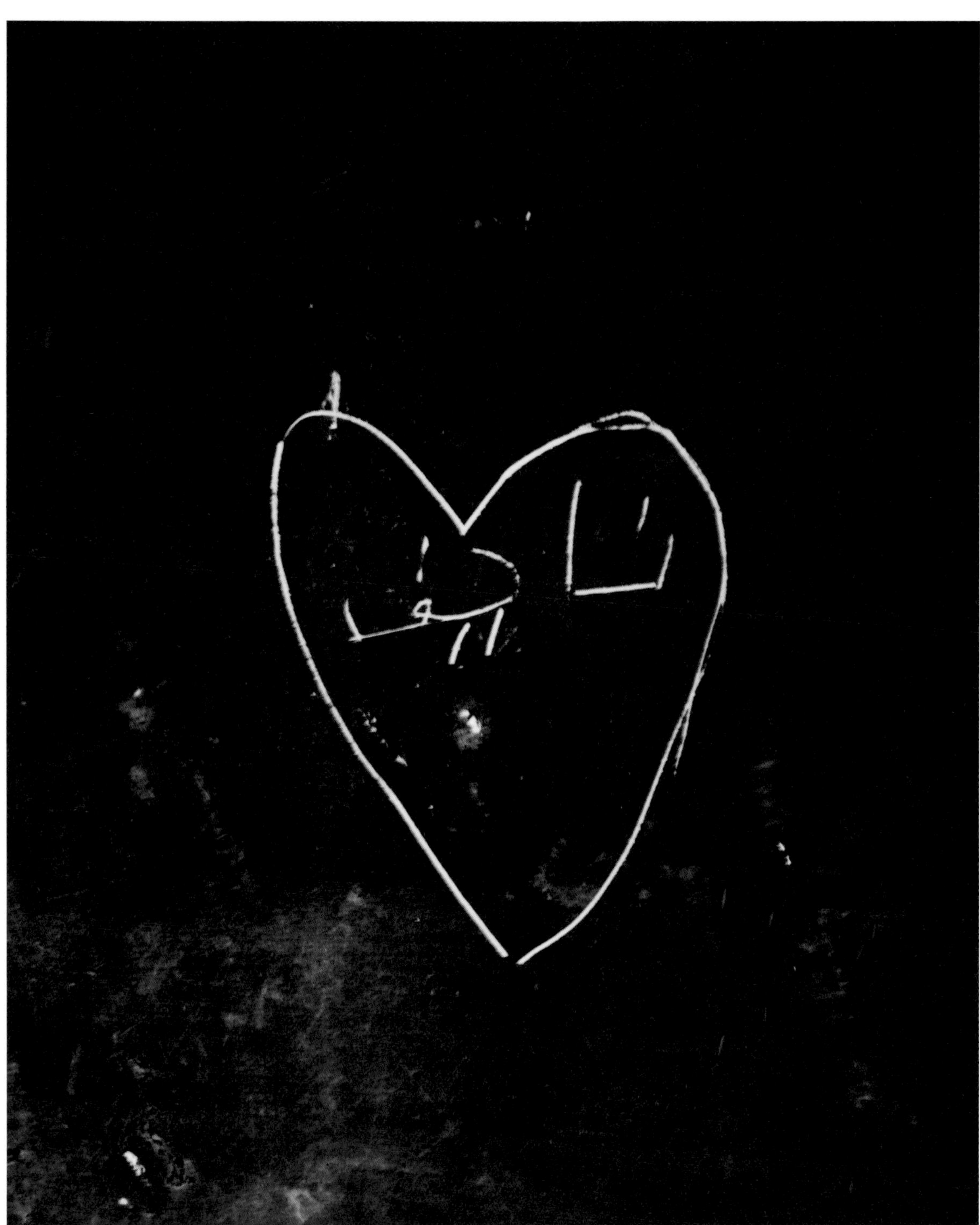

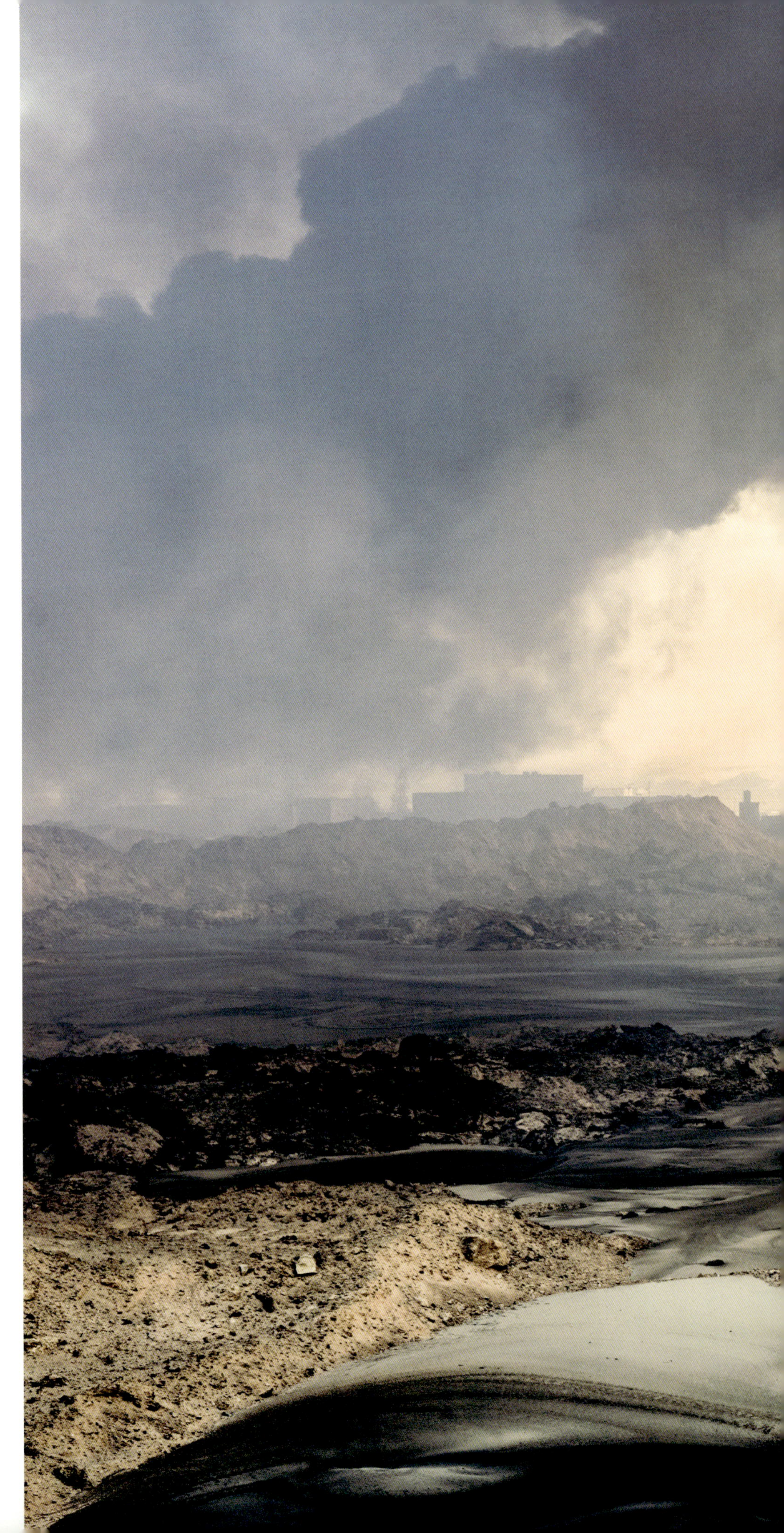

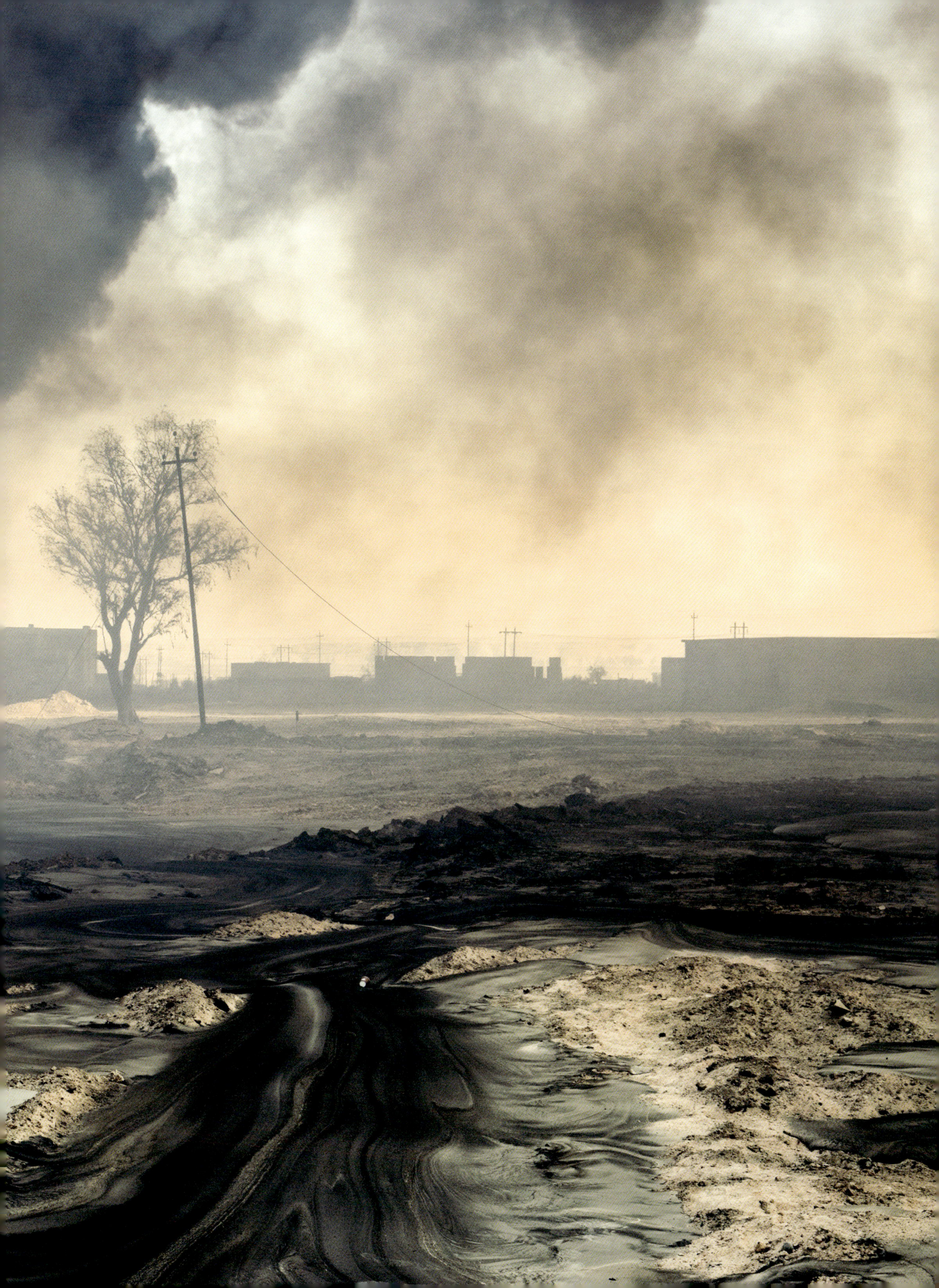

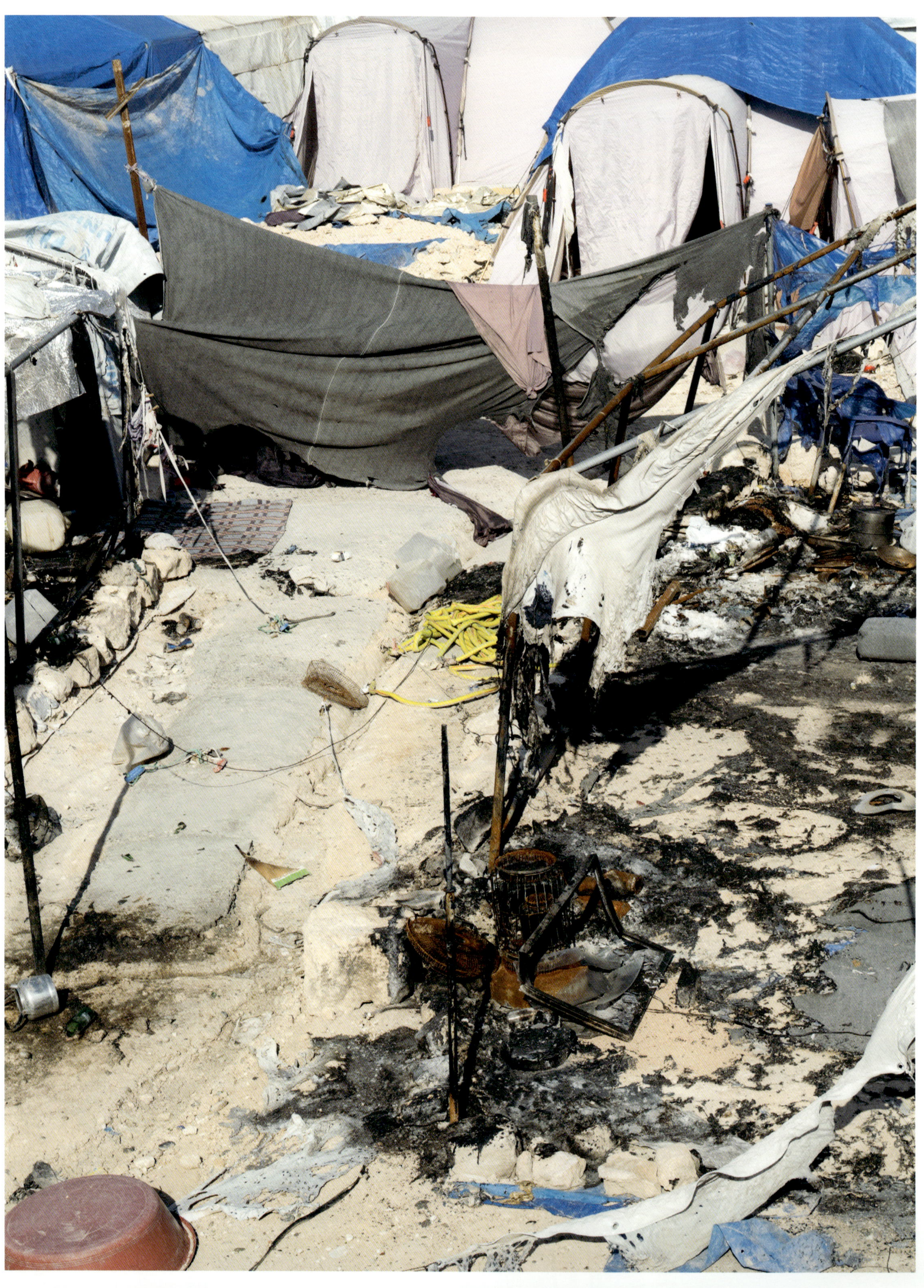

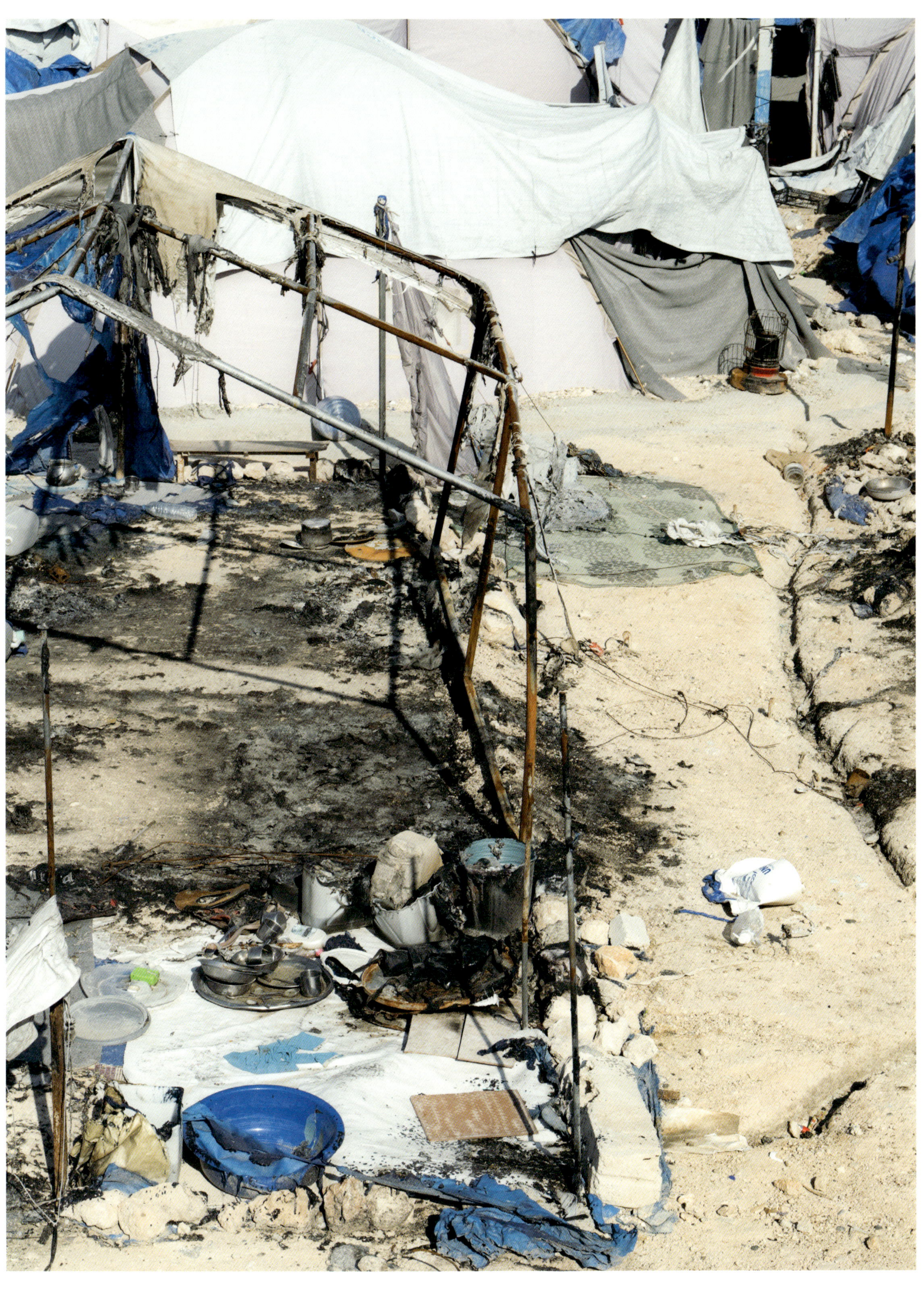

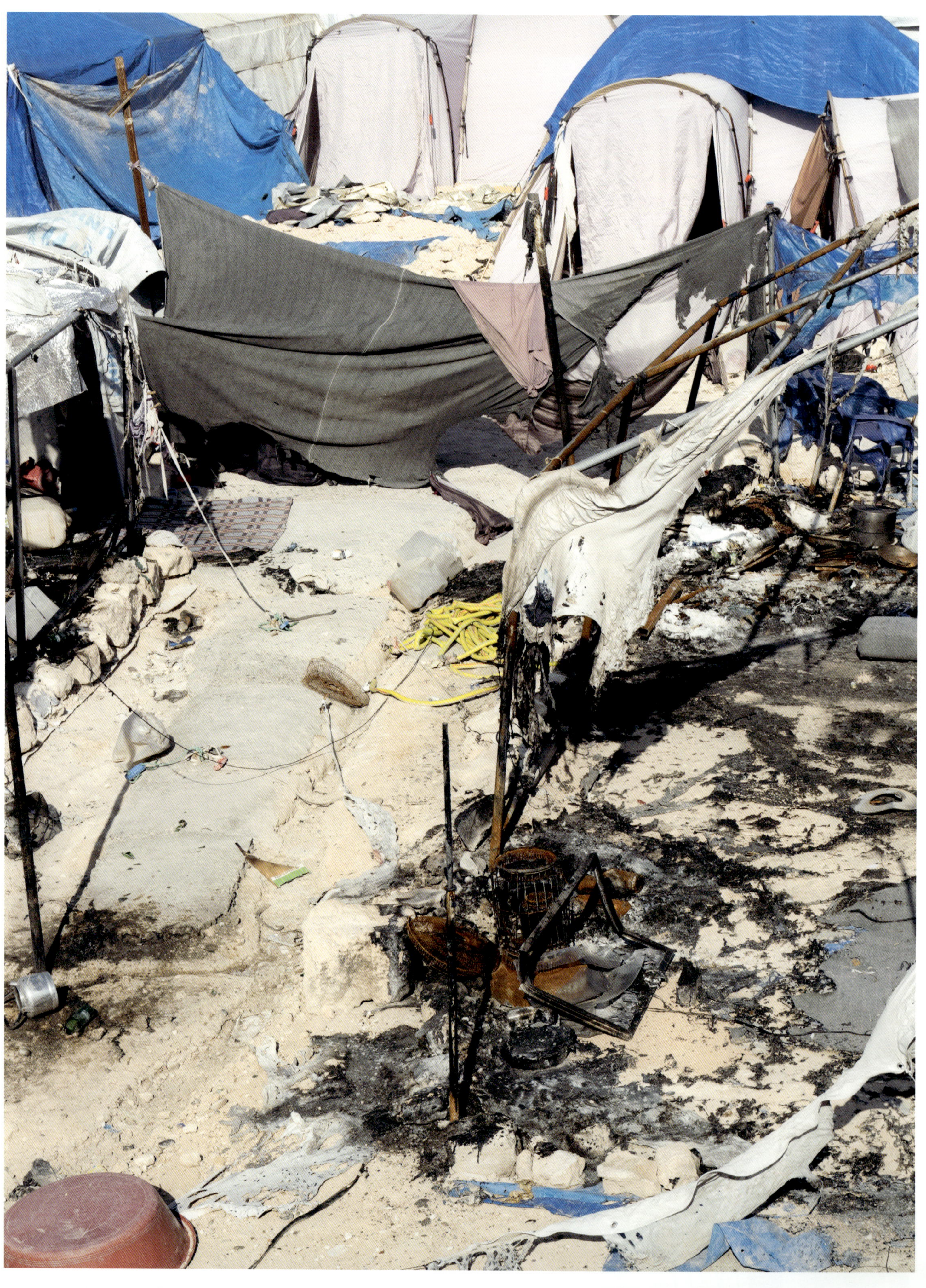

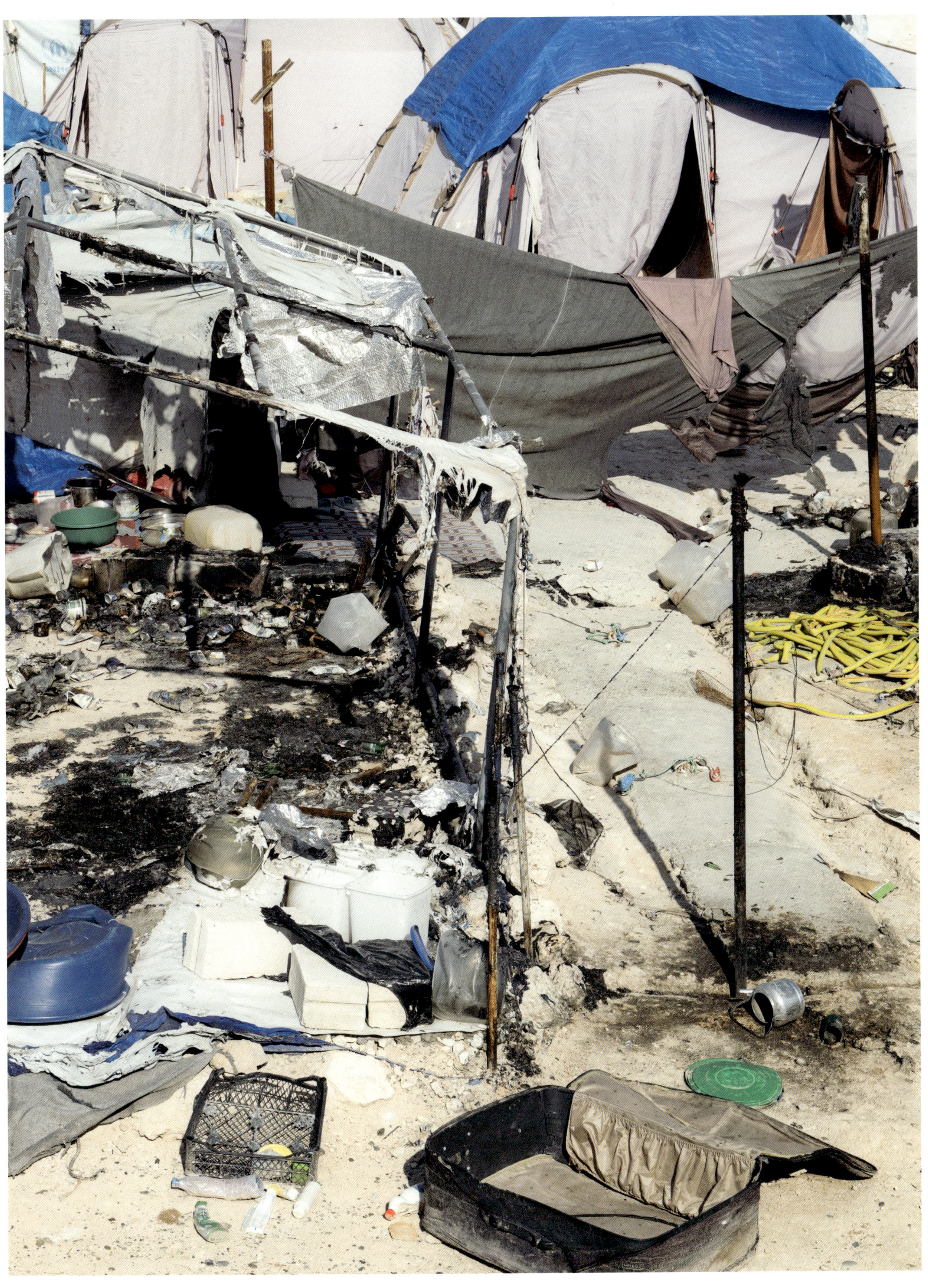

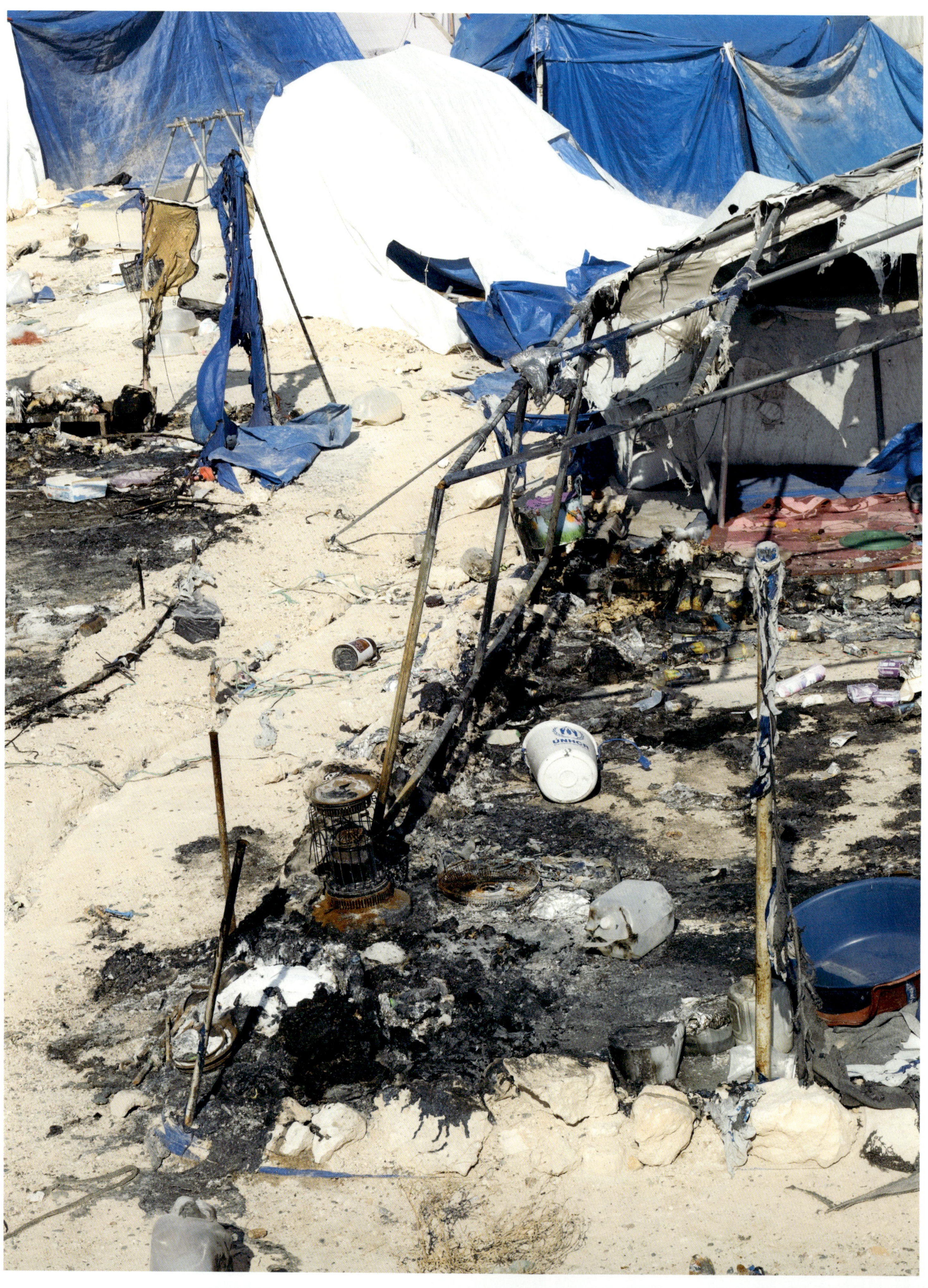
UNHCR

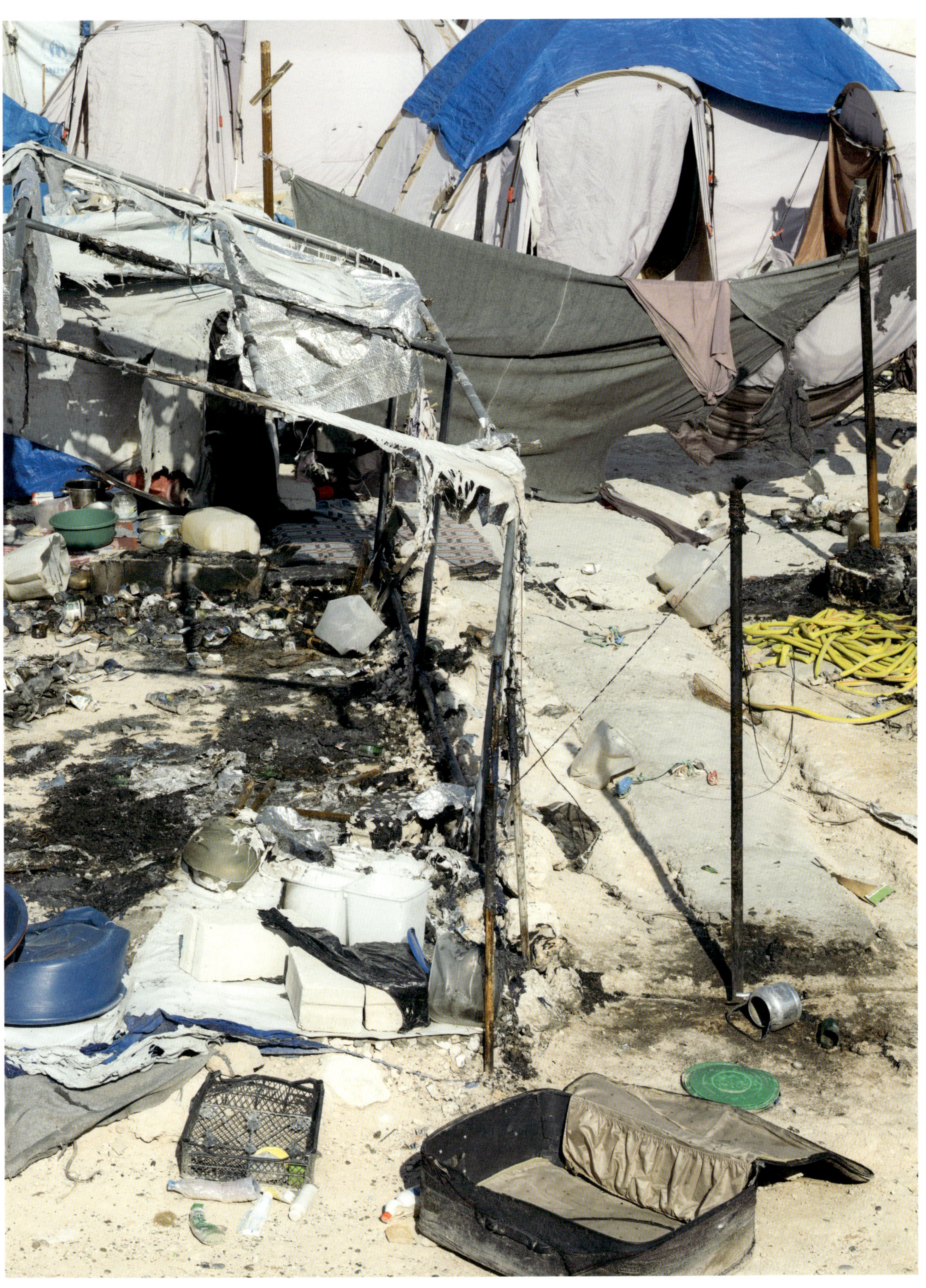

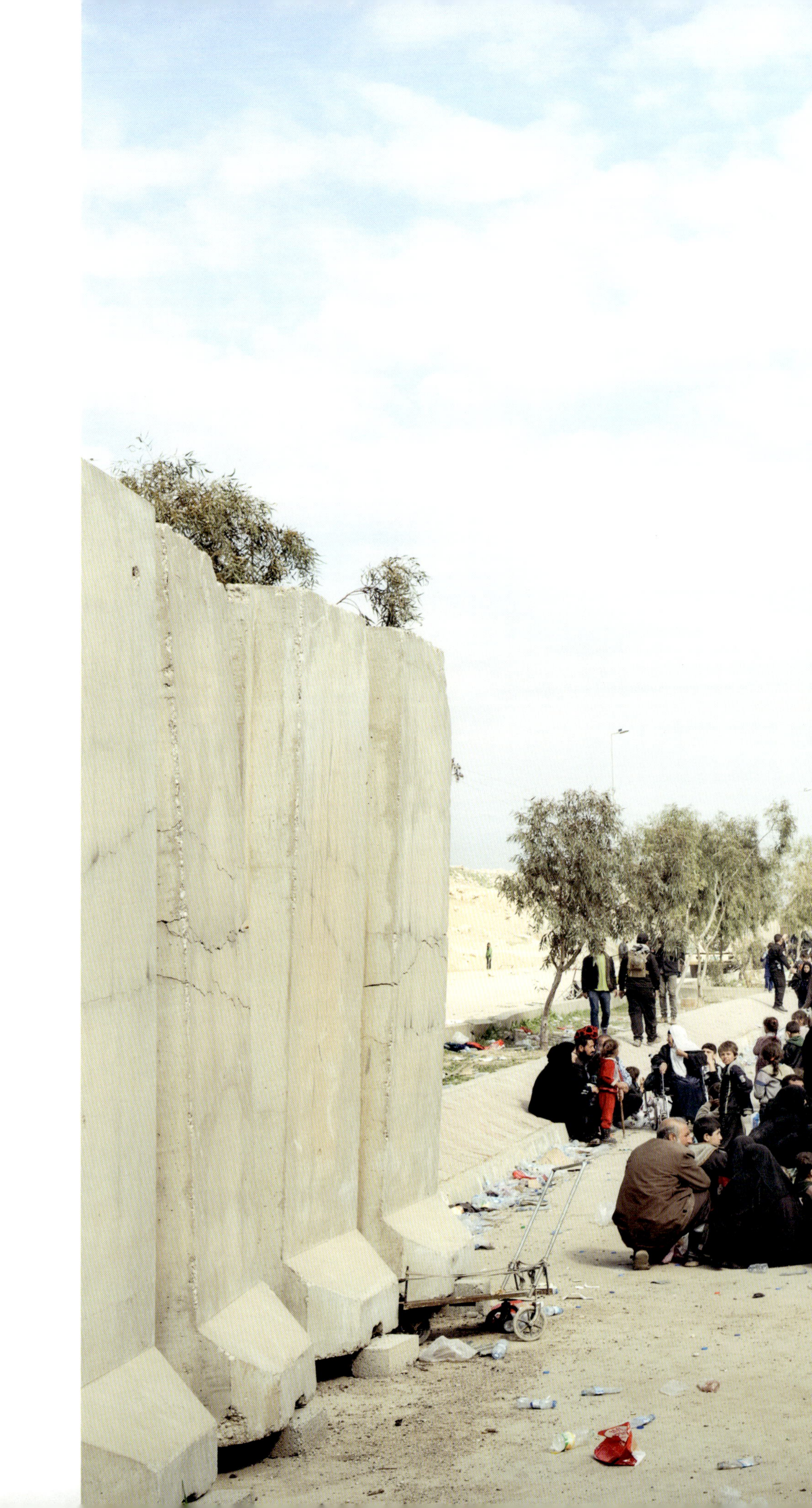

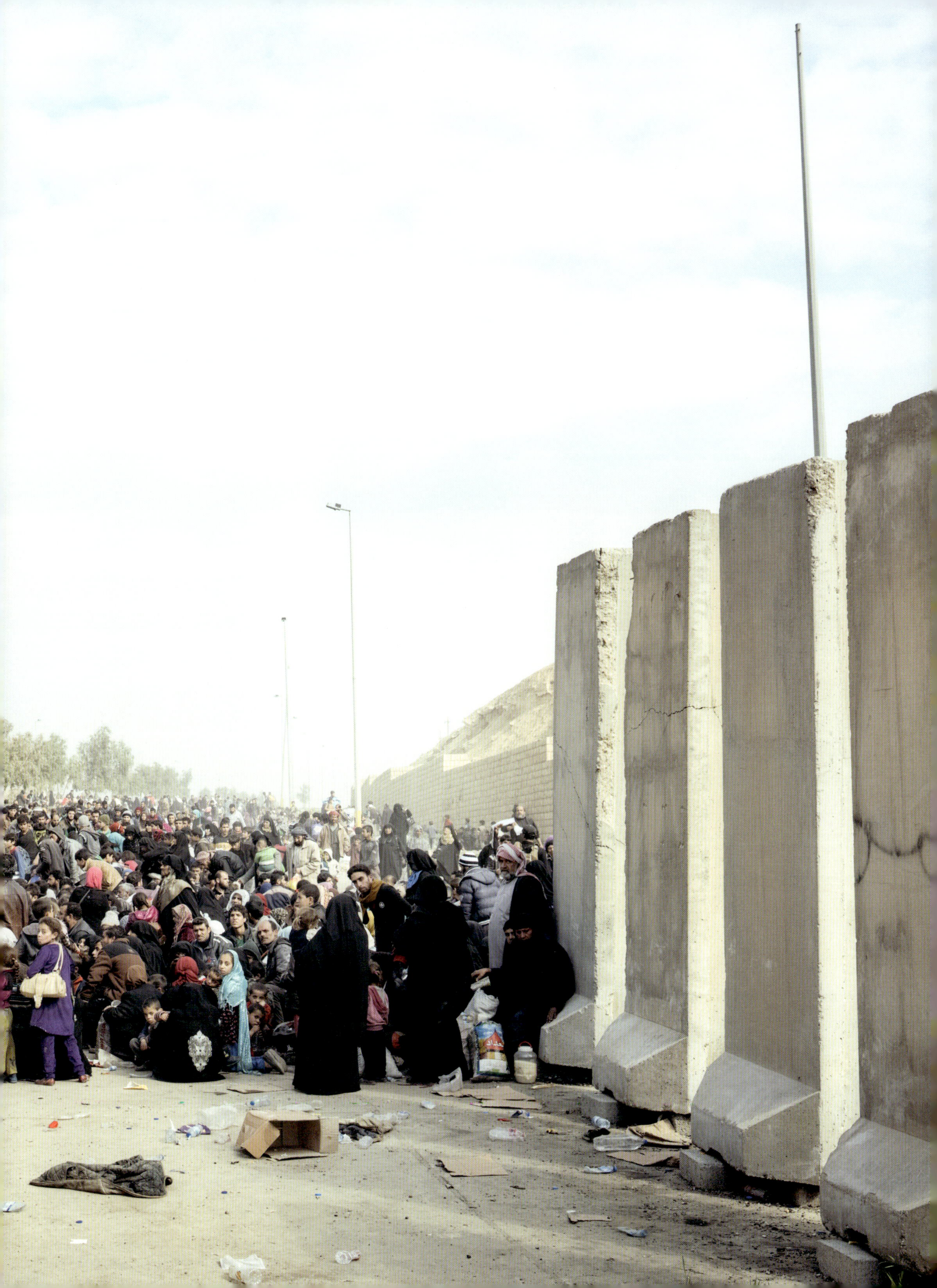

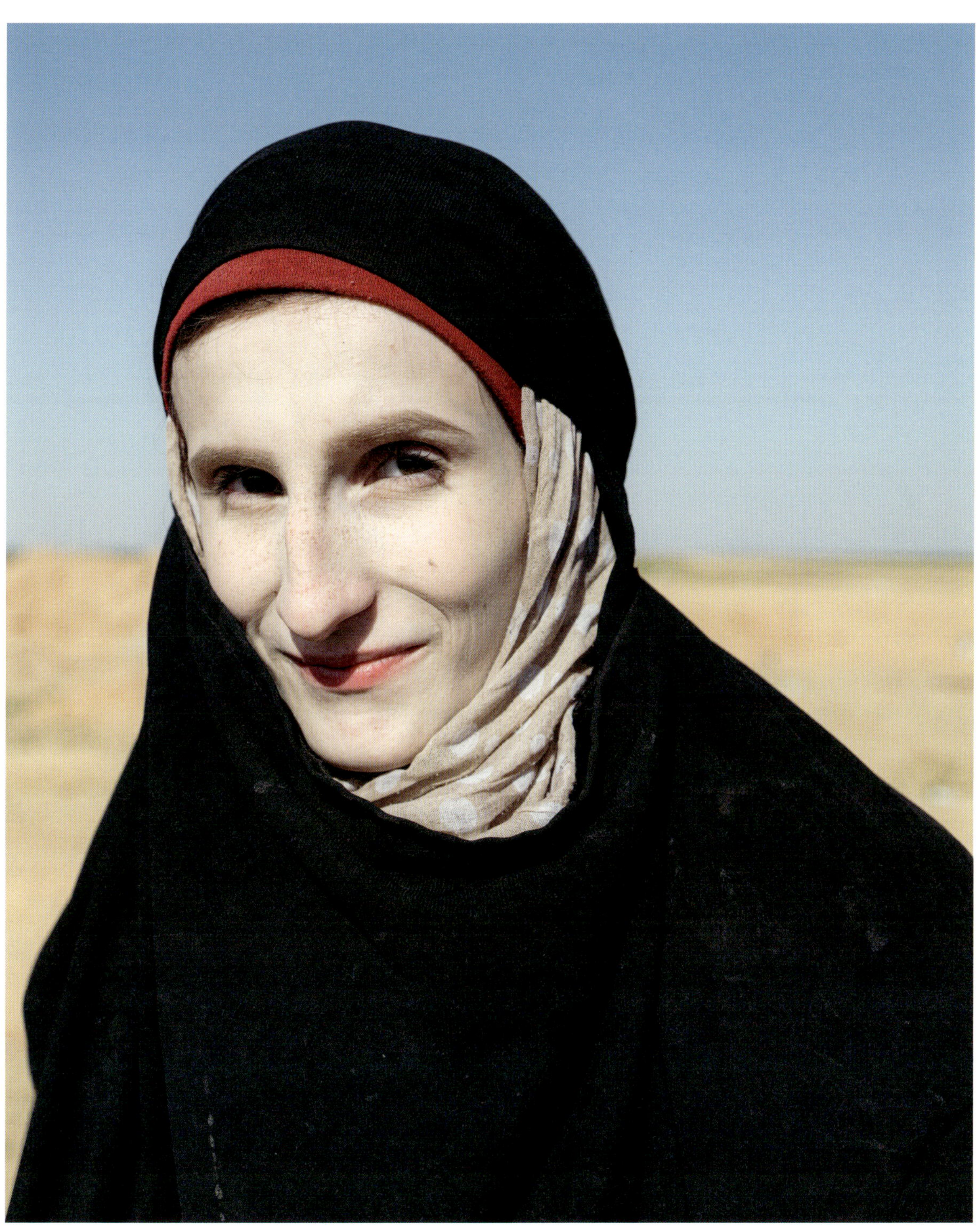

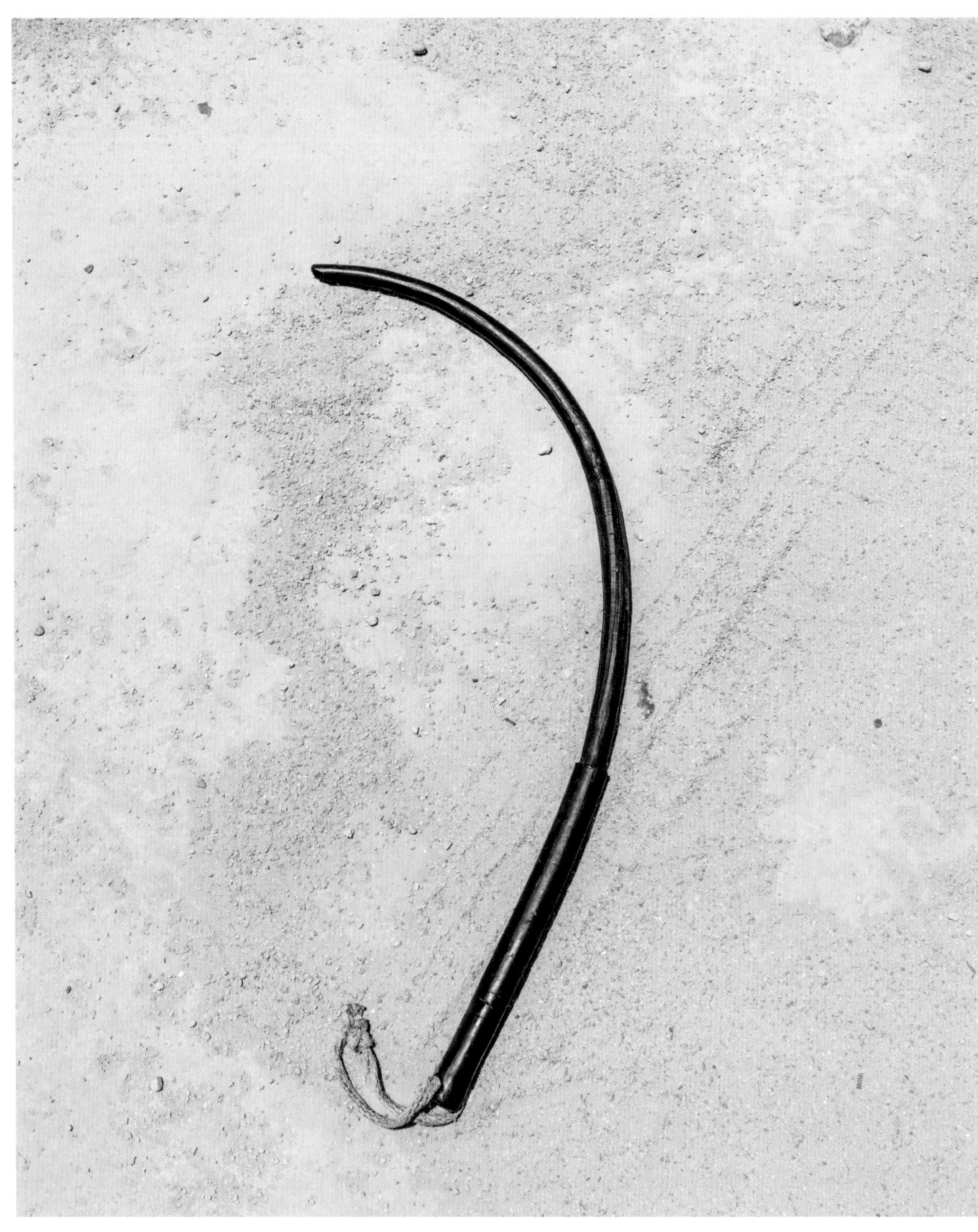

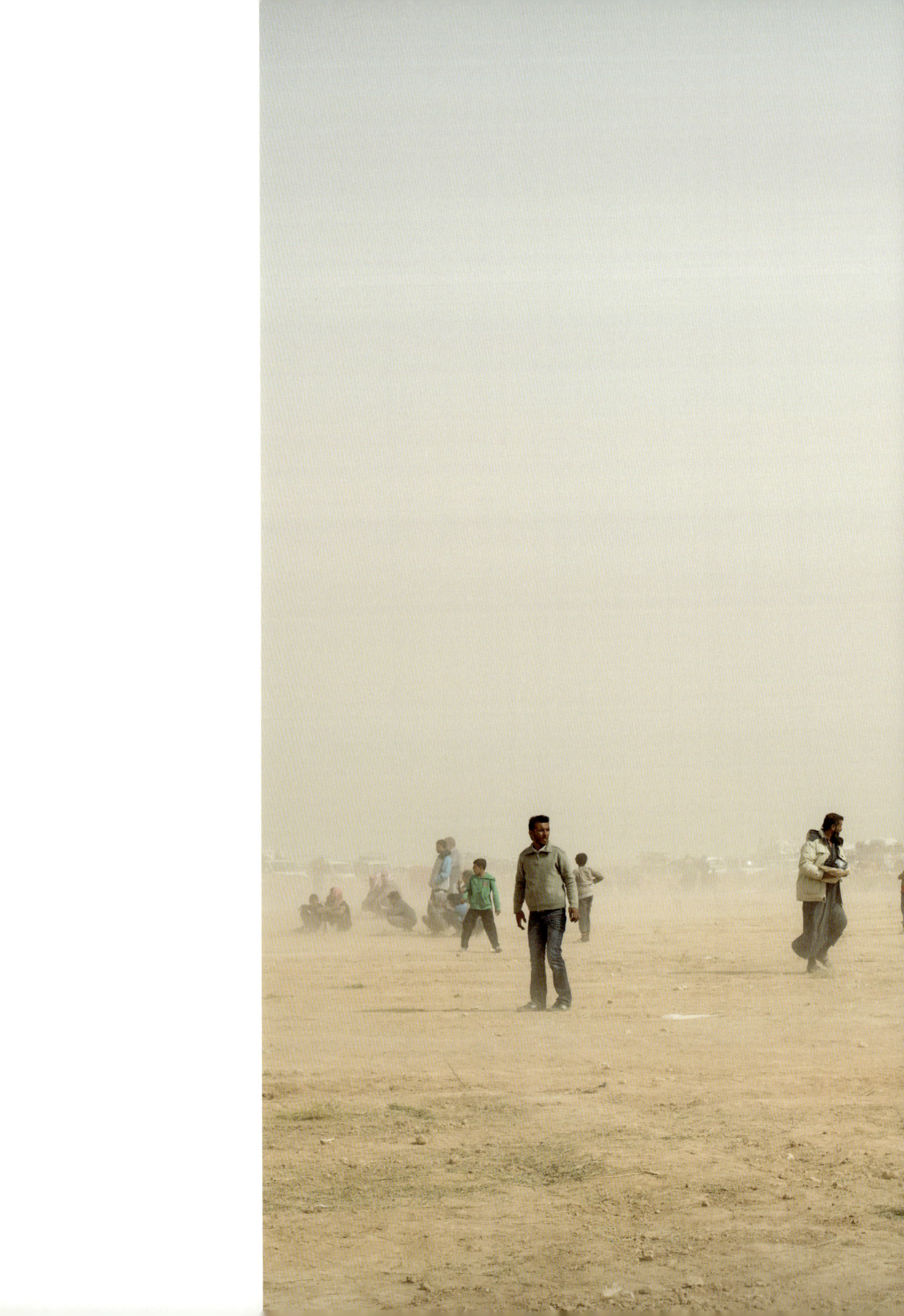

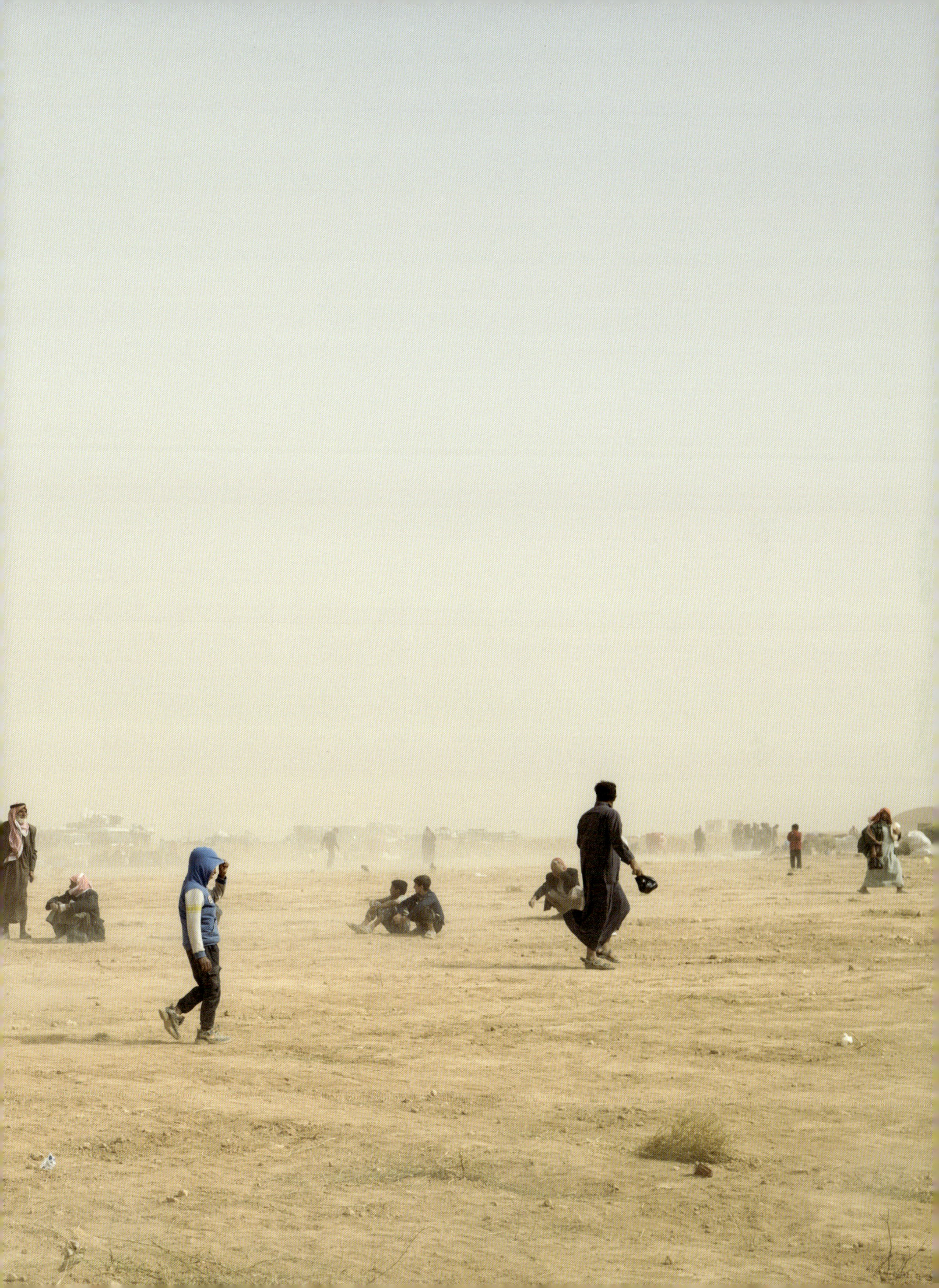

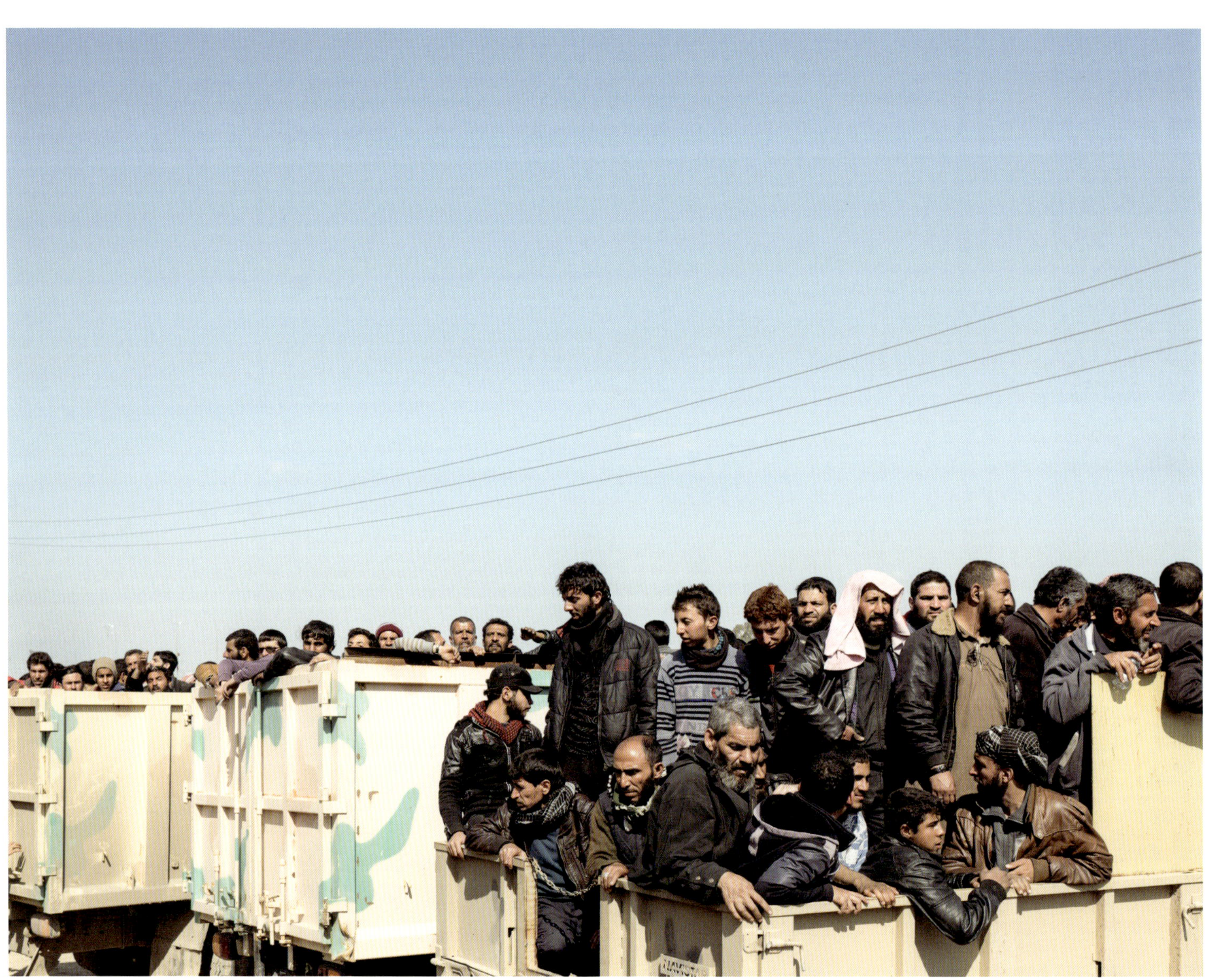

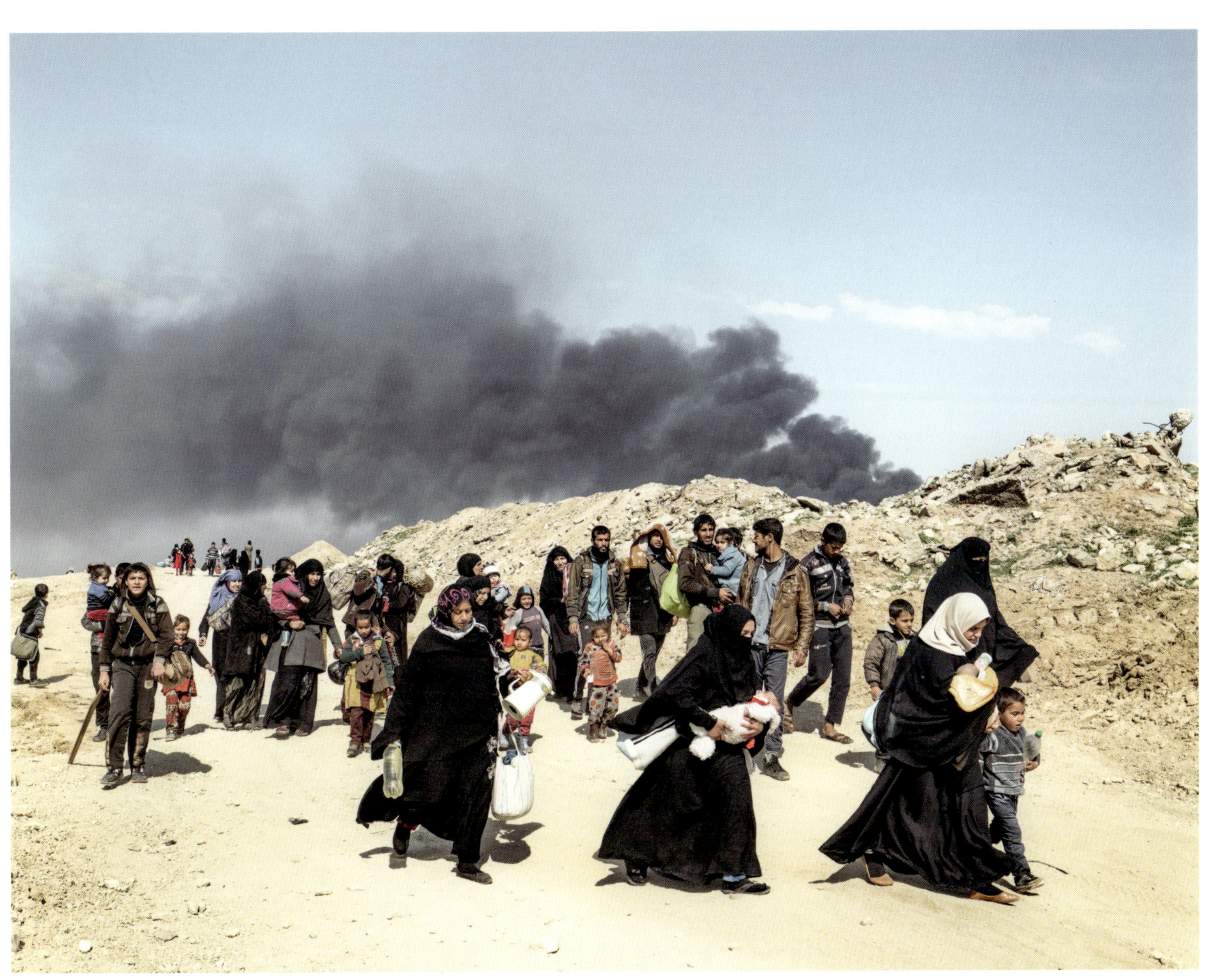

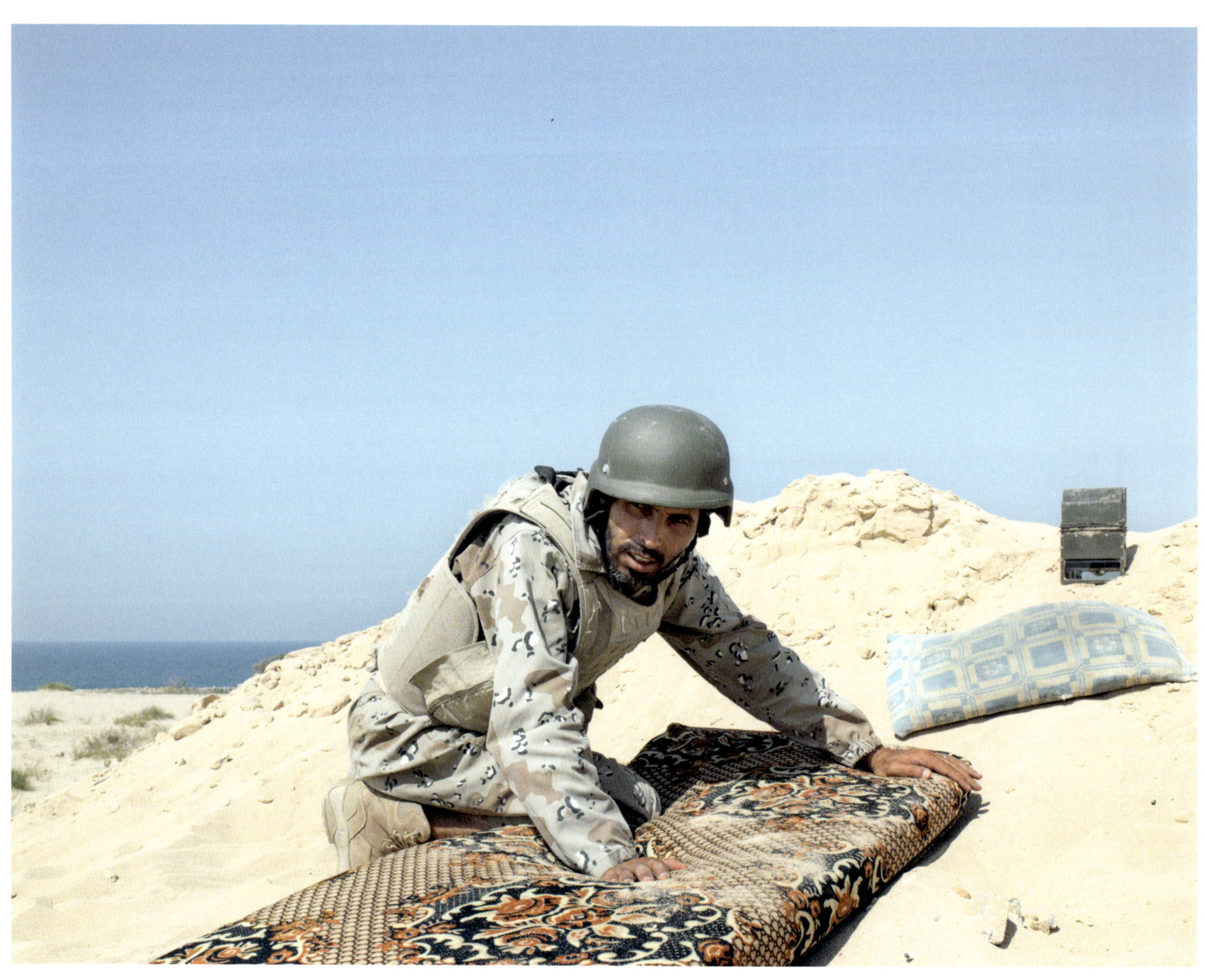

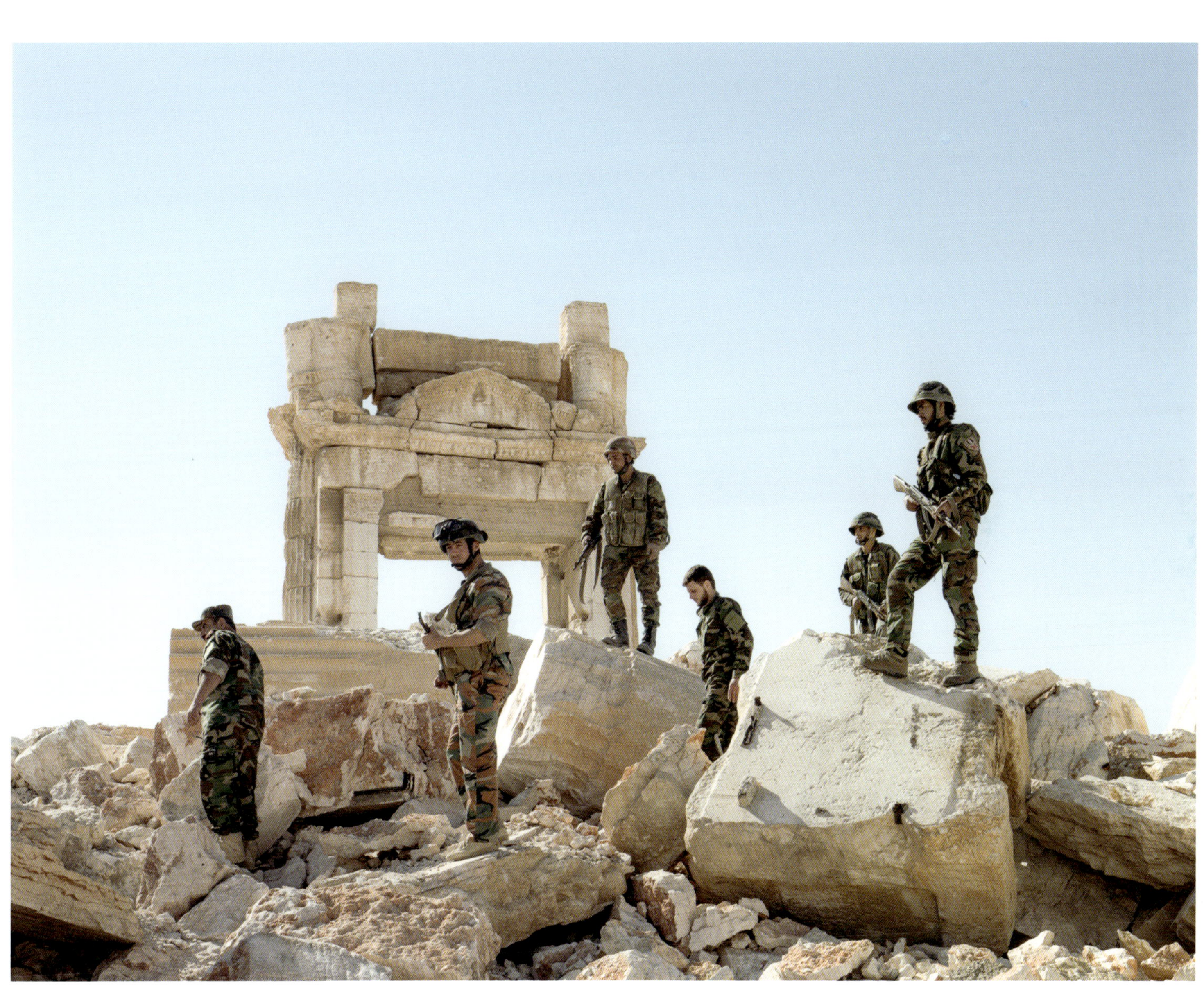

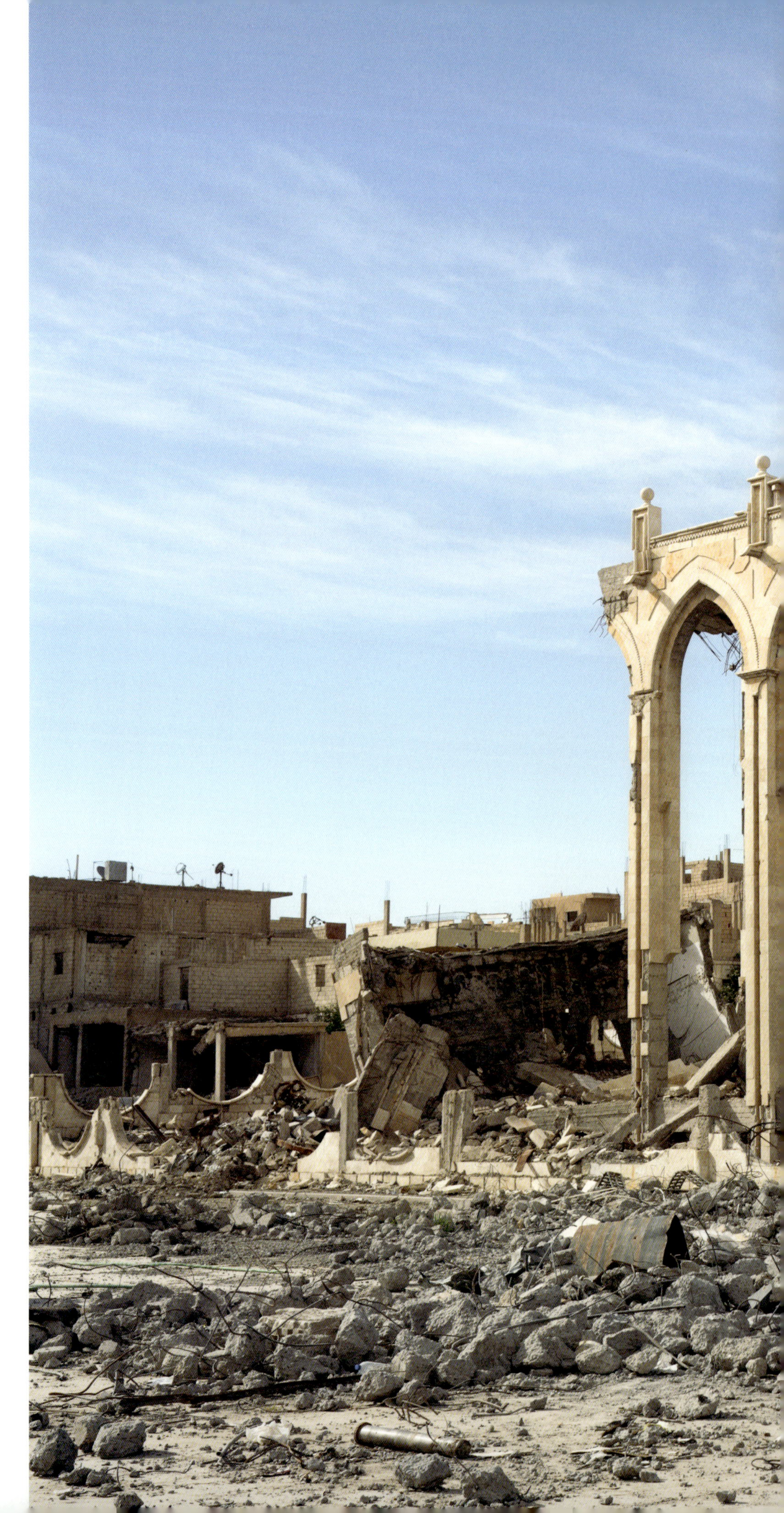

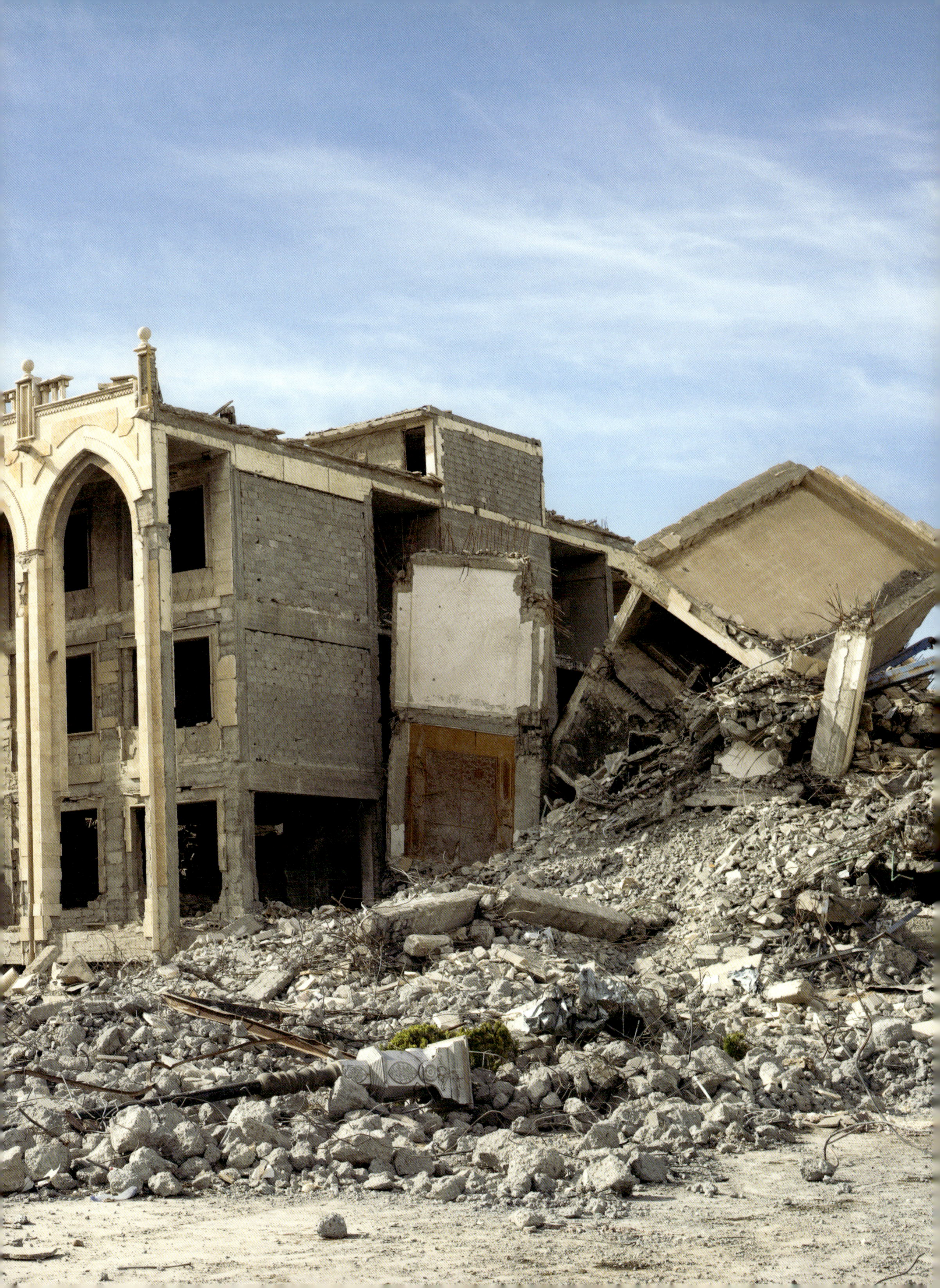

'FROM THE DESERT, THEY CONTINUED TO CARRY OUT ATTACKS. FLEEING FROM BATTLE, AND GOING BACK TO THE DESERT.'

This work started as a journey of hope across the Middle East and North Africa in 2011, during what was expected to be the dawn of a new era of democratisation. It turned out to be my first conflict reportage, which lasted a decade.

The idea was to explore ways of capturing uprisings against totalitarianism and the after-effects of colonial ventures—such as the 1916 Sykes-Picot agreement, which facilitated the creation of the modern day map of the Middle East—by connecting the history of troubled countries with their current events.

While working on the northern Syrian borders in 2012, one of the first battles I photographed took place between Kurdish fighters and Islamist elements of the rebel forces fighting the Syrian government. This was the initial rise to prominence of radical fighters, including al-Qaeda affiliates.

Within two years, extremist tendencies had coalesced in the Islamic State, which proclaimed itself in 2014. My work's focus naturally consolidated on this terror group, which seemed to pull together the disparate narratives I had been working on. Not only did the Islamic State reject the post-1916 border delineations, releasing a propaganda video entitled 'The End of Sykes-Picot,' it brought together many other threads—rising extremism, links between history and the present day, the ongoing impact of powerful countries' foreign policy in the Middle East, and the sectarianism which had long plagued the region.

My work from 2013 to 2019 covered the rise, reign, fall and immediate aftermath of the Islamic State as a territorial entity. I travelled extensively in Syria, Iraq and Libya, covering conflict and the associated humanitarian catastrophes, displaced people and destruction.

During this time, the Islamic State started to preoccupy my thoughts. Not only its activities, but what it really was, what it represented, how it had materialised, and what was going through the minds of its adherents.

Entering newly liberated territories, soldiers or militias often swiftly burned or destroyed Islamic State propaganda, while I instinctively started collecting such physical fragments from the so-called caliphate, feeling these were important, not only to photograph but also to preserve for their historical value.

The Islamic State eluded definitions and still does. When it came to preparing my images for this book, I spread out thousands of pictures across the floor and walls, and thought about how to portray this conflict without oversimplifying it.

The word that kept recurring in my mind was 'fragmentation,' because the countries where I worked were all deeply divided by ethnicities, faiths, tribal factions, territories and political affiliations. 'Fragments' equally seemed to evoke the violence of war, where people are often killed by shrapnel from explosions. 'Fragmented' also seemed to summarise my own view, and visual representations, of the events I had witnessed.

This inspired me to create a sequence where conflict photographs are interrupted by images of items found amongst the rubble of war and excerpts of writing by Islamic State members from letters, graffiti and publications.

Any linear narrative of this work is perpetually interrupted by these fragments of a now-broken territorial entity, another failed state, but one with an ideology which has permeated across the globe and inevitably has not been eradicated with its territories.

The images form a loop—a constant repetition—throughout the book, reflecting my experiences in the field. Despite being perceived as action filled and adrenaline fuelled, war is actually very repetitive and, although working in different countries, I often found myself photographing similar scenarios.

My intent was to try, within the limits of visual language, to understand and rationalise a conflict—its roots and evolution—and thus position it within its historical context. The Islamic State's emergence was a logical development, and I can potentially understand why many young men in Iraq, Syria and Libya decided to join. I asked myself many times: if I had been born Iraqi and my family was killed by US soldiers, what might I have done?

War is often depicted in black and white; good against evil, aggressors versus victims, and eventually the victors and the vanquished. But, in my experience, the reality is much more fluid, and such 'roles' can become interchangeable, often paving the way for a future spiral of violence and revenge.

In this work, I have moved away from such classic polarisations, and also the 'spectacle' of war, to present an alternative view of conflict, from either the frenzy of the battlefield or the intensity of frontline photojournalism.

The visual language aims to deconstruct the 'epic of war'—rejecting the symbolism of the heroic fighter and myths of patriotism—in favour of images reflecting life before and after conflict, underlining the historical repetitiveness inherent in every war and attempting to counter the false presentation of war as a definitive resolution to hostilities.

With the 'suspension' permeating these images, I have tried to harness the expressive power of photography, intended not as a tool of persuasion but rather as a reflection on history and the shared destiny of humanity.

The Islamic State may have appeared to be the embodiment of evil but it is crucial to consider the shades of grey and understand how such an organisation could have evolved, how it attracted adherents from around the world, occupied vast swathes of territory, and has been so challenging to defeat. I believe that, without understanding and rationalising the roots of the 'history-in-motion' we are currently witnessing, there can be little hope for our future.

LORENZO MELONI

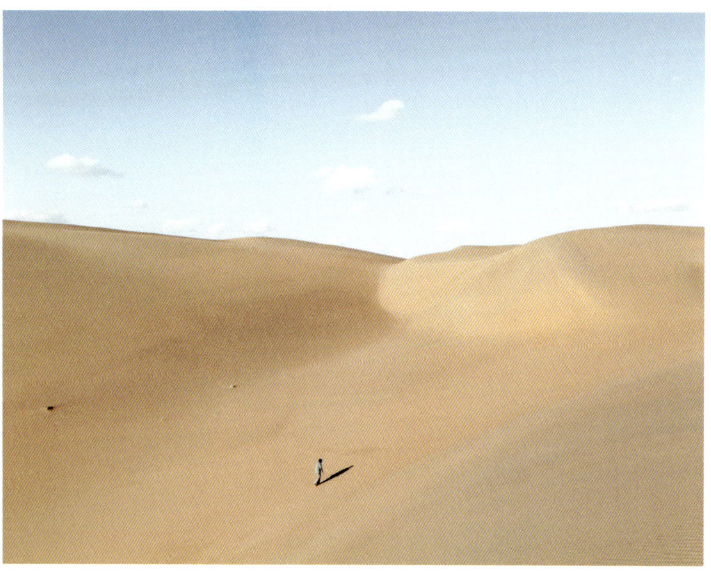

LIBYA The Sahara Desert. December 2015. A member of the Third Force patrols the desert surrounding Libya's el-Sharara Oil facility. Operating under the Tripoli-based government, the Third Force has security mandates in parts of southern Libya.

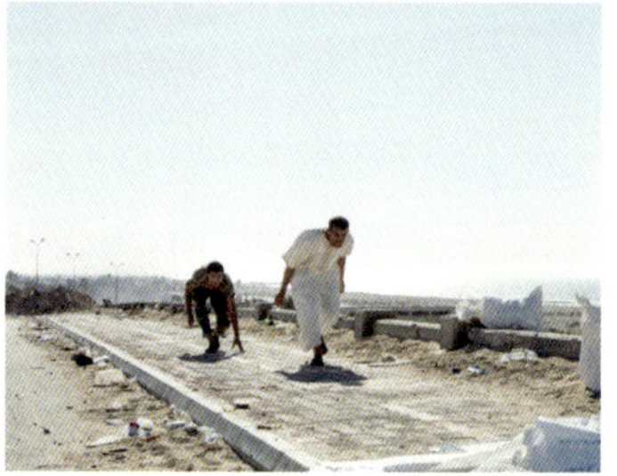

LIBYA Sirte. July 2016. Two Libyan fighters keep low to the ground to avoid Islamic State sniper-fire on the coastal westernmost frontline. Well-trained Islamic State snipers are an impediment to the Libyan forces' advances.

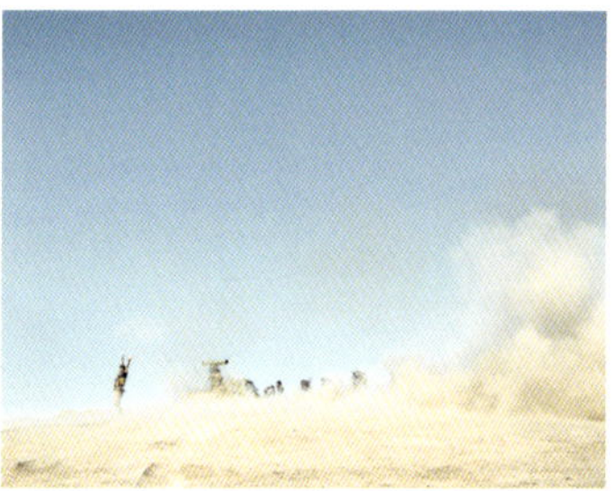

IRAQ Tal Afar. November 2016. Fighters with the Hashd al-Shaabi (popular mobilisation) forces launch an anti-tank rocket towards an approaching Islamic State suicide vehicle-borne improvised explosive device (SVBIED), during the operation to take Tal Afar airport.

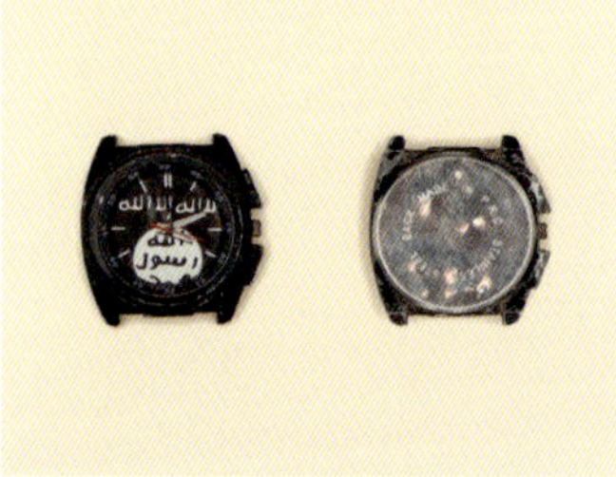

FRANCE Paris. April 2019. A watch featuring Islamic State insignia found in 2019 in the rubble of residential homes in Baghouz, in Syria's Deir ez-Zor Governorate. Baghouz was the last stronghold of the so-called caliphate.

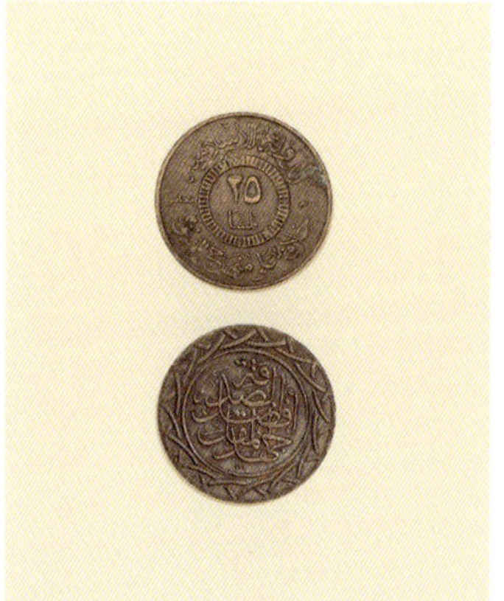

FRANCE Paris. April 2019. Both sides of a low-value Islamic State copper coin, found in rubble in Baghouz, in Syria's Deir ez-Zor Governorate in 2019. The Islamic State created its own currency, minting seven types of coins—two in gold, three in silver and two in copper.

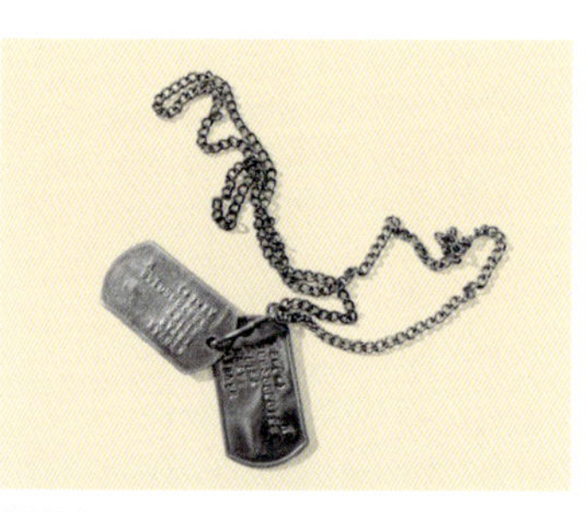

SYRIA Qamishli. November 2014. Turkish military 'dog tags' (identity tags) found on the corpse of an Islamic State fighter.

'PEOPLE CHANGE, ACTORS ARE CHANGED, TOOLS EVOLVE, BUT THE STAGE OF THE EVENTS IS CONSTANT AND THE STORY OF THE CONFLICT IS THE SAME.'

TAKEN FROM 'Important Advice For The Mujahidin (Part 1) By Abu Mus'ab az-Zarqawi' (Rumiyah-Issue 11-Shawwal 1438)

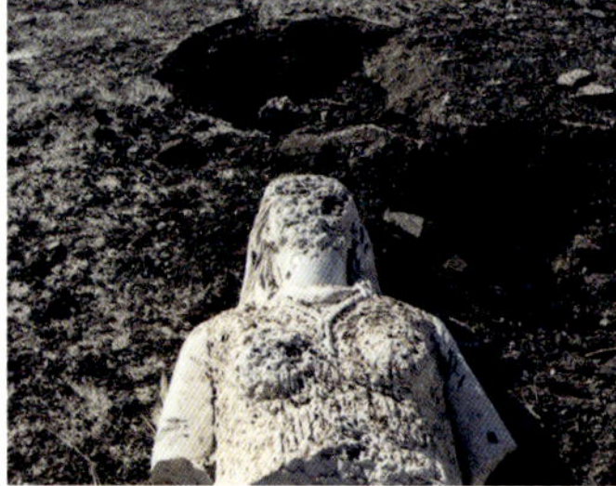

SYRIA Palmyra. April 2016. The broken torso of a defaced statue lies on a road pitted by the controlled detonation of hundreds of mines planted by Islamic State militants in modern Palmyra. Nearby lies the historic town of Palmyra. Both were retaken from the Islamic State days earlier by the Syrian Arab Army.

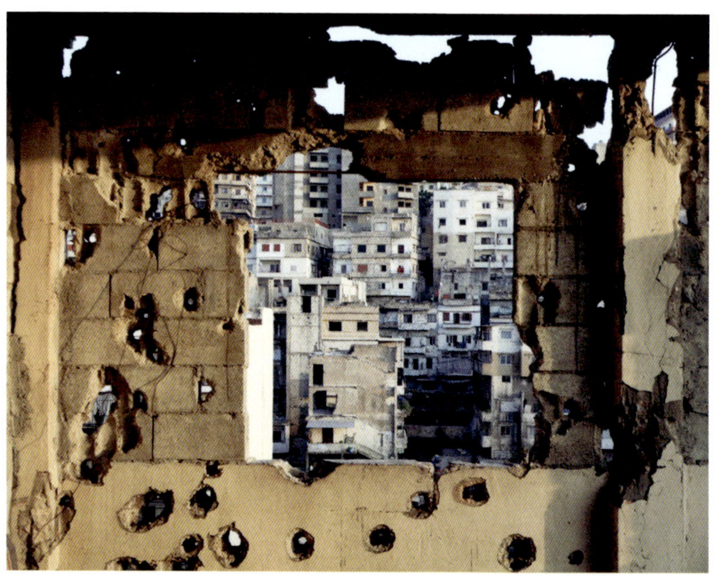

LEBANON Tripoli. November 2013. The view from an apartment on Syria Street in Tripoli's Bab al-Tabbaneh district. Sectarian violence has been rife here for decades. The area also serves as a radicalisation hub for Sunni militants.

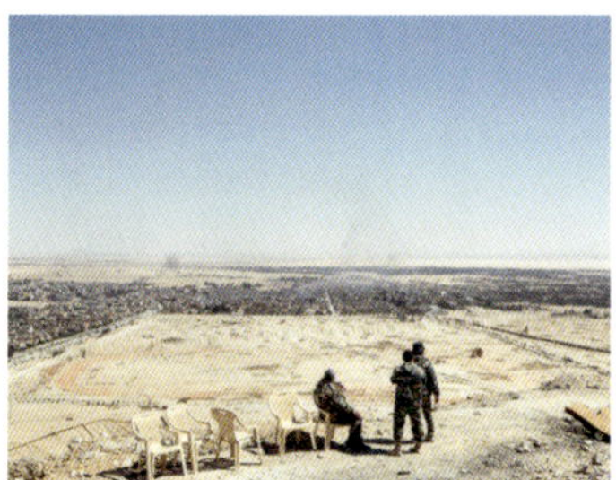

SYRIA Palmyra. April 2016. A Syrian general and two soldiers gaze across modern and ancient Palmyra from the nearby medieval citadel. Gaining control of the strategic citadel was a decisive moment in the battle for Palmyra, which was retaken from the Islamic State days earlier by the Syrian Arab Army.

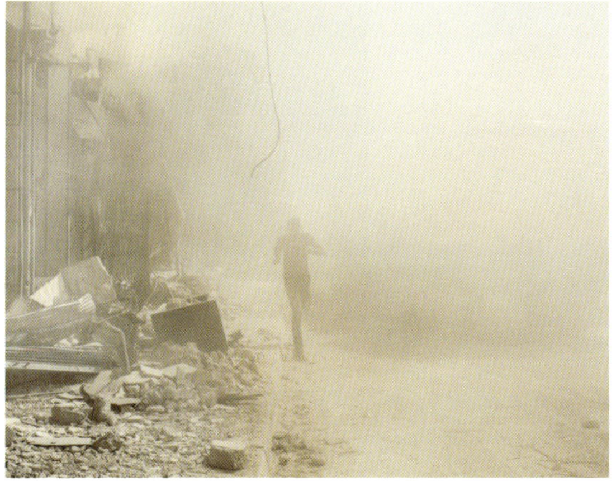

SYRIA Raqqa. April 2018. A man runs from a falling building in Raqqa. Since the Islamic State was defeated here, civilians have slowly started to return, although much of the city still lies in ruins.

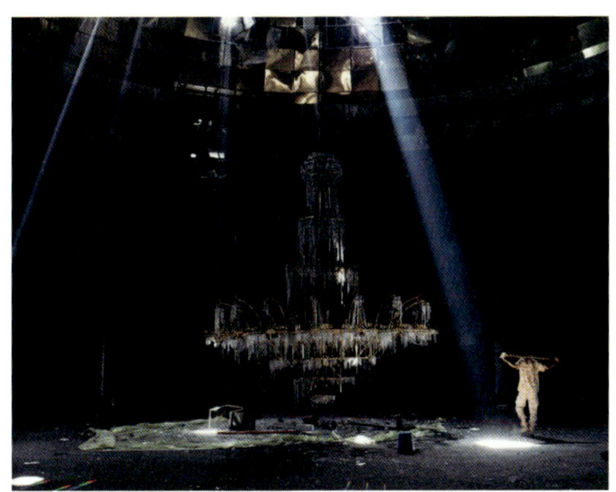

LIBYA Sirte. September 2016. Following its liberation from the Islamic State, a Libyan fighter walks through the Ouagadougou Conference Centre, built during the rule of former Libyan leader Muammar Gaddafi.

'HISTORY REPEATS ITSELF AND THE LOGIC THROUGHOUT THE AGES DOES NOT CHANGE.'

TAKEN FROM 'Important Advice For The Mujahidin (Part 1) By Abu Mus'ab az-Zarqawi' (Rumiyah-Issue 11-Shawwal 1438)

الإدارة العامة للحدود

بسم الله الرحمن الرحيم
الدولة الإسلامية في العراق والشام
الإدارة العامة للحدود

لا إله إلا الله

بيانات مجاهد

1	Name:	
2	Jihadi name:	
3	Mothers name:	
4	Blood type:	
5	Date of birth and nationality:	
6	Marital status:	
7	Address and place of residence:	
8	Level of education:	
9	Level of sharia knowledge:	
10	Job before coming:	
11	Countries you travelled to and duration:	
12	Border post you entered and contact:	
13	Recommended and by who:	
14	Date of entry:	
15	Did you on jihad before and where:	
!6	Fighter/suicide/ingemasi(fight till death)	
17	Specific skills:	
18	Current place of work:	
19	What did you leave at deposit office:	
20	Level of obedience:	
21	Address that we can contact:	
22	Date and place of death:	
23	Notes:	

مسؤول الحدود

الدولة الإسلامية في العراق والشام _ سري _

FRANCE Paris. April 2019. An Islamic State registration form in English, found in Raqqa, Syria in 2017. The so-called caliphate attracted adherents from across the world, some of whom spoke little or no Arabic.

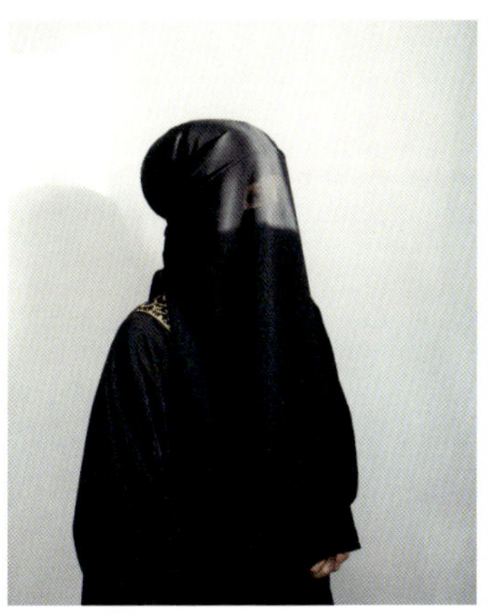

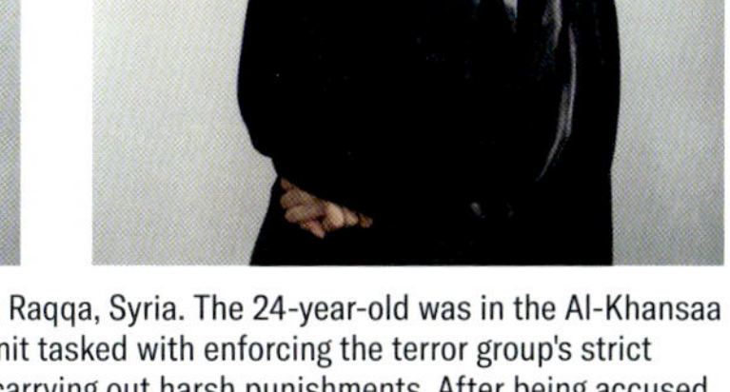

TURKEY Urfa. July 2015. Manar al Hareth from Raqqa, Syria. The 24-year-old was in the Al-Khansaa Brigade, an all-women Islamic State police unit tasked with enforcing the terror group's strict interpretation of Sharia law for women, and carrying out harsh punishments. After being accused of spying for the Free Syrian Army (FSA) and witnessing brutality and executions, she defected from the Islamic State and escaped to Turkey.

'DO NOT WORRY ABOUT MONEY OR ACCOMMODATIONS FOR YOURSELF AND YOUR FAMILY. THERE ARE PLENTY OF HOMES AND RESOURCES TO COVER YOU AND YOUR FAMILY.'

TAKEN FROM 'Important Advice For The Mujahidin (Part 1) By Abu Mus'ab az-Zarqawi' (Rumiyah-Issue 11-Shawwal 1438)

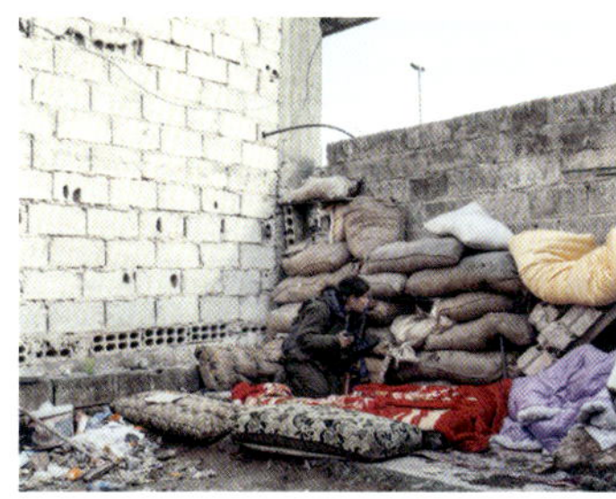

SYRIA Kobane. December 2014. A sniper from the Women's Protection Units (YPJ) keeps watch over the southern frontline. Kobane has been under siege for several months and Kurdish fighters, including the YPJ, are playing a significant role.

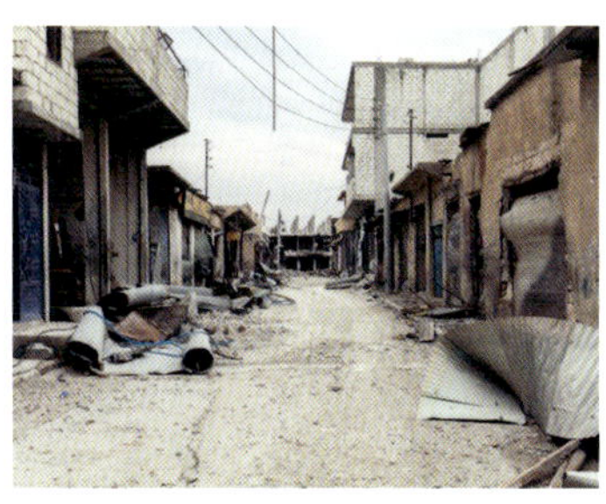

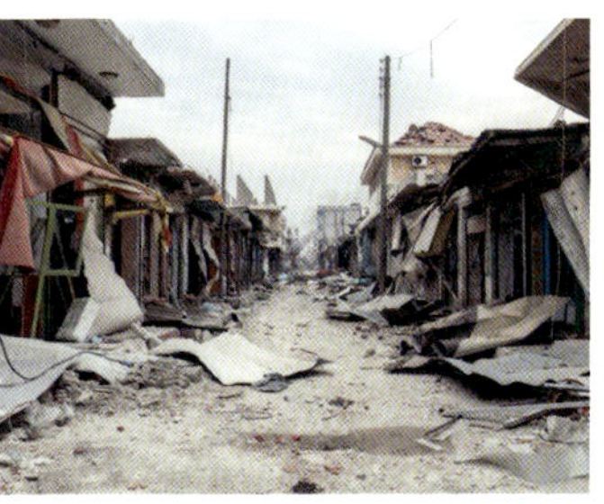

SYRIA Kobane. December 2014. Views of the central market, largely destroyed by Islamic State mortars. Approximately 70 percent of the city is already in ruins from intense fighting between the Islamic State and Kurdish fighters, with US-led coalition support.

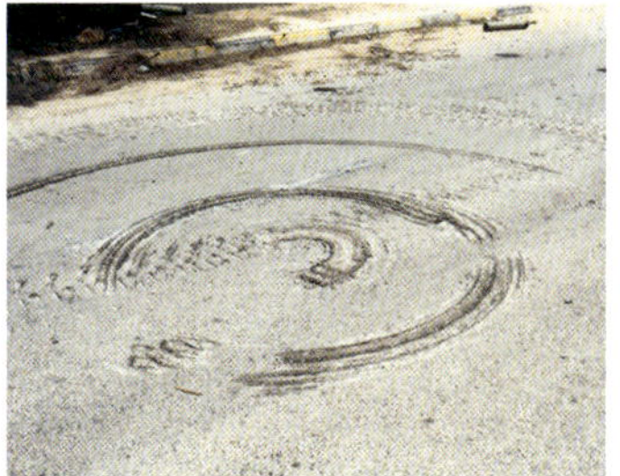

LIBYA Sirte. July 2015. A Sirte road scarred by tank manoeuvres during a military operation against the Islamic State. The Libyan forces rely heavily on outdated Soviet-era equipment.

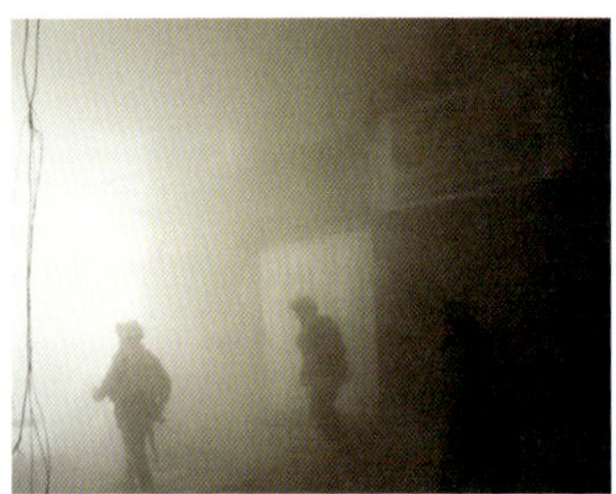

IRAQ Mosul. March 2017. The aftermath of a 'friendly fire' rocket explosion which hit frontline positions held by Iraq's Emergency Response Division (ERD) and Federal Police in Mosul. Well-trained Islamic State snipers have stalled Iraqi military advances on this frontline for weeks.

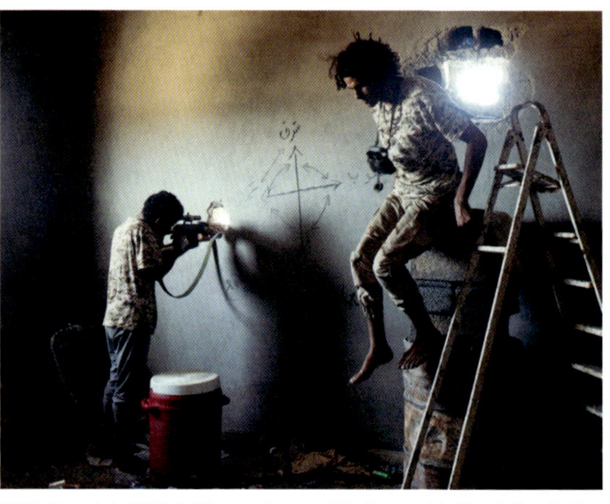

LIBYA Sirte. July 2016. A Libyan sniper and his 'spotter' in Sirte's Hay Dollar neighbourhood. Libyan forces are largely comprised of untrained, often voluntary, militia fighters who gained previous battlefield experience in 2011 or during the country's subsequent civil conflicts.

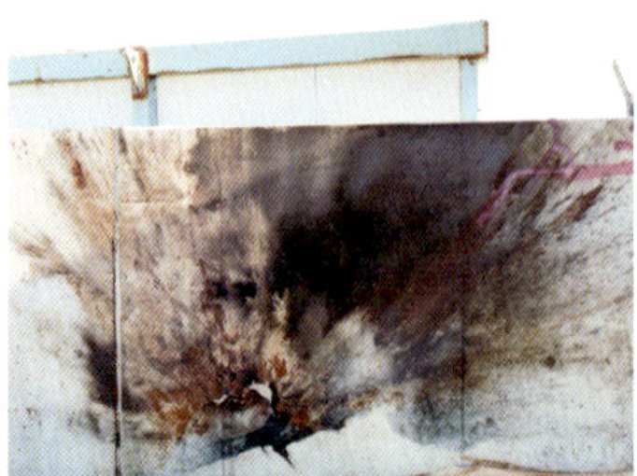

LIBYA Sirte. July 2016. Bloodstains from the commander of a Libyan bomb disposal unit, who was killed when the Islamic State landmine he was trying to dismantle exploded in his hands. Islamic State fighters are creative and experimental with the landmines and improvised explosive devices they make and deploy, which are holding up Libyan forces' advances.

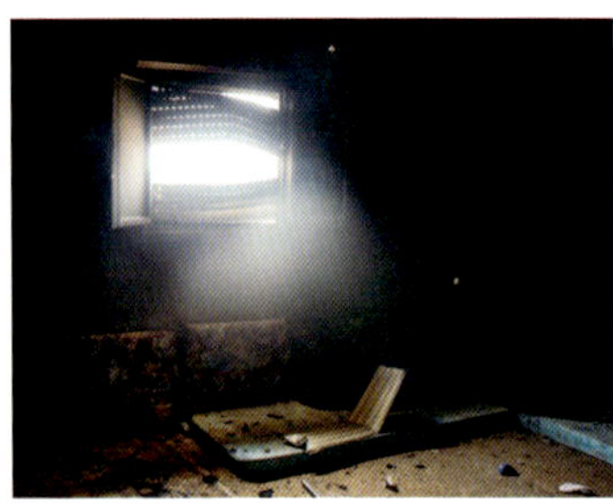

LIBYA Sirte. July 2016. A burned-out room in a civilian home in territory newly liberated from the Islamic State by Libyan forces. Protracted and intense fighting in the city has left many areas extensively damaged.

'HE DETONATED HIS EXPLOSIVE BELT AT THE CHECKPOINT FOR ONE OF THE PRISON'S ENTRANCES AND SUCCEEDED IN KILLING AND WOUNDING AT LEAST FIFTEEN.'

TAKEN FROM 'A Selection Of Military Operations Across The Islamic State' (Dabiq-Issue 11-Dhul-Qadah 1436)

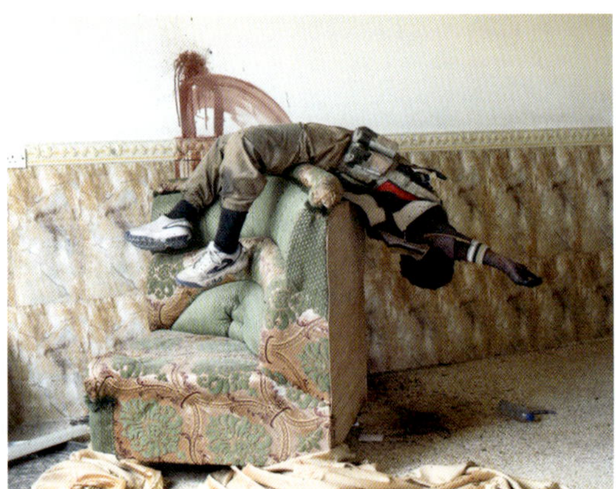

IRAQ Mosul. May 2017. The corpse of a suspected foreign fighter with the Islamic State, who had been holding a sniper position in a luxurious civilian home before he was shot dead by Iraqi special forces.

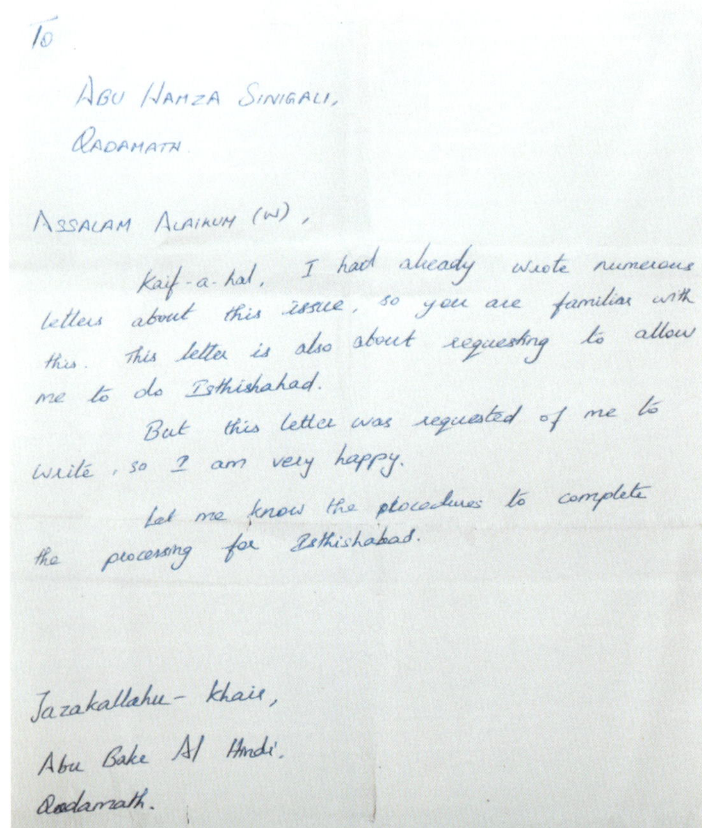

To

ABU HAMZA SINIGALI,
QADAMATH.

ASSALAM ALAIKUM (W),

Kaif-a-hal, I had already wrote numerous letters about this issue, so you are familiar with this. This letter is also about requesting to allow me to do Isthishahad.

But this letter was requested of me to write, so I am very happy.

Let me know the procedures to complete the processing for Isthishabad.

Jazakallahu-khair,
Abu Bakr Al Hindi.
Qadamath.

FRANCE Paris. April 2019. A letter written by an Islamic State fighter from India to his Senegalese superior asking for permission to undertake a suicide mission, found in Sirte, in 2016.

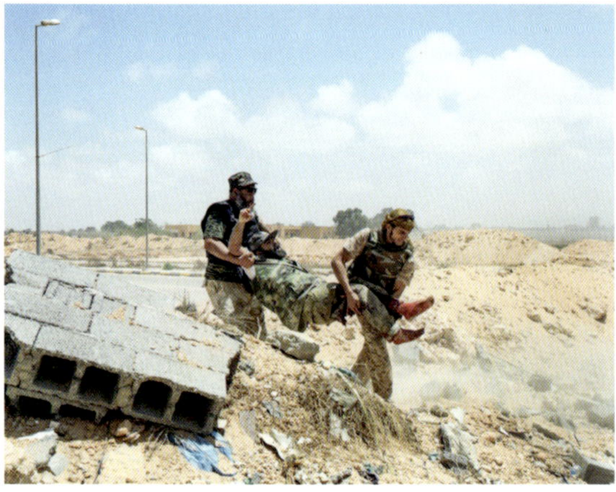

LIBYA Sirte. July 2016. Libyan fighters carry a comrade, injured by an Islamic State landmine, from the battlefield. The Islamic State deploy a wide range of landmines and improvised explosive devices while defending their Mediterranean stronghold of Sirte.

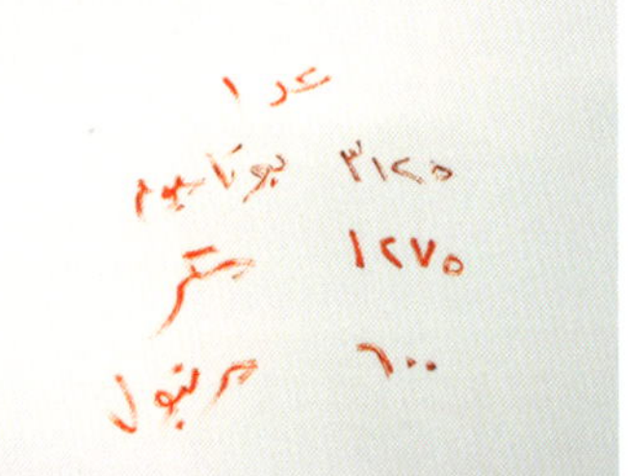

IRAQ Qaraqosh. November 2016. A formula listing the ingredients and quantities needed to make an explosive—3,125 potassium, 1,275 sugar and 600 sorbitol—written on the wall of an Islamic State bomb-making factory, in the grounds of a desecrated church.

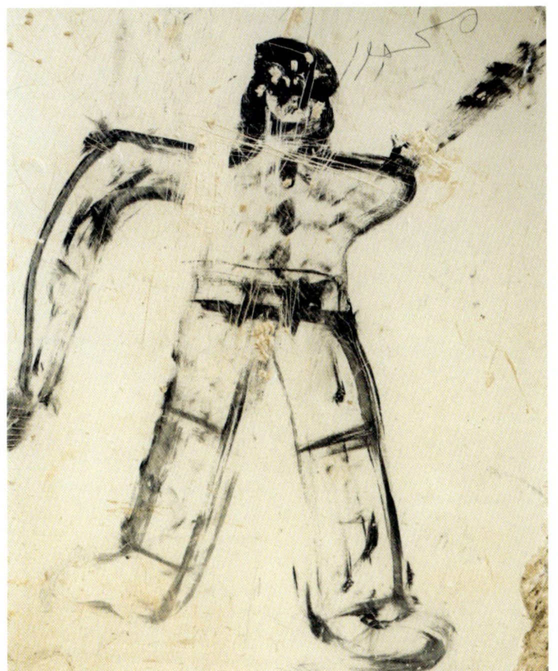

IRAQ Mosul. March 2017. A defaced piece of graffiti, by an Islamic State fighter, in an outhouse used to monitor a nearby main road. The Arabic (possibly unconnected to the drawing) means 'reserved' or 'confined.'

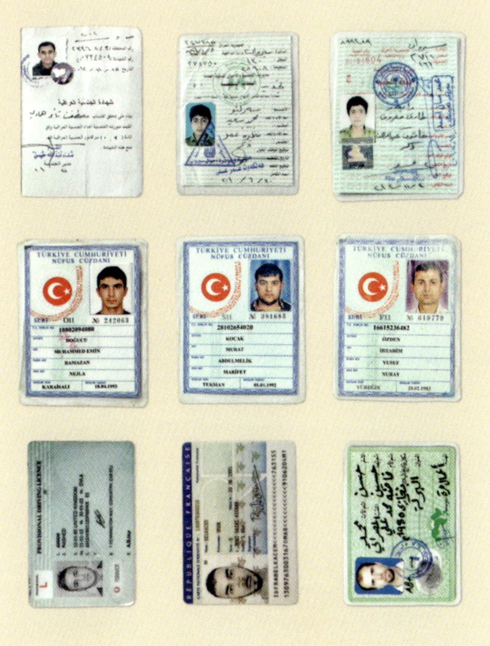

SYRIA Qamishli. November 2014. Identity documents found on Islamic State fighters, including French, Turkish, Iraqi and Libyan identity cards and a British provisional driving license.

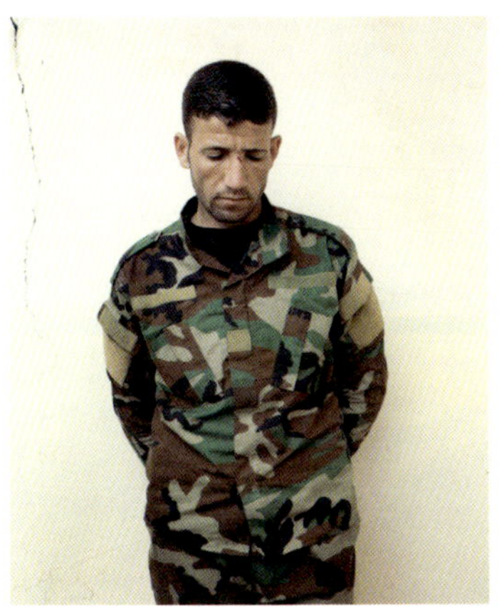

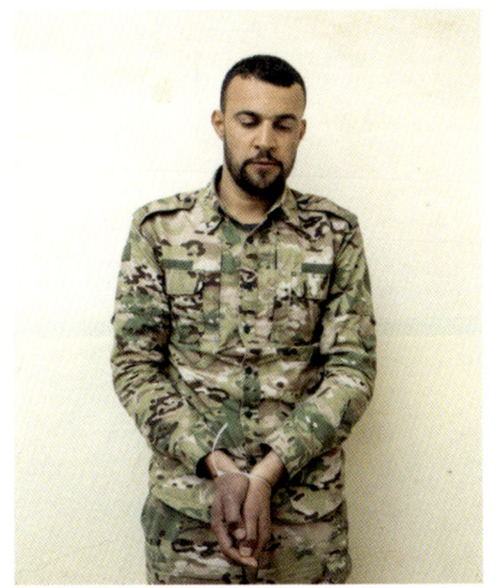

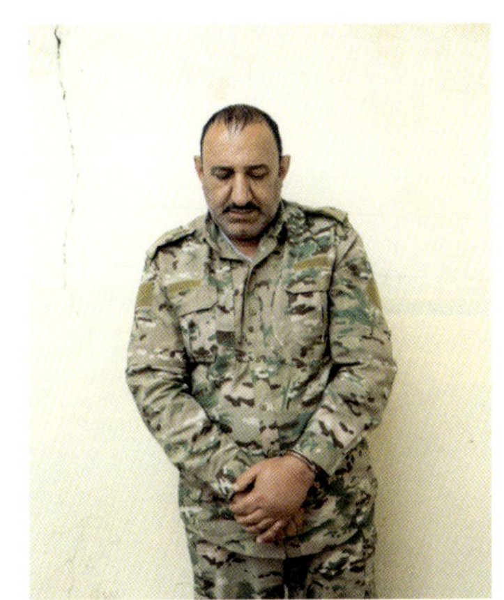

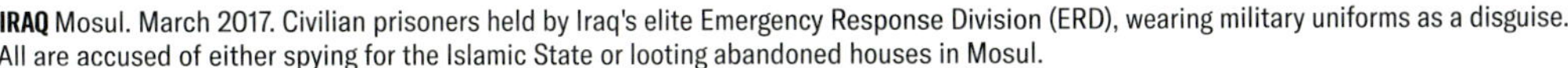

IRAQ Mosul. March 2017. Civilian prisoners held by Iraq's elite Emergency Response Division (ERD), wearing military uniforms as a disguise. All are accused of either spying for the Islamic State or looting abandoned houses in Mosul.

'AND THE PEOPLE SEARCH FOR A SOLUTION IN THE MIRAGE OF THE DESERT OF THE LABYRINTH, WHILE THE SOLUTION IS IN THEIR HANDS...'

TAKEN FROM 'Important Advice For The Mujahidin (Part 1) By Abu Mus'ab az-Zarqawi' (Rumiyah-Issue 11-Shawwal 1438)

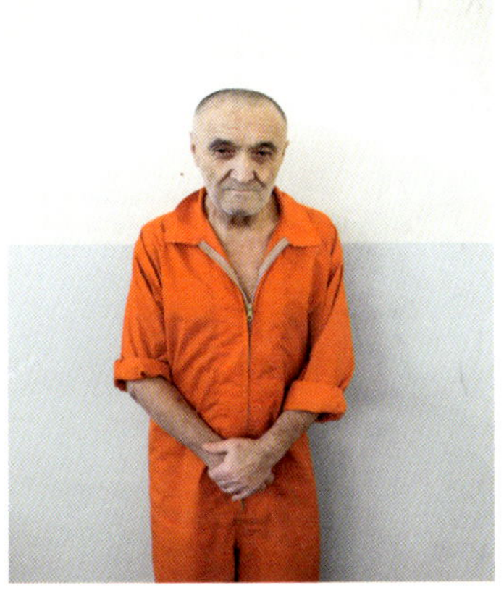

SYRIA Hasakah. November 2019. An Islamic State militant from Chechnya, detained in the Hasakah Central Prison. Many Chechens joined the Islamic State and were believed to be amongst the terror group's most skilled fighters, according to forces who battled the militants.

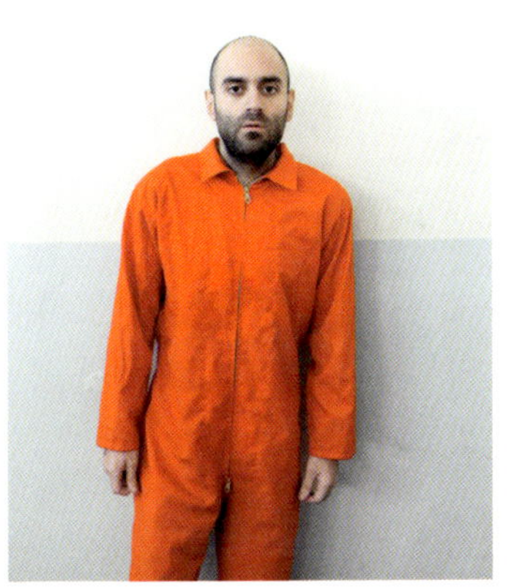

SYRIA Hasakah. November 2019. An Islamic State militant from Turkey, detained in Hasakah Central Prison, which houses around 5,000 inmates of twenty-eight different nationalities. Most were captured during the last offensive against the Islamic State in Baghouz.

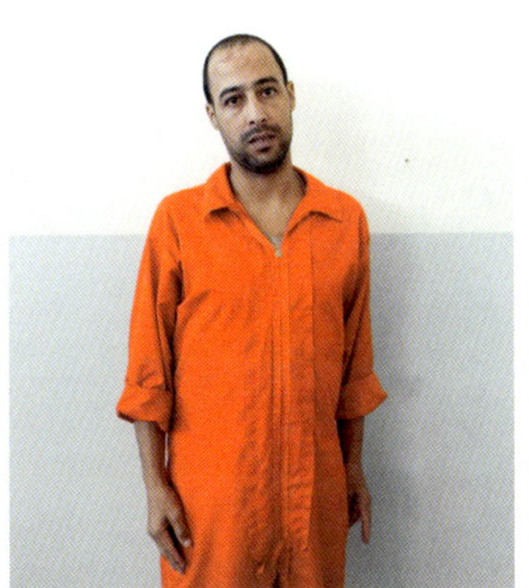

SYRIA Hasakah. November 2019. An Islamic State militant from Italy, who gave his name as Mohamed Koraichi, in Hasakah Central Prison. He later died in the prison.

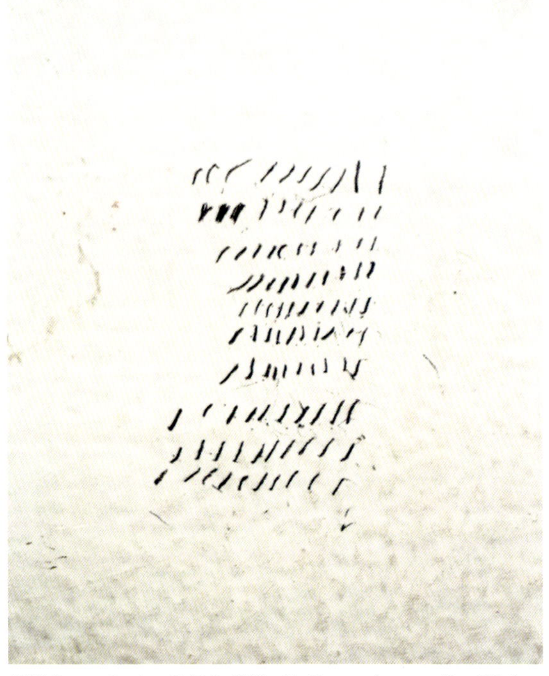

SYRIA Raqqa. October 2017. Graffiti inside Raqqa prison, marking 100 days in detention. The prison, located beneath Raqqa stadium, was used by the Islamic State for members who had fallen foul of their superiors.

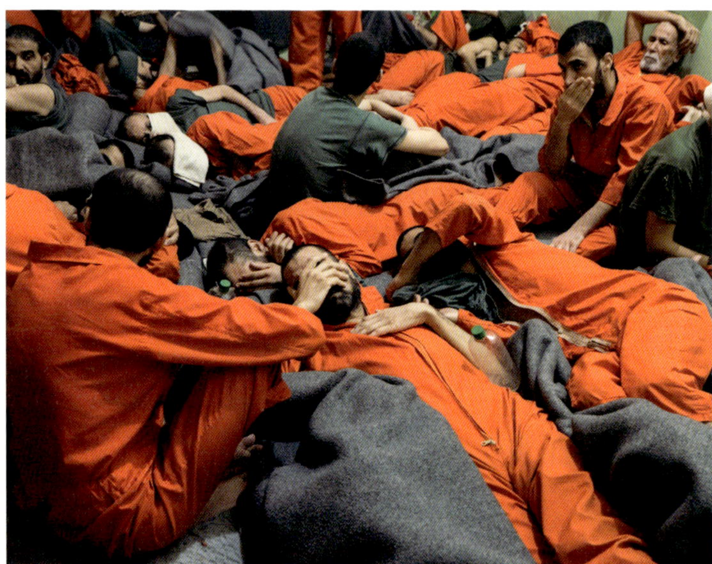

SYRIA Hasakah. November 2019. Inmates in one of the Hasakah Central Prison's cells, where up to 200 prisoners suspected of being Islamic State fighters are held in a room. The prisoners are kept in overcrowded cells in poor living conditions.

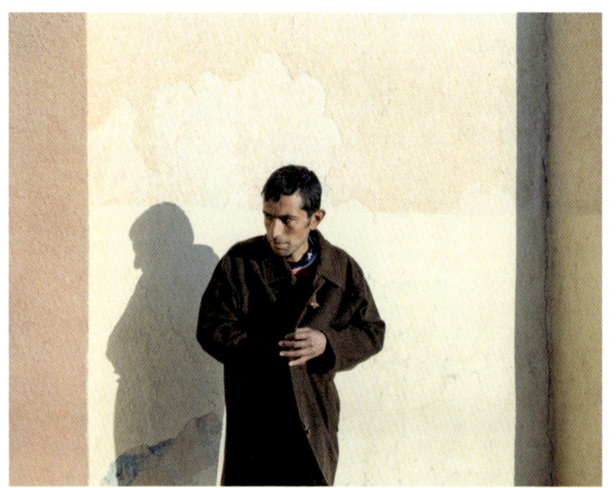

IRAQ Al-Jaraf. November 2016. A civilian working with the Iraqi forces to help identify local Islamic State militants hiding amongst civilians, in the village of Al-Jaraf, near Mosul. Intelligence provided by locals is crucial to both military advances and the capture of hidden Islamic State affiliates.

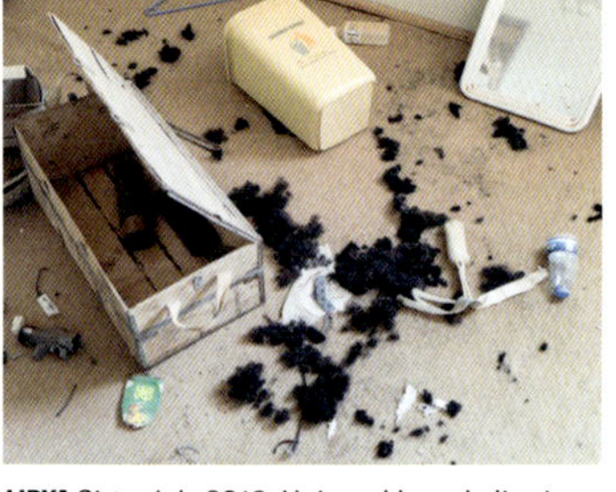

LIBYA Sirte. July 2016. Hair and beard clippings from Islamic State fighters, who adjusted their appearance before fleeing the battle zone, in the hope they could then move undetected amongst ordinary civilians.

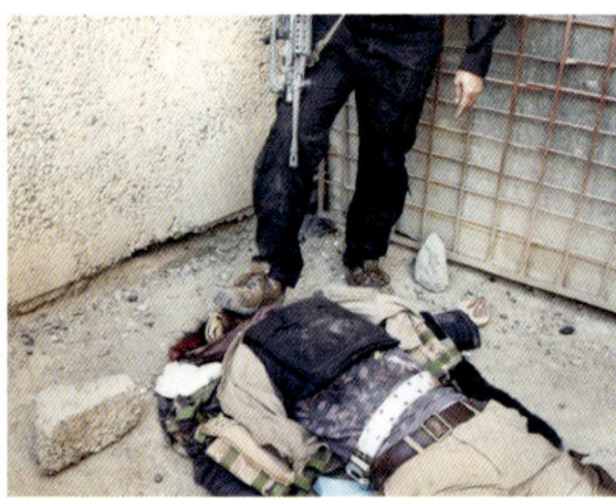

IRAQ Mosul. November 2016. An Iraqi Special Forces soldier stands with his foot on the face of a dead Eastern European Islamic State fighter.

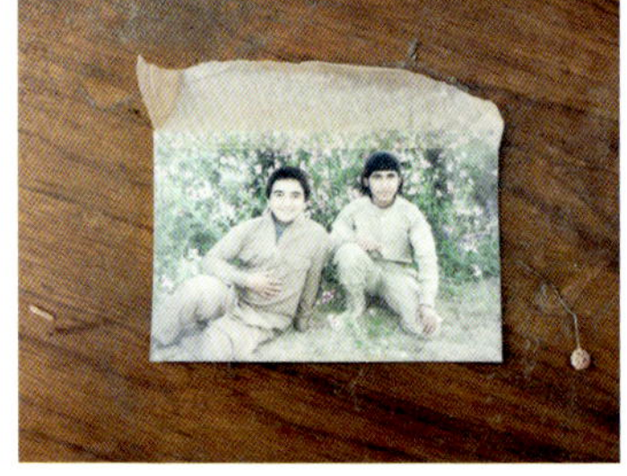

IRAQ Mosul. November 2016. A found photograph of two young Islamic State fighters, found in Mosul. Many local young men eventually joined the Islamic State, lured by promises of money, weapons, power and women.

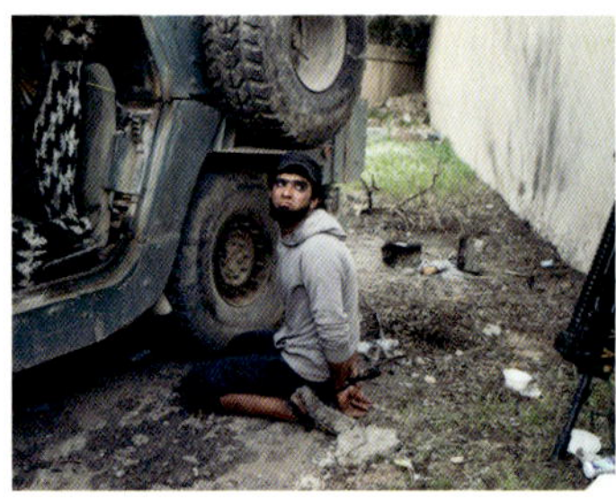

IRAQ Mosul. April 2017. A man suspected of being an Islamic State fighter, arrested by Iraqi forces whilst hiding amongst fleeing civilians near the Mosul Museum. Some Islamic State suspects captured on the frontlines are subject to brutal interrogation practices, before being transferred to prisons.

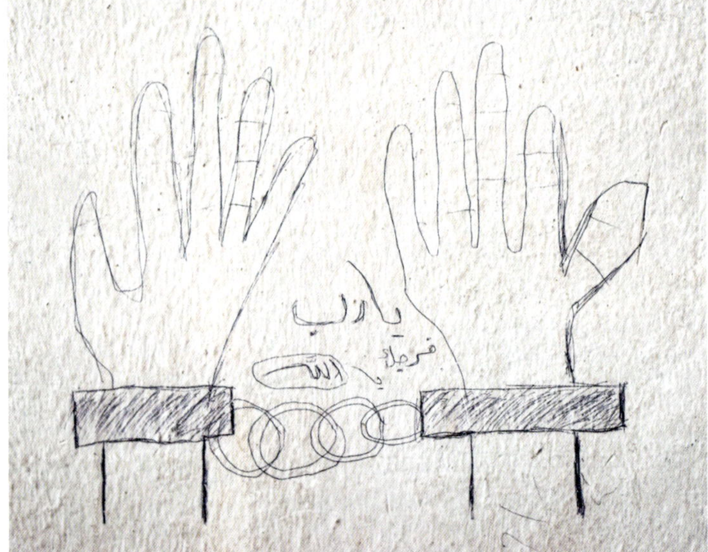

SYRIA Raqqa. October 2017. Graffiti on a wall inside Raqqa prison depicts a pair of hands in shackles, with an Arabic phrase used to beg God for help in desperate situations.

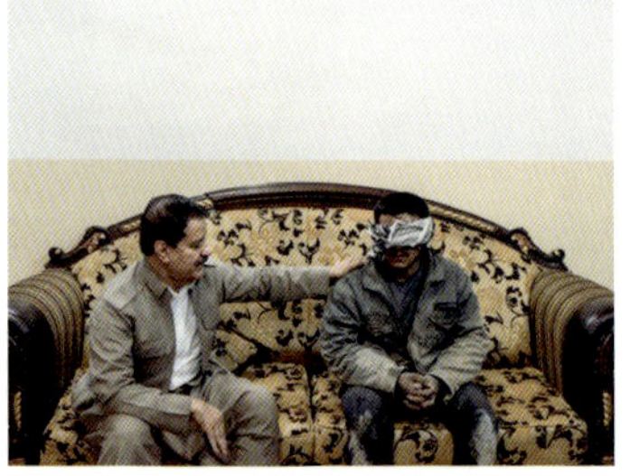

IRAQ Kirkuk. December 2016. Dr. Kemal Kirkuki, a Peshmerga commander and former speaker of the Iraqi Kurdistan Parliament, questions an Islamic State suspect in his offices near the frontline of northwest Kirkuk.

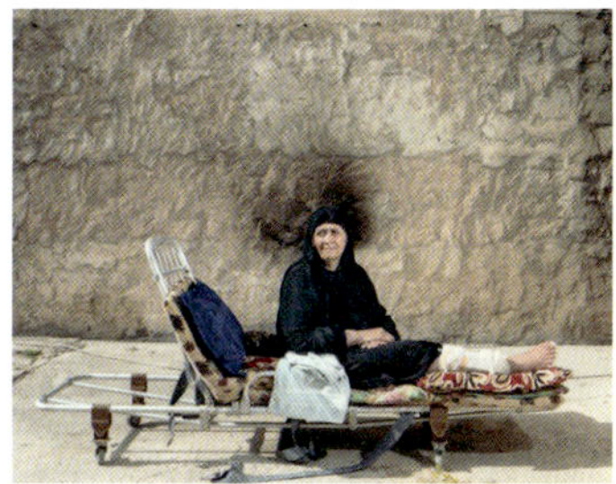

IRAQ Mosul. February 2017. A civilian wounded by shelling sits on a bed outside her home. As the battle against the Islamic State in Mosul progresses, civilian deaths and injuries increase exponentially.

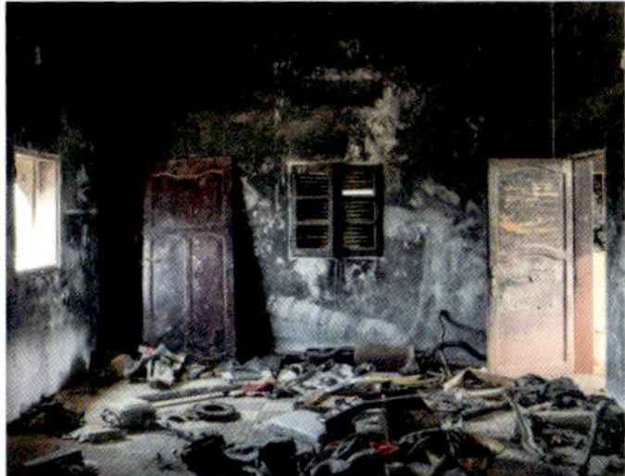

LIBYA Sirte. July 2016. A burned-out room in a premises used by the Islamic State as a manufacturing facility for suicide vehicle-borne improvised explosive devices (SVBIEDs) in an industrial district on the outskirts of Sirte. The Islamic State rely heavily on SVBIEDs whilst defending their Mediterranean stronghold.

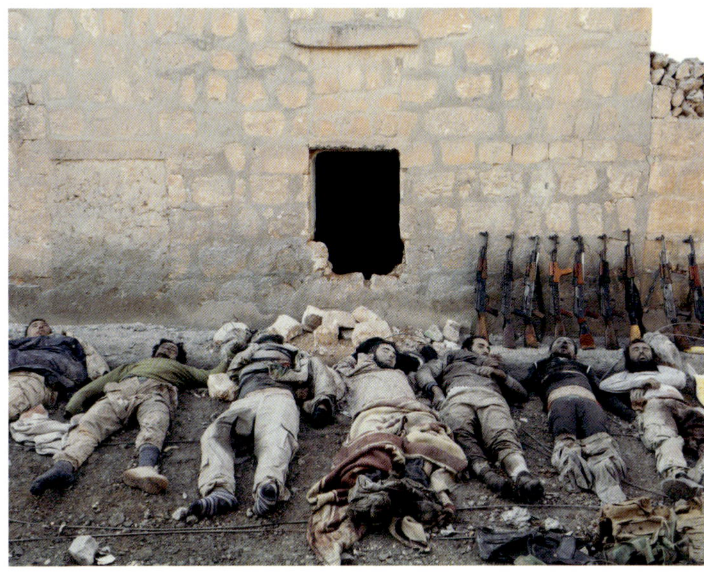

SYRIA Kobane. December 2014. An Islamic State Chechen commander and his unit, killed in action by Kurdish fighters from the People's Protection Units (YPG).

'DURING TIMES OF WAR, TRIBULATIONS, AND HARDSHIP, WORRIES ABOUND AND HEARTS REACH THE THROATS.'

TAKEN FROM 'Be A Supporter Not A Demoralizer' (Rumiyah-Issue 10-Ramadan 1438)

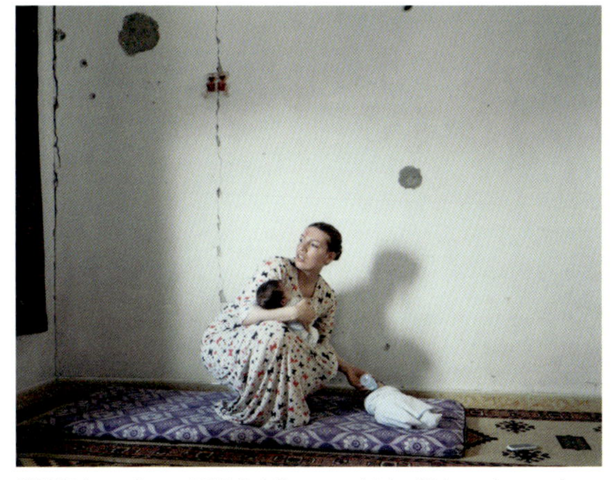

SYRIA Kobane. August 2015. A civilian named Arin with her twin sons, four months after returning to Kobane. An estimated 70 percent of the city was left in ruins from intense fighting and US-led coalition airstrikes.

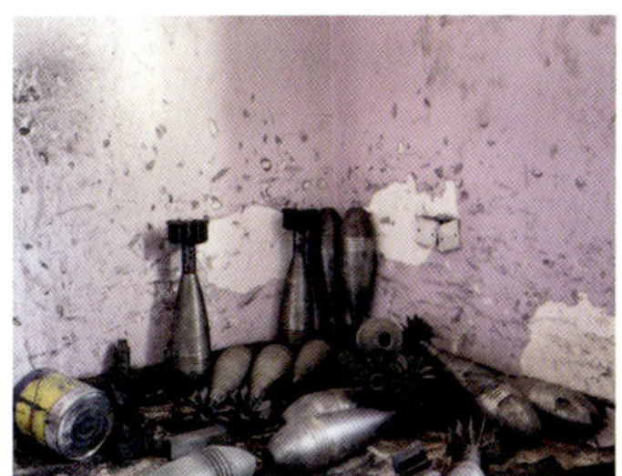

IRAQ Mosul. March 2017. A stockpile of mortars used by the Islamic State in suicide vehicle-borne improvised explosive devices (SVBIEDs). The Islamic State rely heavily on SVBIEDs, which can be as small as civilian cars or as large as bulldozers or lorries, as part of their defence strategy.

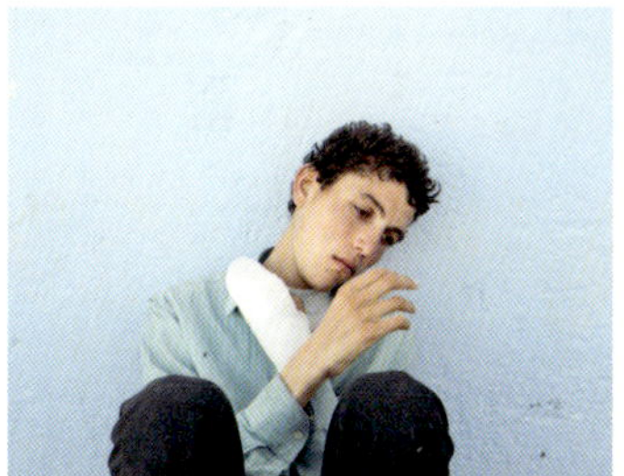

SYRIA Ain Issa. October 2017. A wounded boy in a camp for internally displaced persons near Raqqa. Although this camp holds people displaced from across Syria, the majority are from Raqqa, Aleppo and Deir ez-Zor.

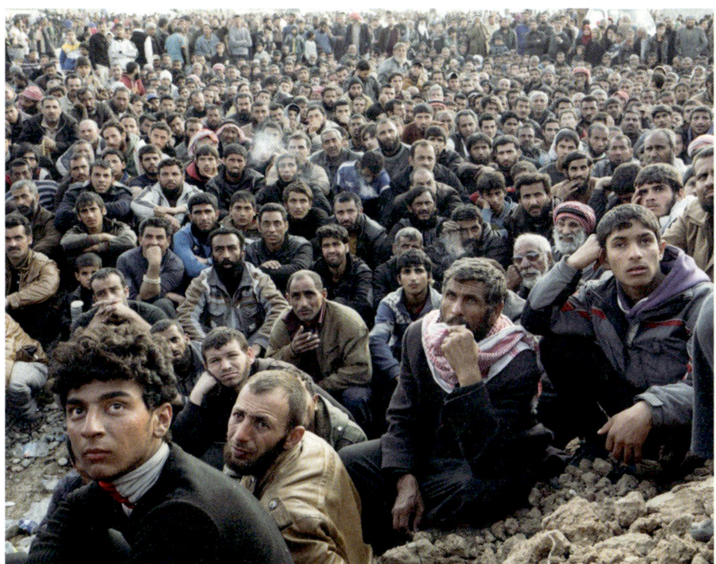

IRAQ Hammam al-Alil. March 2017. Civilians wait in a screening area at a camp for internally displaced persons in Hammam al-Alil. The Iraqi forces hold an extensive database listing Islamic State members and all men leaving Mosul have their identities checked against this.

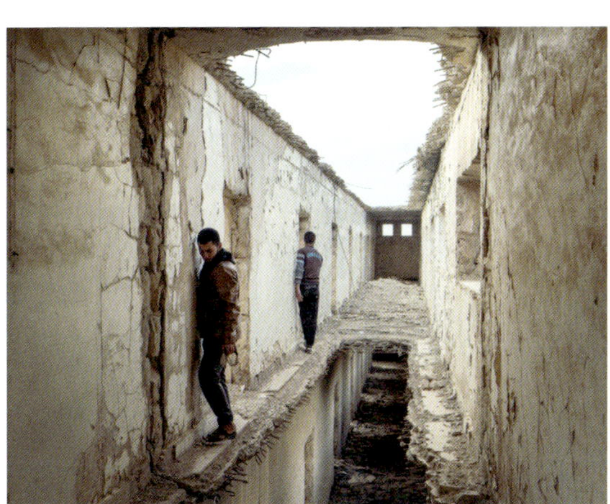

IRAQ Hammam al-Alil. December 2016. Two boys hunt for birds inside a building formerly used by the Islamic State as a military base, which was targeted by an airstrike carried out by the US-led coalition.

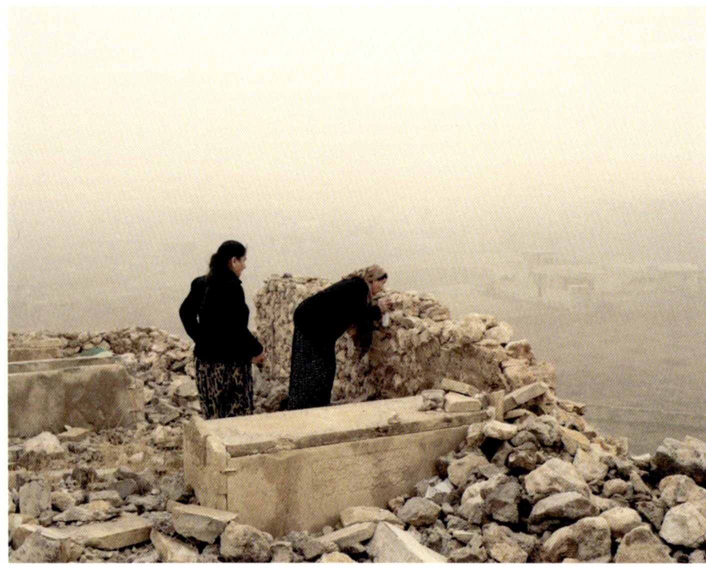

IRAQ Bashiqa. December 2016. Yazidi women in a cemetery destroyed by the Islamic State. Because of their ancient faith, Iraq's minority Yazidis have been singled out by the Islamic State for particularly harsh treatment.

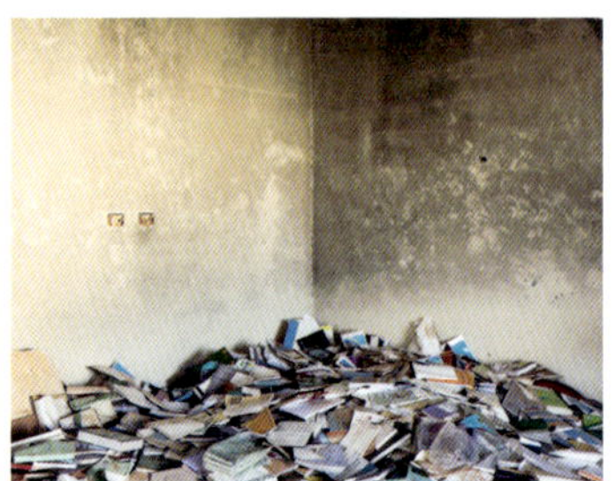

LIBYA Sirte. September 2016. Books piled into one room in a civilian house in a newly-liberated Sirte neighbourhood. Libyan forces claimed this was the former home of Ahmed Gaddaf al-Dam, a cousin of the late Libyan leader Muammar Gaddafi.

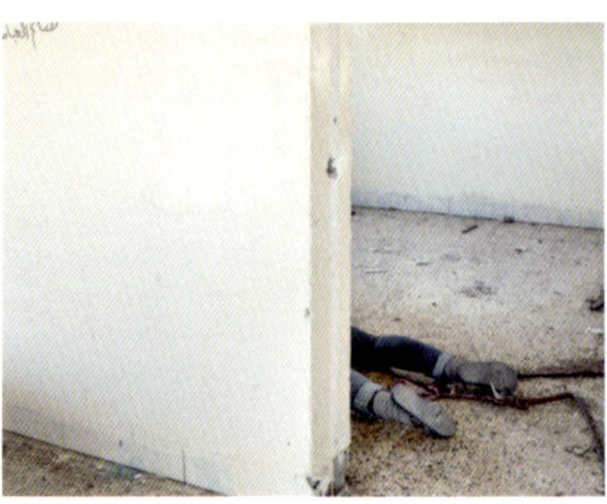

IRAQ Mosul. March 2017. The body of a man in civilian attire, killed by a head wound, lies in a building near Mosul's former train station.

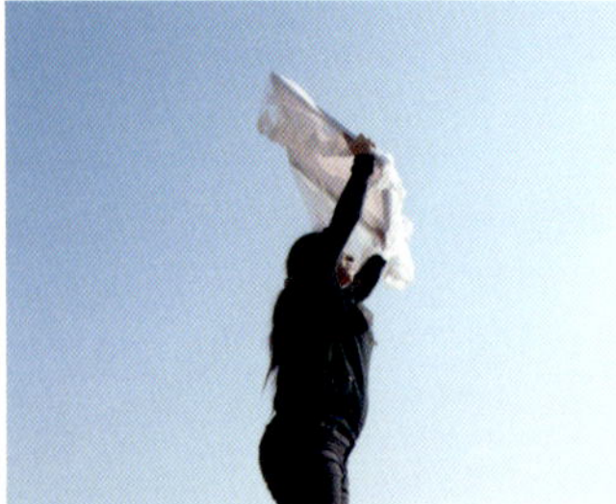

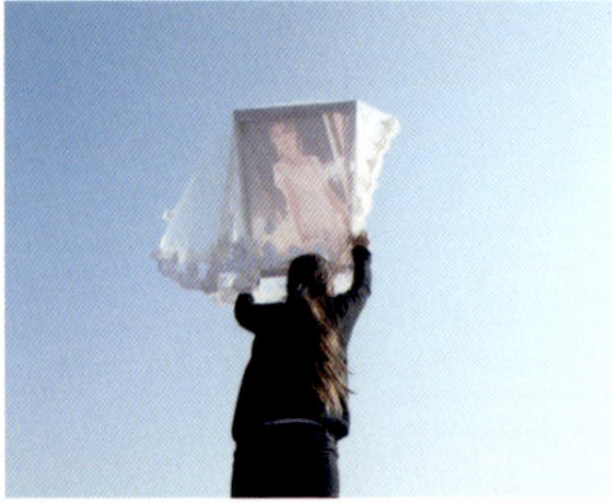

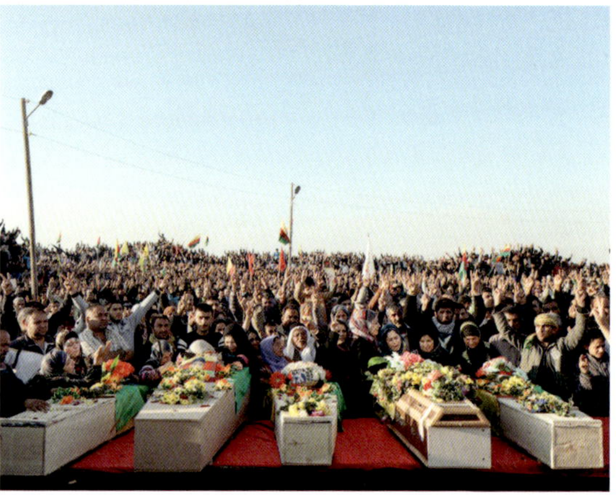

SYRIA Ras al-Ayn. November 2012. Relatives mourn their dead at the Martyrs' cemetery. Kaled Omar Hamou and Sala Ayo (members of the Kurdish intelligence agency), Sipan Sino and Ahmed Kawas (YPG fighters), and the head of Ras al-Ayn's Popular Council Abdid Xelil. All were killed during fighting between the YPG and Jabhat al-Nusra, apart from Hamou and Ayo, who were kidnapped and killed early in the battle.

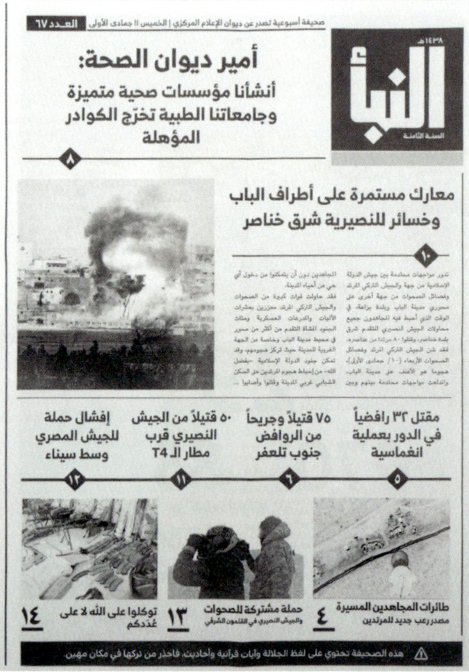

صحيفة أسبوعية تصدر عن ديوان الإعلام المركزي | الخميس ١١ جمادى الأولى | العـدد ٦٧

النبأ
١٤٣٨هـ
السنة الثامنة

أمير ديوان الصحة:
أنشأنا مؤسسات صحية متميزة وجامعاتنا الطبية تخرّج الكوادر المؤهلة
٨

معارك مستمرة على أطراف الباب وخسائر للنصيرية شرق خناصر
١٠

مقتل ٣٢ رافضياً في الدور بعملية انغماسية
٥

٧٥ قتيلاً وجريحاً من الروافض جنوب تلعفر
٦

٥٠ قتيلاً من الجيش النصيري قرب مطار الـ T4
١١

إفشال حملة للجيش المصري وسط سيناء
١٢

طائرات المجاهدين المسيرة
مصدر رعب جديد للمرتدين
٤

حملة مشتركة للصحوات
والجيش النصيري في القلمون الشرقي
١٣

توكلوا على الله لا على عُدَدكم
١٤

هذه الصحيفة تحتوي على لفظ الجلالة وآيات قرآنية وأحاديث، فاحذر من تركها في مكان مهين

FRANCE Paris. April 2019. An Islamic State newspaper found in East Mosul, Iraq in 2017. The Islamic State published magazines, newspapers and leaflets as part of a major propaganda drive.

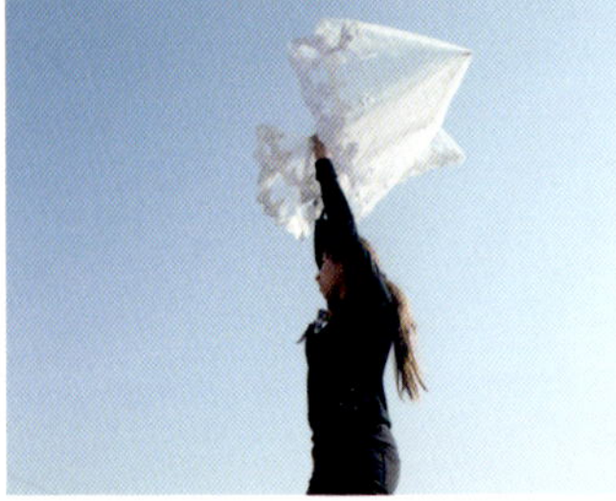

SYRIA Qamishli. November 2019. At a funeral, a woman holds a photo of her sister, one of the victims of two Islamic State suicide vehicle-borne improvised explosive devices (SVBIEDs), which exploded in Qamishli's city centre. Five civilians and a member of the local Kurdish intelligence department were killed.

'AS MUCH AS SOME LIBERAL JOURNALIST WOULD LIKE YOU TO BELIEVE THAT WE DO WHAT WE DO BECAUSE WE'RE SIMPLY MONSTERS WITH NO LOGIC BEHIND OUR COURSE OF ACTION, THE FACT IS THAT WE CONTINUE TO WAGE AND ESCALATE A CALCULATED WAR.'

TAKEN FROM 'Why We Hate You & Why We Fight You' (Dabiq-Issue 15-Shawwal 1437)

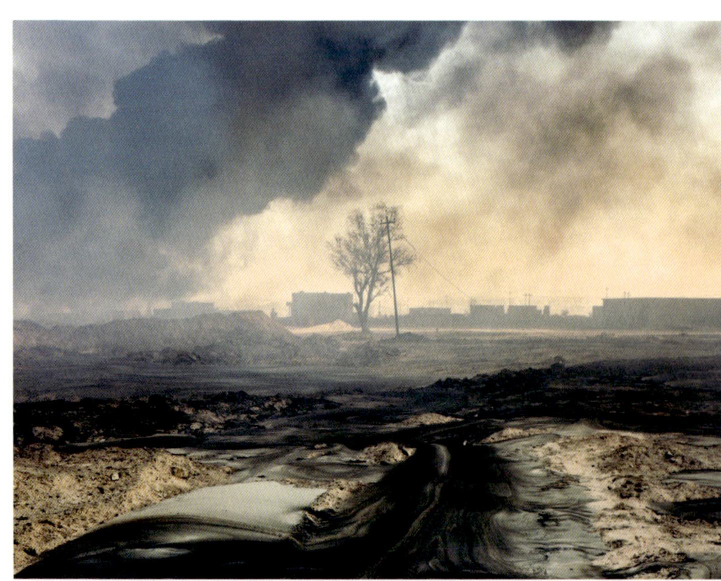

IRAQ Qayyarah. November 2016. Islamic State fighters set fire to oil wells near Qayyarah, to provide cover from Iraqi Air Force and US-led coalition airstrikes.

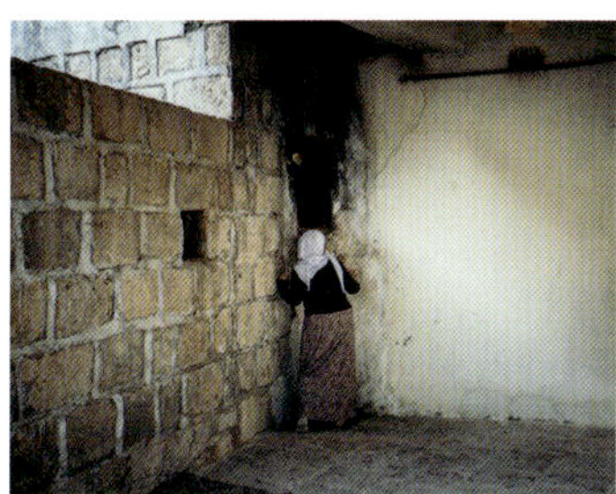

IRAQ Lalish. November 2017. A Yazidi woman prays in Lalish, the sacred religious centre for Yazidis. Because of their ancient faith, Iraq's minority Yazidis were singled out by the Islamic State for particularly harsh treatment, and many Yazidis displaced from Sinjar now live near Lalish.

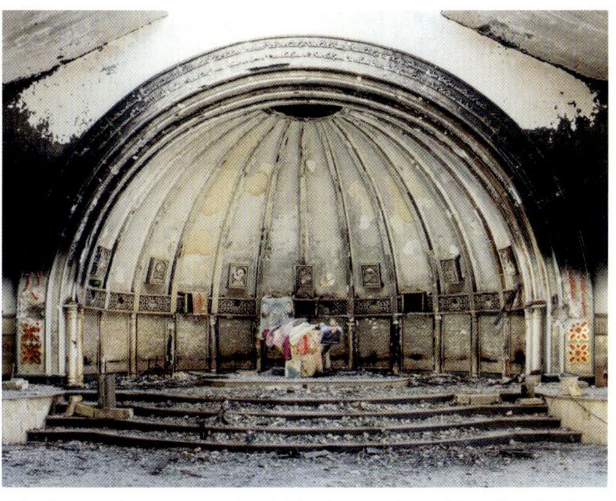

IRAQ Qaraqosh. November 2016. The former altar of the Church of Mar Behnam and Mart Sarah Church set ablaze by the Islamic State in the Christian-majority town of Qaraqosh. Almost all the local inhabitants fled when the Islamic State neared the town, leaving militants to desecrate churches, topple steeples and use religious statues for target practice.

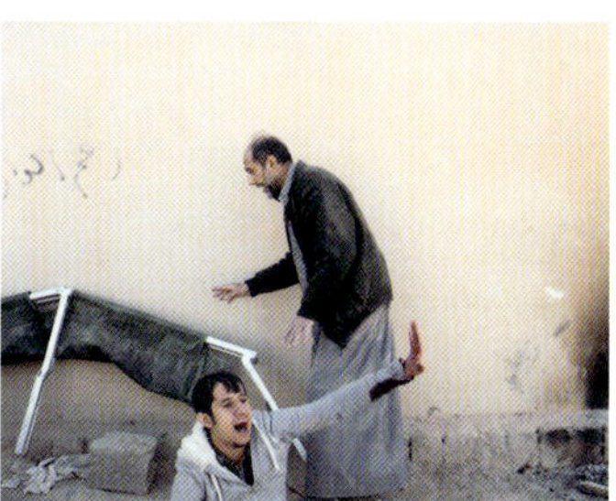

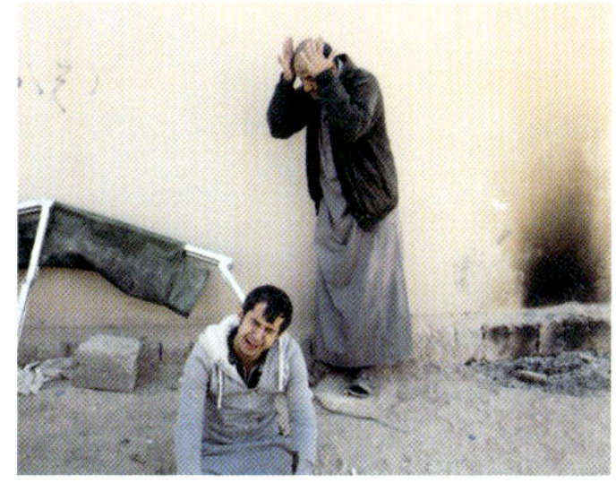

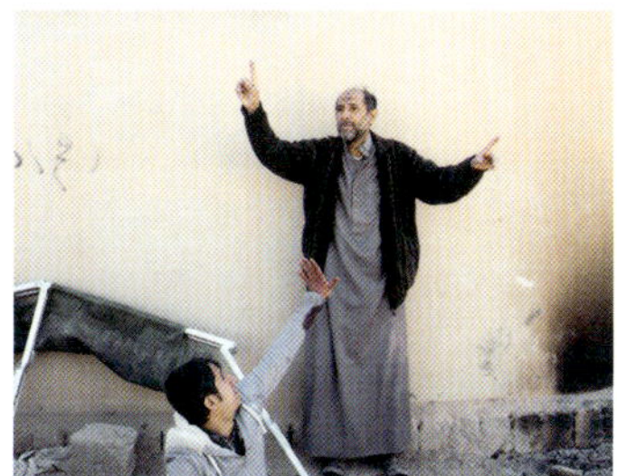

IRAQ Mosul. November 2016. Civilians grieve the loss of their entire family, killed by mortar fire, outside a field hospital on the outskirts of Mosul. Mortars are being deployed extensively by both the Islamic State and the Iraqi forces.

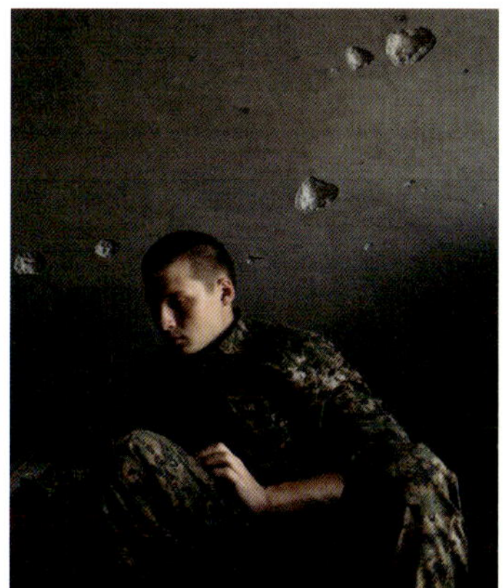

SYRIA Sarrin. August 2015. A German fighter with the Kurdish People's Protection Units (YPG) in a military base. Many foreign fighters joined the so-called caliphate but others came to Iraq or Syria to join Kurdish forces fighting against the Islamic State.

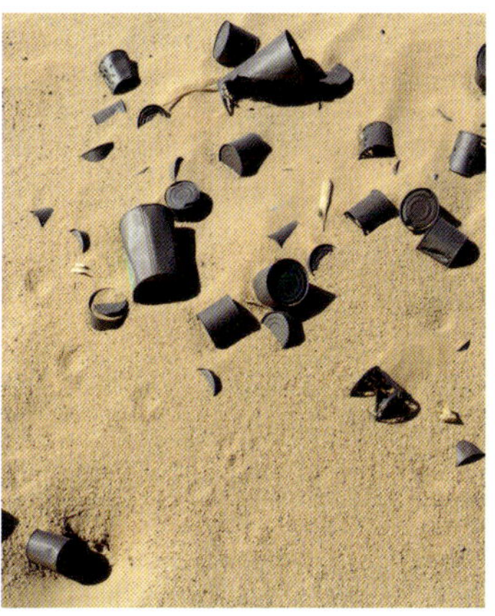

LIBYA The Sahara Desert. November 2015. Food cans abandoned by fighters in the desert. Approximately 90 percent of Libya is desert, and the Islamic State were able to grow there unchecked, before they announced their Mediterranean branch in the city of Sirte.

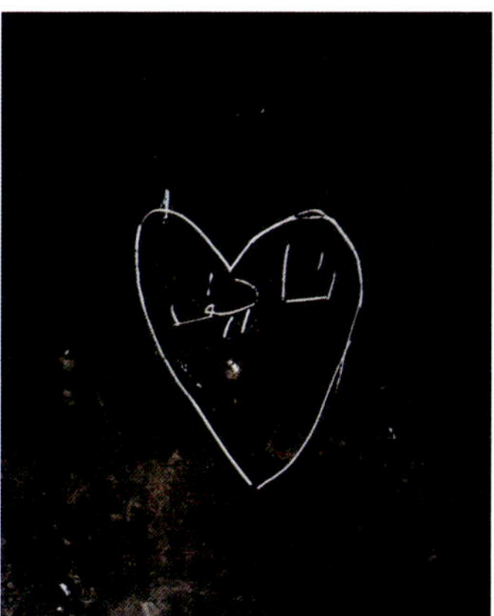

IRAQ Mosul. April 2018. Graffiti in Mosul Old City with the name 'Naef,' a name more common in Gulf countries than Iraq. The Old City was the last bastion of Islamic State resistance in Mosul.

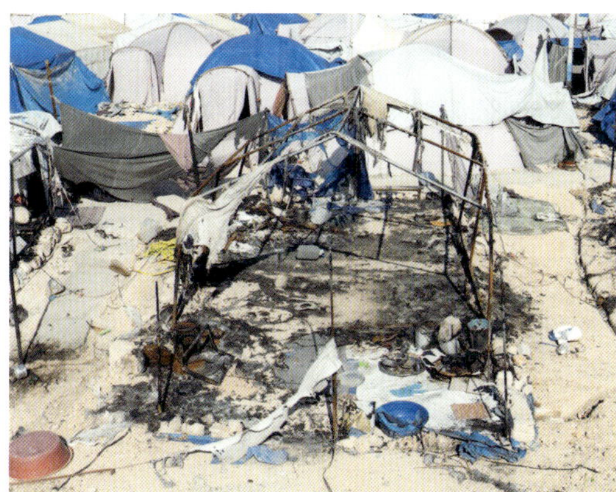

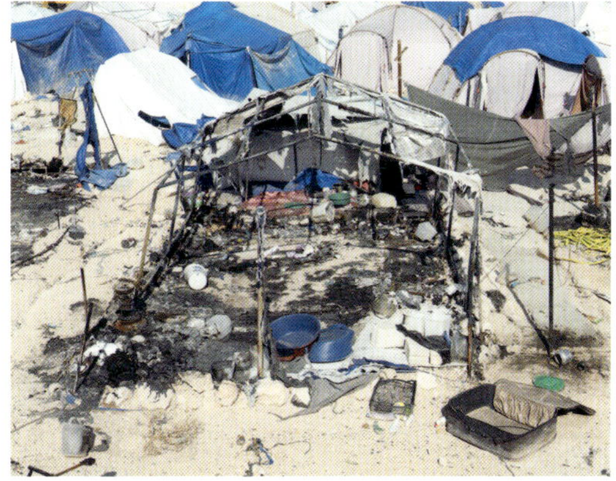

SYRIA Ayn Issa. November 2019. Housing around 9,000 internally displaced people, including families of Islamic State members, the Ayn Issa camp is run by the Syrian Democratic Forces (SDF). During an attack by the Turkish Armed Forces and the Turkish-backed Free Syrian Army (TFSA), Islamic State families reportedly set fire to their tents, creating panic inside the camp and facilitating the escape of at least 750 people suspected of having links to the Islamic State.

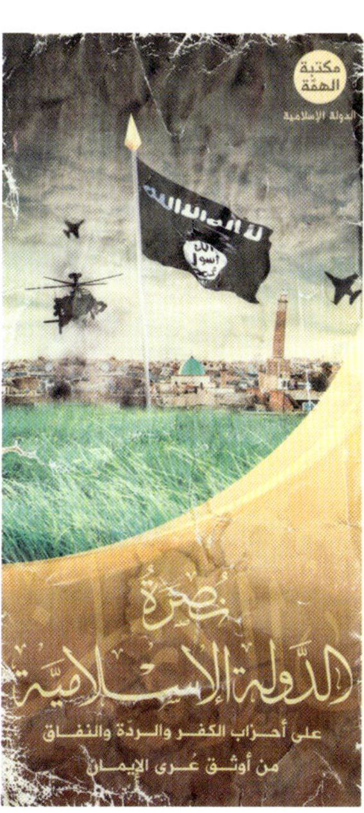

FRANCE Paris. April 2019. A propaganda pamphlet found in East Mosul, Iraq in 2017, burnishing the image of the Islamic State and depicting it as superior to 'infidels, hypocrites and liars.'

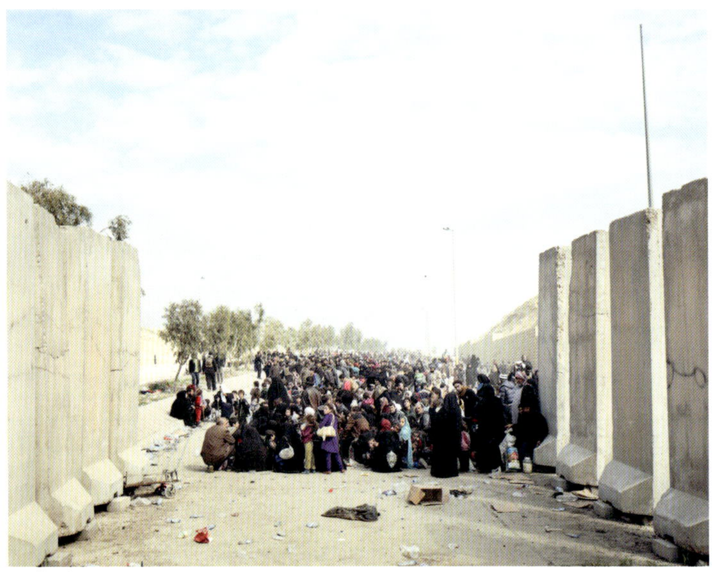

IRAQ Mosul. March 2017. A group of civilians wait to be taken to a screening centre, where their identities will be checked against an Iraqi Army database listing Islamic State members. Those with no known links to the Islamic State will then be taken to camps for internally displaced persons.

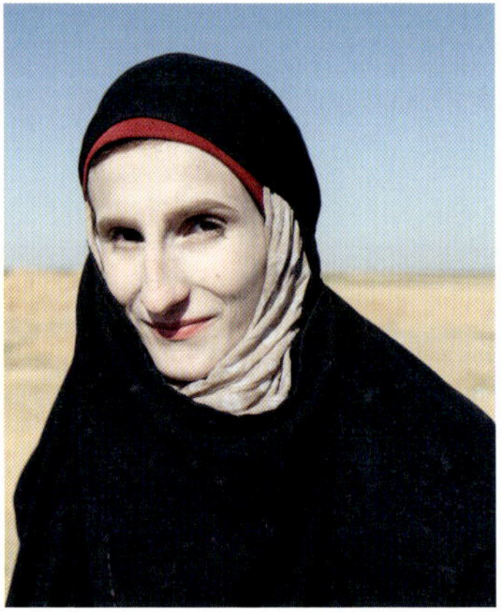

SYRIA Deir ez-Zor province. February 2019. Leonora, aged 19, from Germany, just outside Baghouz, where she was handed back to the Syrian Democratic Forces (SDF) by US intelligence after being questioned. She joined the Islamic State when she was 15-years-old and married Martin Lemke, a member of the *Islamic State's Amniyat* (intelligence). Lemke was also taken in for questioning by US intelligence but was not released.

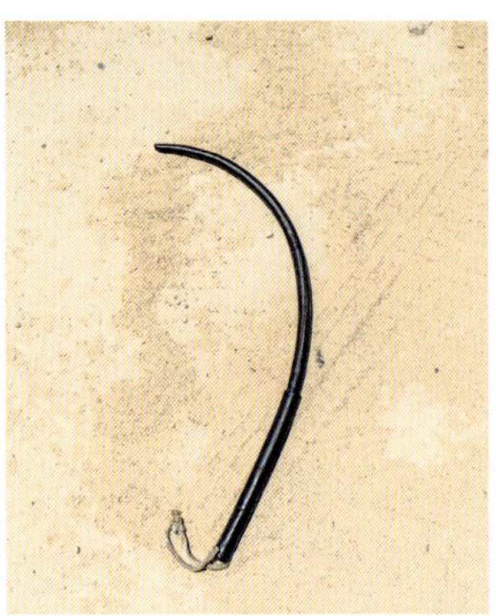

LIBYA Sirte. July 2016. A whip lying on a road during fighting in Sirte. The Islamic State carry out punishments according to their own strict interpretation of Sharia law, which specifies some criminals must be lashed with a whip.

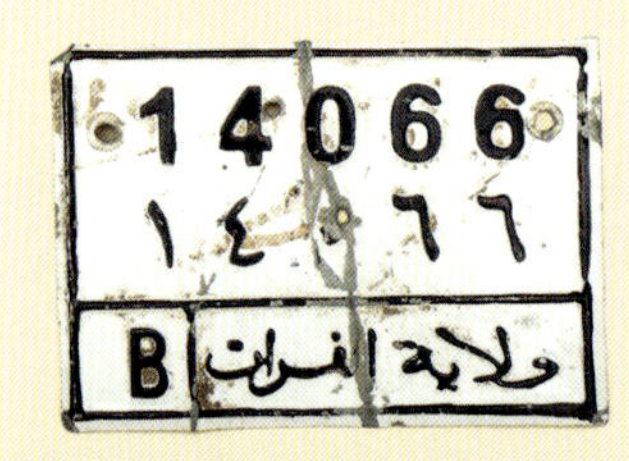

FRANCE Paris. April 2019. An Islamic State number plate found in Baghuz, Syria in 2019 from a province of the so-called caliphate Wilayat al-Furat, which is part of Syria's Deir ez-Zor Governorate.

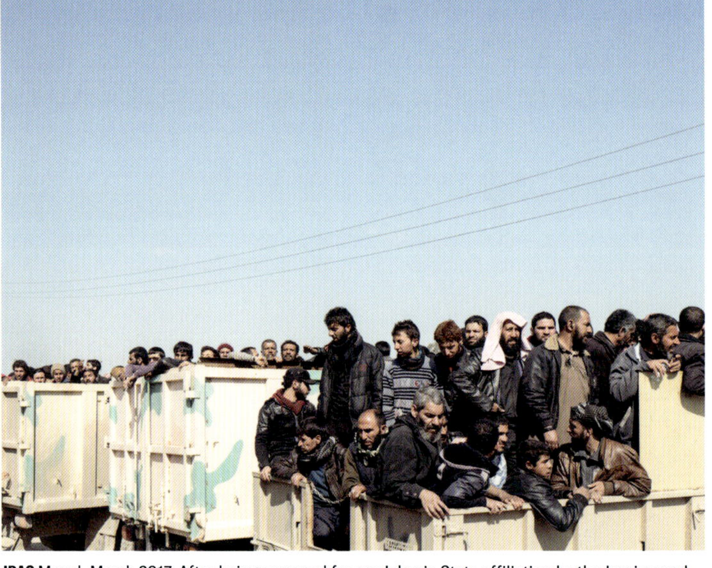

IRAQ Mosul. March 2017. After being screened for any Islamic State affiliation by the Iraqi armed forces, men cram into military trucks, ready to be transported to nearby camps for internally displaced persons.

'THE HISTORICAL ORIGIN OF THE "ARAB SPRING" BANNERS— IS A FLAG DESIGNED BY THE BRITISH CRUSADER MARK SYKES. YES, MARK SYKES OF THE SYKES-PICOT AGREEMENT, WHICH DIVIDED THE MUSLIMS' LANDS INTO NATIONALIST STATES.'

TAKEN FROM 'From the pages of History: The Flags of Jahiliyyah' (Dabiq-Issue 9-Sha'ban 1436)

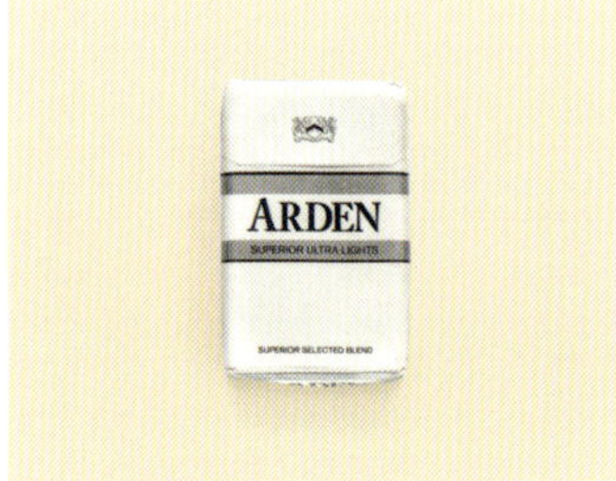

FRANCE Paris. September 2021. A pack of Arden cigarettes, a popular brand smoked on the Syrian and Iraqi frontlines. Cigarettes, food and water are among the most requested supplies, to help pass the time during long days on the frontlines.

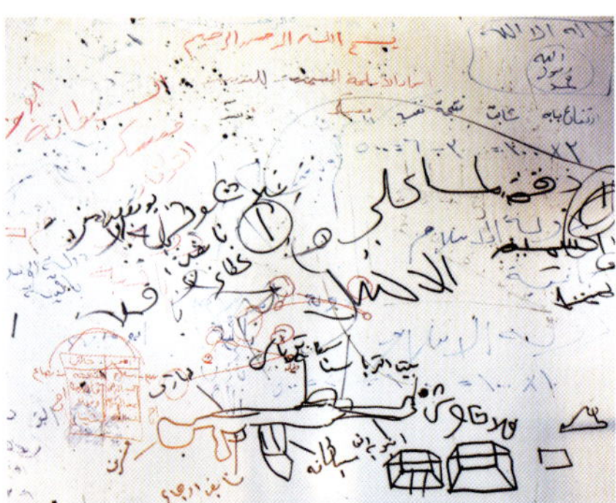

IRAQ Qaraqosh. November 2016. A whiteboard used for weapons training with a labelled drawing of a Kalashnikov, in the courtyard of the al-Tahira (Immaculate Conception) Church. The courtyard was used as a firing range for Islamic State militants to practise their shooting, and Christian statues were used for target practice.

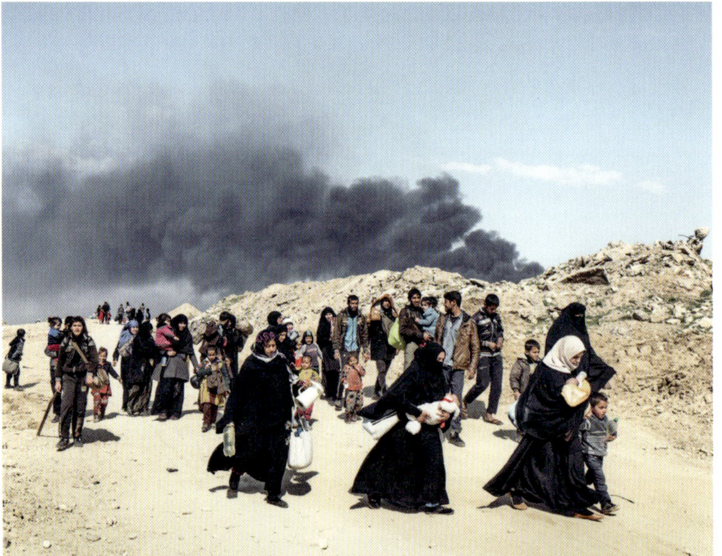

IRAQ Mosul. March 2017. Civilians flee intense fighting in Mosul. The city has been under siege for six months, and the remaining inhabitants are close to starvation, subject to abuse from the Islamic State which has also been using them as human shields, and under daily bombardment from Iraqi and US-led coalition forces.

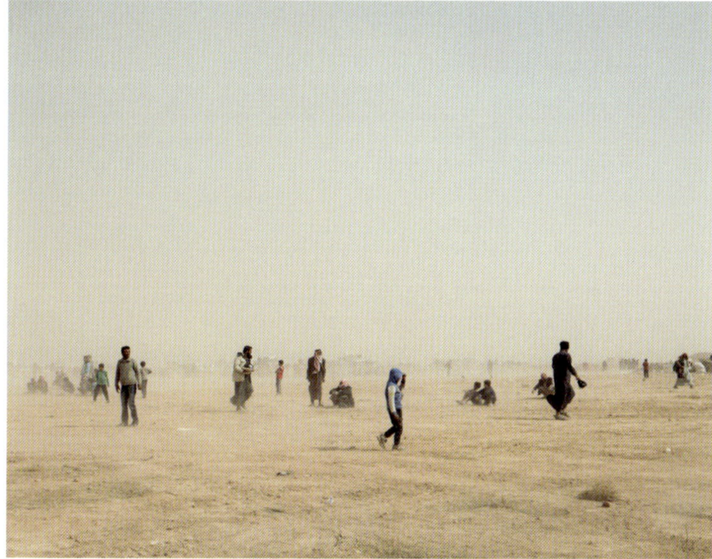

SYRIA Deir ez-Zor. October 2017. Civilians flee from Deir ez-Zor through the Syrian desert. After escaping from fierce fighting between the Syrian Arab Army, supported by Russian airstrikes, and the Islamic State, they have been blocked in the desert, without water, by the Kurdish People's Protection Units (YPG), who suspect Islamic State militants may be hiding amongst them.

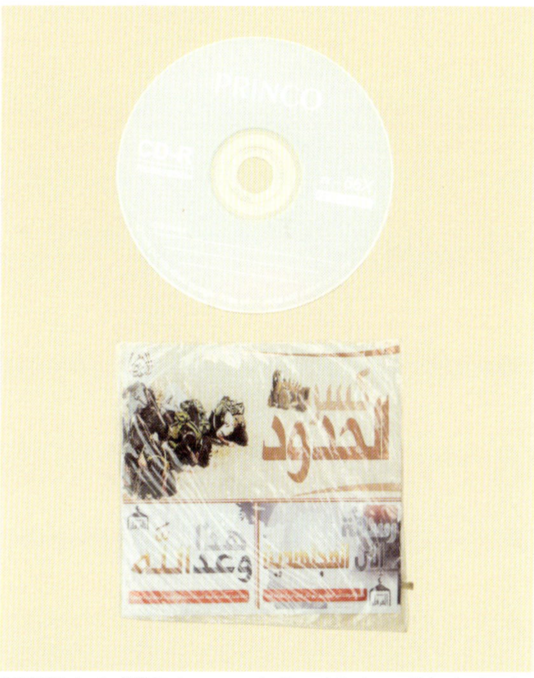

FRANCE Paris. April 2019. A propaganda disc, of the type widely-circulated by the Islamic State to attract new recruits, found in Sirte, Libya in 2016. It features three videos, entitled: 'Break the Borders,' 'Mujahideen Suffer' and 'This is God's Promise.' Such violent video propaganda, showing beheadings and battle scenes, was used to target vulnerable young Muslim men.

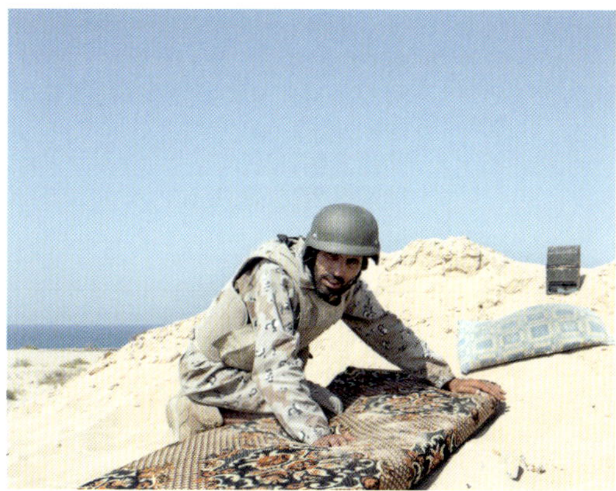

LIBYA Sirte. July 2016. A Libyan 'spotter' identifying Islamic State positions on Sirte's seafront, the westernmost frontline of the battle. Sirte is the Islamic State's Mediterranean stronghold, and the only coastal territory held by the otherwise landlocked so-called caliphate.

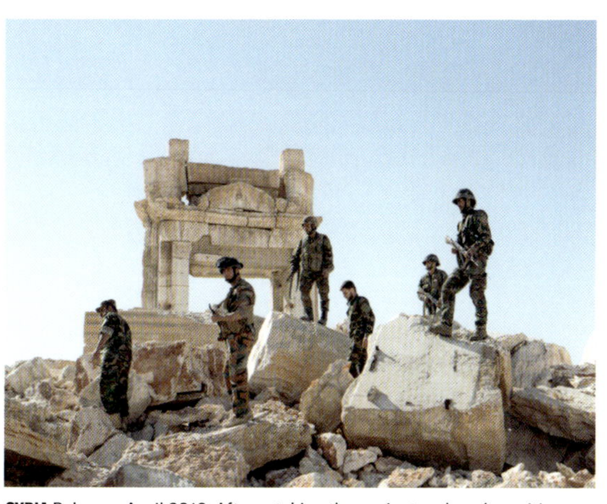

SYRIA Palmyra. April 2016. After retaking the ancient and modern cities of Palmyra days earlier, victorious Syrian Arab Army soldiers climb over rubble. A section of a portico is all that remains of ancient Palmyra's Temple of Bel after it was blown up by the Islamic State.

'FROM THE DESERT, THEY CONTINUED TO CARRY OUT ATTACKS. FLEEING FROM BATTLE, AND GOING BACK TO THE DESERT.'

TAKEN FROM 'From Hijrah To Khilafah' (Dabiq-Issue 1-Ramadan 1435) & 'The Danger Of Abandoning Darul-Islam' (Dabiq-Issue 11-Dhul-Qa'dah 1436)

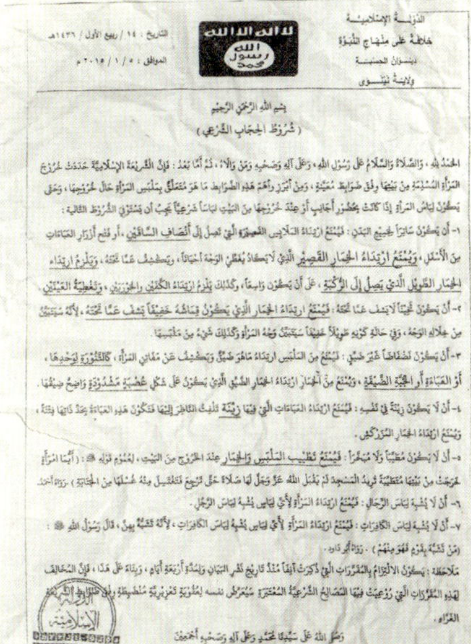

الدولة الإسلامية
خلافة على منهاج النبوة
ديوان الحسبة
ولاية نينوى

بسم الله الرحمن الرحيم

(شروط الحجاب الشرعي)

الحمد لله، والصلاة والسلام على رسول الله، وعلى آله وصحبه ومن والاه، ثم أما بعد: فإن الشريعة الإسلامية حددت خروج المرأة المسلمة من بيتها وفق ضوابط معينة، ومن أبرز وأهم هذه الضوابط ما هو متعلق بملبس المرأة حال خروجها، وحتى يكون لباس المرأة إذا كانت بحضور أجانب أو عند خروجها من البيت لباساً شرعياً يجب أن يستوفي الشروط التالية:

FRANCE Paris. April 2019. An Islamic State 'code of conduct' document, found in West Mosul, Iraq in 2017. The Islamic State appears to have been fairly bureaucratic, as part of efforts to make its so-called caliphate into a proper 'state.'

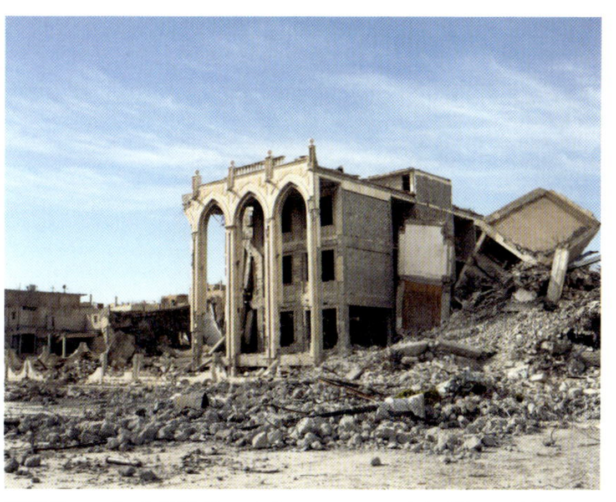

SYRIA Raqqa. April 2018. Raqqa's former governorate building, which the Islamic State later converted into its headquarters and central command for the entire so-called caliphate. An estimated 70 percent of the city was left in ruins, from intense fighting and US-led coalition airstrikes.

LIBYA The Sahara Desert. December 2015. A member of the Third Force patrols the desert surrounding surrounding Libya's el-Sharara oil facility. Operating under the Tripoli-based government, the Third Force has security mandates in parts of southern Libya.

I WOULD LIKE TO THANK

My family, for giving me the freedom to make my own mistakes.

My grandmother, who supported me despite wisely stating: 'photography is not a job.'

Giulia Tornari, for believing in me when I was starting out as a photographer, and for always being there with honest criticism.

Gian Micalessin, for the passion, perseverance and dedication to work on frontlines for some forty years.

Giulio Piscitelli, for the long waits together in remote places, hoping to take a photo.

Gabriel Chaim and Jana Andert, because we live for today not for tomorrow.

Gabriele Micalizzi, for always showing up on some frontline and making me laugh with a joke... but not for making me search all the field hospitals in Baghouz.

Livia Regali, for being a companion in adventures, from artichoke batter to the life and death of an image.

Irene, for being my beast forever.

Imma Vitelli, for speaking to me about love on a frontline.

Max Pinckers, for his good advice.

Melane Wenger, for all the love and wisdom.

Michele Palazzi, for the endless discussions about the end of photography, photojournalism, democracy and cataclysms.

Samuel Forey, for being among those who want to be there at any cost.

Samuel Gratacap, for making me wait for him on a Sirte frontline, so that now we can enjoy aperitifs together in Paris.

Tom Westcott, for running free in the desert, and for polishing the text of this book with her royal British English.

Veronique Rautenberg, Jan Desloover and Andrew Katz, for their support with publications in *L'Obs*, *De Standaard* and *TIME*.

Wendy Federici, who humbly said: 'This book would not exist without my patience, my credit card, my pilgrimages to Western Union, my translations and my distractions.'

My Roman friends: Nicola, Federella, Federica, Karim, Pekora, Yoann, Gillian, Cibba, Bobby, Alice, Silvia, Diana, Adriano and Bruno.

All the people photographed in this book: the so-called good, the so-called bad and those who had no choice. I hope they have a better future. For those who have no future, I hope they rest in peace, at least with themselves.

AT MAGNUM

Abbas, for the sense of 'history' and because god is too busy—a master.

Alex Majoli, because in the Middle East the sky is not always bluer.

Antoine d'Agata, because too much is still not enough.

Antoine Kimmerlin and Natalie Ivis, for their dedication to the 'cause.'

Gilles Peress, for being a constant inspiration.

Giulietta Palumbo, just for being, and for giving me strength and energy even when nothing goes as it should.

Clarisse Bourgeois, for her accurate eye.

Jerome Sessini, for sharing the few joys and the many pains of this profession.

Josef Koudelka, for his dedication and devotion.

Larry Towell, because 'dirty hands, clean heart.'

Mark Power, for being a photography lord.

Moises Saman, because the picture is here.

Paolo Pellegrin, for his help and support.

Patrick Zachmann, because photography is a passport to others.

IN LIBYA

Ahmed Droughi, for those days in a Benghazi prison.

Commander Mohammed Issa, thanks to whose pointless frontline speech against Haftar I was wounded by mortar shrapnel, and who later took me to the field hospital.

Hafed Makhlouf, for helping me navigate Libyan bureaucracy in the most complicated of times.

IN IRAQ

Ahmed Algalibi, from the Emergency Response Division (ERD), for being my darling on the frontline.

Rebin Rozhbayane, Makeen Mustafa, Halan Shekha, Sangar Khaleel and Lina Issa, for their courage and help in Mosul.

Bewar Abdulqader, for making me feel part of a family in Iraq.

Major Ali, from the ERD, for cooking me fries on the frontline and for sharing the last pack of cigarettes of his life with me.

IN SYRIA

Asya, for being the most generous and beautiful fighter I have ever seen.

Adel Judi, commander of the Qamishli brigade during the battle of Baghouz, because 'we don't say goodbye.'

Mustafa Bali, Mustafa Alali, Serbest Ali, Perwer Muhammad Ali, Farhad Shami and Mahmoud Bali, for those days under siege in Kobane, smoking cigarettes tasting of chocolate or mint and sharing the same canned meat for weeks, while dreaming of Gauloises.

Talal Khrais, for finding a way to get me a visa even though I was blacklisted, enabling me to document the liberation of Palmyra.

Jac Holmes, for those days together during the fall of Raqqa. I should have told you even more firmly that it wasn't a good idea, but you wouldn't have listened anyway.

REGARDING THIS BOOK

Incite Project, for supporting living photographers. Harriet Logan and Tristan Lund, for their friendship, insightful and valuable suggestions, and for the support without which this book would have been much harder to produce.

Stuart Smith, for the beauty of the 'non finito' and the perfection of consistency.

Brian Paul Lamotte, for his valuable help, time and patience in designing this book.

Claudia Paladini, for creating order amongst the chaos, and for taking such precious care of the production of the book.

Gert Verbelen, for helping me create a first dummy book. His creativity and editing skills put me on the right track, and are responsible for some of the nice spreads in this book.

Fabio Barile and Davide Di Gianni, for taking care of my photos and prints.

ARDEN
SUPERIOR ULTRA LIGHTS
SUPERIOR SELECTED BLEND

We Don't Say Goodbye
First published in 2021 by
GOST Books, London

info@gostbooks.com
gostbooks.com

Design: Brian Paul Lamotte and GOST
Edit: Lorenzo Meloni

GOST: Katie Clifford, Gemma Gerhard, Justine Hucker, Allon Kaye, Eleanor Macnair, Claudia Paladini, Ana Rocha

Printed in Italy by EBS

British Library cataloguing-in-publication data.
A catalogue record of this book is available from the British Library.

ISBN 978-1-910401-44-6

Supported by
THE INCITE PROJECT

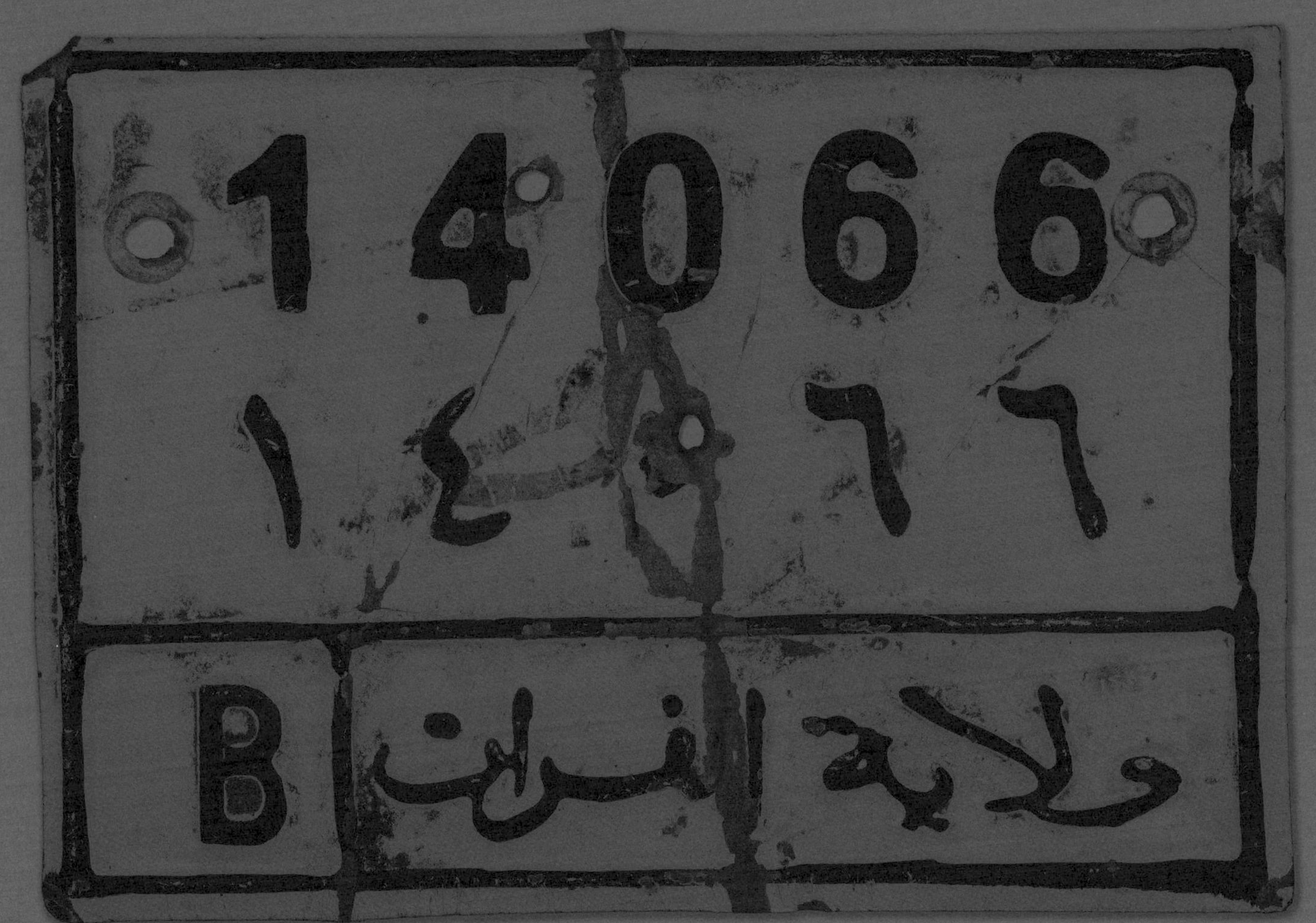
14066
١٤٠٦٦
B
ولاية الفرات

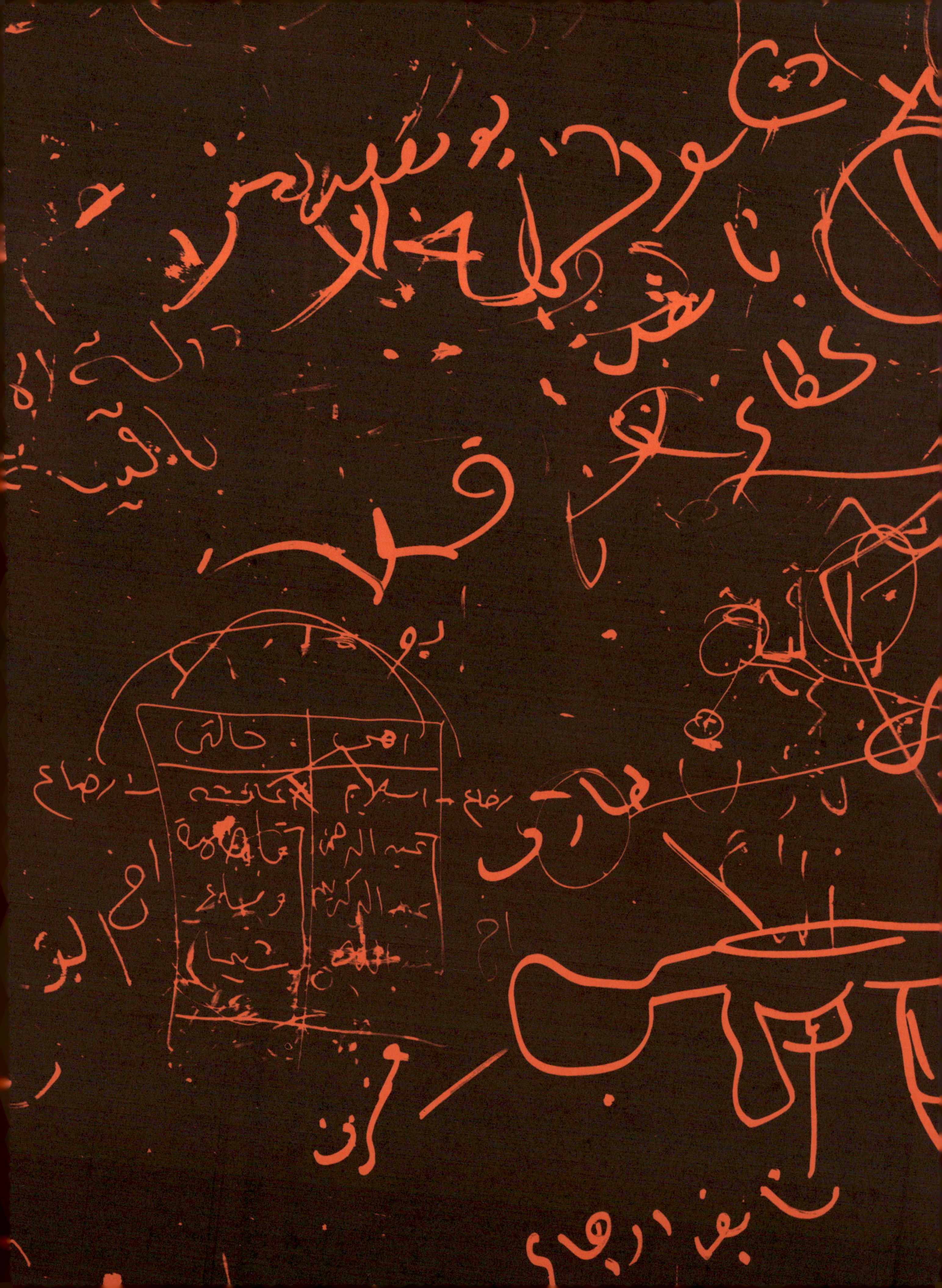